COACH

COACH

THE PAT BURNS STORY

ROSIE DiMANNO

DOUBLEDAY CANADA

Doubleday Canada and colophon are registered trademarks

Library and Archives Canada Cataloguing in Publication

DiManno, Rosie
    Coach : the Pat Burns story / Rosie DiManno.

Issued also in electronic format.
ISBN 978-0-385-67636-6

1. Burns, Pat, 1952-2010. 2. Hockey coaches—Canada—
Biography. I. Title.

GV848.5.B88D54 2012   796.962092   C2012-902434-1

Cover image: Michael Stuparyk/GetStock.com

Printed and bound in the USA

Published in Canada by Doubleday Canada,
a division of Random House of Canada Limited

Visit Random House of Canada Limited's website: www.randomhouse.ca

10 9 8 7 6 5 4 3 2 1

For Our Fathers

Domenic DiManno

&

Alfred Burns

Contents

The Running Man

"They've all had that gun out for me."

IT'S WELL PAST MIDNIGHT, sleeting, and Pat Burns is halfway home.

There's a six-pack on the seat next to him, a duffel bag containing a few articles of clothing, and a cell phone stamped with the Toronto Maple Leafs logo. Just outside Kingston, the vacancy sign of a Super 8 motel beckons. Burns is tired right down to his bones—so weary, eyes puffy from sleeplessness, spots blurring his vision—so he prudently pulls his pickup off Highway 401 and into the motel's parking lot. At the front desk, the bored clerk doesn't recognize the dishevelled guest who checks in for just the one night, and Burns is grateful for that. Anonymity is what he craves at this moment, not an autograph-seeker and definitely not an armchair expert with advice for a hockey team that has been imploding spectacularly. All the world's a coach when it comes to hockey in Canada.

But the Leafs aren't Burns's problem anymore. He's not their coach anymore. It's March 4, 1996.

Only a handful of people are aware of this development, however. It's a secret, a hush-hush contrivance that was the final gesture of mercy offered to Burns by the franchise where he'd been as much a Leaf luminary as Doug Gilmour, his beloved Dougie. In the fight-or-flight response common to all creatures faced with stress and fright, Burns has chosen to flee. He is running, in the middle of the night. A man who has always prided himself on never dodging any challenge or ordeal has lammed it while the city sleeps.

So many times, Burns had made this trip between Toronto and the Eastern Townships of Quebec, by truck and by Harley. Three and a half years earlier, he'd set out in the opposite direction on a hot summer's day, music blasting on the CD player, the future unfolding as brightly, as welcoming, as the open road, signposts whizzing past. Now he'd shifted gears into reverse, the Big Smoke disappearing in his rear-view mirror, all that anxiety and amassed failure left behind, along with twenty-five suits, hundreds of ties and two Harleys stored at a Richmond Hill dealership.

In the spartan motel room that's illuminated by the flash of headlights from the highway, Burns shucks out of his parka, kicks off his hand-tooled cowboy boots, sinks onto the bed, fires up an extra-mild cigarette and flips the cap on his first beer. The brew is unpleasantly warm. Burns isn't much of a beer drinker anyway—he prefers scotch or wine, the expensive stuff. Once, when taken to dinner by a reporter who was working on a Burns profile, he'd blithely ordered a $400 bottle of California Opus One as the journalist gagged over an expense that would never be approved by the office. Burns could be mischievous that way, or thoughtless.

In his solitude now, the coach who's no longer a coach sips intermittently and ponders events from a whirlwind forty-eight hours, the last gasps of a job that had seemed so secure at midseason, when he'd been offered, and accepted, a provisional contract extension by Leafs general manager Cliff Fletcher. The kicker is that Burns was still being paid a deferred salary from his earlier tenure as coach of the Montreal Canadiens, a dream gig that had ended just as precipitously, though less ignominiously, at the end of his fourth season behind the bench. A four-year coach with a three-year act—the rap that would be pinned on him again, Burns frets. He picks up the phone and dials a friend. "I'm gone," he says, ever so softly.

At 10 p.m., unseen even by security guards, Burns had slipped into his office in the bowels of Maple Leaf Gardens and cleared out his desk, tossing a few personal items into the duffel bag. In the eerie quiet of the dressing room—the dank venue where, on one memorable occasion during his first season in Toronto, he'd conducted a blistering postgame media scrum deliberately staged so that his players would get an earful of the diatribe aimed specifically at them—Burns scribbled a departing message on the blackboard, GOOD LUCK BOYS, and signed it "BURNSIE." He left a well-wishing note also for the interim coach, Nick Beverley, who would replace him. Then he jumped in his truck and pointed it towards his rustic off-season cottage on the shore of Lake Memphremagog, ten miles north of the Vermont–Quebec border.

That he'd got his ticket punched in Toronto was inevitable, if agonizing in the long goodbye—six weeks of lurching through mounting losses, first one tailspin and then, after a brief respite, another. Fletcher had been adamant that he wouldn't fire his coach—indeed, had never in his lengthy and distinguished career as a hockey executive canned a coach in midseason. On February 6, Fletcher assured reporters that the coach's job was not in jeopardy. "Pat Burns is our coach for next year, too, if he should decide to return. His future is no different now than it was when he got us to the final four two years in a row. It's not an issue." Burns, flailing, appreciated that Fletcher had his back, though suspicious that some players were stabbing knives in it, even as he publicly denied rumours of team dissent. "I don't feel the players have quit on me and I'm not going to quit on them." On February 25, with the club plummeting in the conference standings, Fletcher issued another vote of confidence to quell the media masses: "It's Pat's job—period. That isn't even an issue." Seven days later, he gassed him.

Everybody watching had sensed the omega moment of the alpha-dog coach approaching. A roster tailored to suit Burns's personnel desires had gone off the rails and Gilmour's aching back couldn't bear the burden anymore. Players generously rewarded for past performances seemed to have lost interest; certainly, they'd lost the motivating fear of Burns that the coach had instilled in them. The team was a shambles as

February gave way to March, caught in a downward spiral that put them in danger of missing the playoffs for the first time in four years. For public consumption, Burns remained stalwart, if sounding increasingly defensive and peevish. "More than ever, everything that has been written and said has made me want to come back next season even more. If Cliff will have me back, I'll be back and I'll win again. I didn't get dumb in three months."

Shock therapy was looming, though.

The Leafs were on the road that final week. On the Saturday, in Burns's 600th game as an NHL coach, they were beaten in Dallas. On the Sunday, they lost 4–0 to the Colorado Avalanche, their eighth consecutive defeat— they had won only three of their past twenty-two matches. Since mid-January, the NBA-expansion Toronto Raptors had won more games than the Leafs.

They tried group meetings, individual meetings, psychologist sessions, scoldings, avuncular chats, trades, yet nothing reversed the descending trajectory. In desperation, Fletcher tapped alumnus Darryl Sittler, the one-time captain and franchise hero of the '70s, latterly a "consultant" for the club, to facilitate communication between the dressing room and the coaching staff. Burns had deeply resented that; he believed Sittler was functioning as de facto spy for management. One of Sittler's first moves as part of his increased role with the Leafs was to corral Gilmour for a heart-to-heart, and that also irritated Burns, who was proprietary about his captain. But he was a profoundly paranoid coach by that point.

On the road, Burns has been reading *The Art of War* by Sun Tzu.

He spoke frequently with his closest buddy back in Magog, Quebec, Kevin Dixon. "He'd say, 'It's coming, it's coming. Fuck, it's going to be coming any day, any day.' He thought Mike Gartner was against him, Jamie Macoun was against him, guys he believed were telling Cliff that he had to go. Think about it, what it was like for him: the team was digging itself a bigger hole every night. He'd get behind that bench and after every first period, he'd look up at the scoreboard and the Leafs were trailing. They're down, he's down. Honest, he should have been on antidepressants, that's how bad it got. Then he called from Phoenix and it was just, 'I'm done.'"

Before that Avalanche game in Denver—with key player Mats Sundin out of the lineup—Burns told his players that they had a ready-made excuse for yet another loss. Don't accept that alibi, he pleaded. "I stood in the middle of the dressing room for a long time. I looked in their faces. Only about five of them could look me in the eye. I knew it was over."

Peppered with questions afterwards, Fletcher told the travelling media that Burns would definitely be standing on the riser behind the Leaf bench—designed to give the home coach a subtle height advantage over his opposing number—for Toronto's next game on Wednesday, back at the Gardens, against the Stanley Cup champion New Jersey Devils. Unusually, the team didn't leave immediately following the Denver game, remaining overnight at their Mile High hotel.

Early Monday morning, Fletcher summoned Burns to his room. The two men conferred briefly. It was a painful meeting, with Burns actually consoling the older man, his friend and benefactor, in a puddle of tears now as he took away the job he'd bestowed with such hopefulness at the start of their adventure together. Fletcher had been weighing the decision for two days, praying the team would pick up at least one victory on the road trip, something positive to go home with. "We can't go back to Toronto without a win," he'd warned. Didn't happen, and that forced Fletcher's hand, which trembled. "I told Cliff I won't quit. But I understood that this is what he had to do. I said, 'Cliff, I know you've never fired a coach in midseason and I know this isn't easy for you. Don't worry. I understand. You've been great to me.'"

Burns professed to be most concerned about who would be taking up the reins and approved the choice of Beverley, who'd never coached a day in the NHL, as interim. He'd been Toronto's director of player personnel. "I was happy to hear it was Nick. He's a good man." Eventually, the position went to Mike Murphy, who'd been through three campaigns as an assistant coach with Burns over the years. Burns had never trusted him. "He wants my job," he'd confided to a friend, and he was right. Burns was not offered a lateral movement within the Leaf franchise and wouldn't have accepted one anyway. And he did not offer to resign. He was axed. But he did stretch out his neck, inviting the blow.

In truth, with the deed done, Burns could exhale. "It was like, 'Whew, take the gun away from me, don't point that thing this way no more,'" recalls his confidant, Dixon. "He said, 'They've all had that gun out for me—"Shoot him!"' Oh yeah, he was relieved."

Each swearing to keep his lips sealed, Burns and Fletcher shook hands, embraced in an awkward hug, then proceeded to the airport and boarded their flight, poker-faced. The con was on.

It might seem atypical for Burns to, essentially, skulk out of town. He'd claimed to have never run away from a fight. Actually, he'd been a runner all his life—from a bad marriage and crumbling relationships, from parental responsibilities, from commitment, from jobs that no longer inspired or suited, from the risk of failure, from wreckage. None of this made him a bad man—far from it. But, like many complicated people, he was so much not what he often appeared—not tough and hardened to his marrow, but sensitive and easily wounded; not forthright, but secretive; not brimming with self-confidence, but frequently insecure; not honest, but . . . deceptive. He was, in fact, his own greatest invention: a persona crafted over the years to hide what really lay beneath—all the doubts and vulnerabilities and hurts, the fatherless boy who learned by his wits to become a man of substance and was still learning on the day he died.

In his motel room that icy March night in 1996, these were the demons pressing in on Burns, relieved as he genuinely was about being released from the horror that coaching the Leafs had become through a fifty-three-day ordeal of compounding disasters, withering behind the bench, perspiring in front of the media glare. He was too stricken to show his face to the media, and that's why he'd fled, why Fletcher had consented to the all-is-fine ruse.

Burns told only a handful of intimates, calling Gilmour to thank him "because that guy gave his heart and soul to this team and I'll always remember that," informing his cousin and agent, Robin Burns, and breaking the news to his two kids, daughter Maureen inconsolable.

By mid-morning the following day, word had begun to leak, however, and the Leafs called a press conference, Fletcher visibly shaken as he addressed the media. Reporters were bitter at having been duped. They wanted a carcass to pick over and accused Fletcher of duplicity. The absent ex-coach was unapologetic for leaving his media scrutineers, some of whom had believed themselves close to Burns, in the lurch.

"I spoke to everybody I wanted to speak to," he would say later. "Isn't it my choice now? They had the chance to say I was a no good, rotten son of a bitch for four years and I never objected to talking to anyone on the job. But now it's my time. I walked away. I shut my mouth. I took my pill and I went home. I never said anything to hurt a player's career. I didn't throw darts. I still have great respect for Cliff, and I don't blame him for what happened because he was always fair with me. They made the change and that was it. But was it better after I left? How far did they go in the playoffs? Is that my fault, too? I gave four years of my life to the Toronto Maple Leafs. I emptied my guts. And we proved something. Maybe we didn't prove the whole thing, because we didn't win a Stanley Cup. But we proved something."

On the road home that morning, the weather had cleared, the sky was blue and Burns's spirits lifted somewhat. Like a wounded bear, he was going to a place where he felt safe—"I'll hide in the woods for a while"— though never anticipating his hibernation would last quite so long, a full season to come out of the game that was his only real passion. In Magog, because his own lakeside retreat was rented out until the end of the month, he took refuge in a friend's cedar-shingled house across the frozen pond, a twenty-five-acre property with all the conveniences of city life, a soapstone fireplace and a fat tabby called Li'l Bastard. Looking out the window, he could occasionally spot deer emerging timidly from the bush. "I'm just going to relax and let things go by. I certainly don't plan on leaving the game. I still think I'm a good coach. I think I've proven that. I don't think I'm a bum now because I've been fired. I'll be back somewhere."

He'd been down this road before and would travel there again. Seven years further on, he'd reach his ultimate destination—holding aloft that ungainly silver trophy bequeathed by Lord Stanley—the boy from St. Henri who'd willed himself to triumph, from cop to NHL coach to championship parade in a dreary New Jersey parking lot, not quite as he'd imagined it. Still, fate had smiled on Pat Burns. And then it delivered a death rattle.

Chapter One
The Fatherless Boy

"This big, big hole that never got filled."

PATRICK JOHN JOSEPH BURNS was born April 4, 1952, in St. Henri, Montreal, the lively working-class francophone and Irish-immigrant neighbourhood immortalized by Gabrielle Roy in *The Tin Flute*. But this was St. Henri in its pre-gentrified era, grungy and grasping and insular.

So proud was Alfred Burns, Sr. of this new addition to the family, a second son who would be the last of six children, that he immediately set about planning a future immersed in hockey, as did thousands of other fathers in Quebec, dreaming about the National Hockey League for their squealing boy infants. Alfred Burns was such an ardent Montreal Canadiens fanatic that, upon returning home from the hospital to the family's upstairs flat at 819 Laporte Avenue, he bought two hockey sticks and nailed them, in an X-shaped cross, above the baby's crib. The family may not have been able to afford fancy layettes and mobiles to amuse their newborn, but from the first days of his life, Baby Patrick's hazel eyes would open on a sacred hockey montage.

Paternally, the Burnses were Catholics who hailed originally from Scotland, tracing their history to a town called Burnshead in the county of Cumberland, during the reign of Edward I. The Burnses had their own coat of arms: a hand holding a hunting horn—symbolizing power—surrounded by three white fleur-de-lis, signifying peace. The clan's motto: "Ever ready."

From genealogical research undertaken by Patrick's sister Diane, the family's ancestors abandoned Scotland for Ireland around the time of the Great Potato Famine that began in 1845, an inauspicious move, since destitute Irish families were fleeing starvation by the boatloads for America. Plenty of Burnses joined the mass emigration, but this branch of the family hung on. It was Alfred Burns's grandfather who sailed to Canada from County Cork.

His progeny fared adequately; a hard-working lot from which eventually sprang Pat Burns, one of the NHL's most respected coaches, three times winner of the Jack Adams Award as coach of the year, and among the highest paid in his profession. None of that, of course, could have been envisioned when Louise Geraldeau Burns brought her baby home to a cramped apartment. Of Louise's heritage, little is known except that her forebears had lived in the region of rural Calumet, Quebec, for as far back as could be traced.

Alfred Burns was a strapping fellow, baldish, with a gift for the gab and a rollicking sense of humour, traits his son would inherit. "My father was Irish right to the bone," Pat would say. His hefty dimensions came from Alfred, too, but otherwise Pat physically resembled Louise. Diane, next youngest to Pat and seven years his senior, idolized her dad. "He was a very good father. Taught me how to put a worm on a hook. He called Patrick his chum. He was so pleased to have another son. Dad was a great fisherman; he loved boats. Pat took that up quite a bit from him."

When Louise met Alfred, they were both working at Imperial Tobacco in Montreal. She was living in a boarding house, drawn to the big city from Calumet in pursuit of gainful employment, first as a cleaning lady, then babysitting for a "high-class" family, before moving on to the tobacco company. Her given name was Giralda, but Alfred couldn't even pronounce that, and everybody called her Louise. Alfred was a master electrician and Louise was on the assembly line, churning out cigarettes. She spoke no English; he spoke no French. The women at the plant all wore trousers, not for fashion but for comfort and utilitarian purpose. One hot afternoon, she was sitting in the park across the street from the sprawling factory and rolled up her pant legs. Alfred spotted the young lady's shapely calves and thought, appreciatively, "Hmm." They were married within a year, and the babies starting coming.

The flat on Laporte Avenue, a fifteen-minute walk from Imperial Tobacco, was long and narrow. A hallway led to a living room, dining room, the couple's bedroom, a bedroom for the older children, and another, in the back, with bunk beds, to be shared years later by Pat and Diane. First born was Violet, now in her late seventies, then Alfred Jr.—called Sonny— then Lillian and Phyllis and Diane, and then no pregnancy for seven years. "Pat came along really late," recalls Diane. "He wasn't a planned baby. I don't know whether it was a fluke or not. Mom says she would have had more had my father not passed away."

In St. Henri, the children—though not Pat, still a toddler—attended St. Thomas Aquinas School and worshipped at the attached St. Thomas Aquinas Church every Sunday. But the family left Montreal and moved to Châteauguay before Pat's third birthday. A lovely profile written by then Montreal *Gazette* columnist Michael Farber in 1988, just as Burns was beginning his NHL career, would become the biographical template, resurrected as a requiem and widely reproduced twenty-two years later. Farber, trailing the coach through his old neighbourhood, could not possibly have grasped that even then Burns was burnishing an invented childhood, making up chunks of a sweet past as he undoubtedly wished it had been.

Burns recounted how his father had taken him to Canadiens games every few weeks, the two sitting in the whites at the Forum, peering around posts that blocked their view, the boy in his number 9 Maurice "Rocket" Richard sweater. "One of those big woollen ones, eh? With the turtleneck. During the fall and spring, they'd start scratching you, eh? Somebody in my family bought me a Blackhawks shirt. I don't know who—an aunt, I guess. I cried my eyes out. I couldn't wear it here. I couldn't wear it here."

Though not yet three years old at the time, Burns claimed to remember his father and brother, Sonny, listening to reports on the radio one evening about a commotion developing outside the Forum. It was March 17, 1955, St. Patrick's Day, and this would become the politically and culturally defining Richard Riot in Quebec. NHL president Clarence Campbell, long at disciplinary odds with hockey icon Rocket Richard, had suspended the fiery superstar for, in his view, deliberately injuring an opponent during a game against Boston and then punching a linesman. Richard was suspended for the remainder of the season and the playoffs. With Richard's chance at a scoring title and the team's first-place standing in jeopardy, to say nothing of their postseason fortunes, Quebecers were incandescent with rage. Foolishly, after imposing the suspension, Campbell decided to attend Montreal's very next home game. Spectators at the Forum could not restrain themselves, pummelling their Public Enemy No. 1 with food and garbage. The game was suspended and the arena evacuated, which dumped thousands of fuming fans onto the street. In the ensuing melee, windows were smashed and somebody set off a tear gas bomb. The riot marked a seminal moment in the evolution of Quebec's modern nationalist movement.

Teased out of a memory likely formed from the retelling rather than the actual event witnessed, Burns recalled father and brother walking up Atwater Avenue to investigate the scene. "There was a story going around the neighbourhood that Dad was up there breaking windows, that the old man had gone up there to cause trouble. That was ridiculous. Years later, he would talk about it and say, 'I remember back in 1955, they were throwing stuff at Mr. Campbell and . . .'"

In fact, there would be no "years later" for Alfred Burns, who died in 1957, aged forty-nine. The truth is more poignant than any improvised reminiscence.

"In the papers, when he first became coach in Montreal, they said his father took him to games, but that never happened," says Diane, setting the record straight. "Not that Dad wouldn't have done that, but he just never got the chance."

When the family picked up and moved to Châteauguay, with Pat three years old, an uncle married to Alfred's sister permitted them to reside in a "house" he owned there. Actually, it was no more than a garage on a piece of property where the uncle's family lived in a large separate house. But Alfred was handy and converted it into a decent home for his brood. "Dad turned the garage into a house for us," says Diane. "But we never had papers or anything to prove that the house belonged to us. When he passed away, my uncle kicked us out."

It was around Christmas. Alfred had been attempting to unclog a frozen well on the property using a blowtorch. He tried lighting the torch several times, to no avail. Nothing happened. As Alfred was peering over the edge of the well, gas fumes from the torch ignited and the torch exploded, the blowback striking him smack in the face. Amazingly, he wasn't killed—nor, it seemed, seriously injured. He called for Lillian to bring him a towel. She wanted to call a doctor, but Alfred said no.

Louise and Diane had been shopping in town, walking home because they had no car, when they discovered a dazed Alfred. Despite what Pat would later say, he didn't witness the accident, either. "The explosion burned Dad's face, singed his eyebrows and his eyelids," says Diane. "He actually looked okay except for the singes and the fact he had no eyebrows. But he refused to go to the hospital, because it was around Christmas and he wanted to be with the family. At least that's what he said."

Within a few weeks, however, Louise noticed that something appeared wrong with Alfred. He was weak and unsteady on his feet. A doctor was summoned. "The doctor came to the house, took one look at Dad and said, 'Oh no, he's got to go to the hospital.'" His brother drove him. "When Dad got there, he bent down to take his shoes off, had a massive heart attack and died."

Speculation after the fact was that Alfred had a bad ticker, some undisclosed pre-existing condition biding its time until triggered fatally by the blast. There was no history of heart problems in his family; his father died of cancer, while his mother lived to a ripe, old age. "He may have had a cholesterol problem," muses Diane. "He was a man with a big appetite— big pie eater, big egg eater. He never went to doctors. You would never know there was anything wrong to look at him. Not at all."

For the youngster Pat, the sudden loss of his father lacerated his psyche, ripping open a wound, a throbbing ache that would never heal. Even before he could process what had been lost, the ever-after absence of Alfred Burns had marked him. Thus would begin a lifelong search for male mentors, a quest for kindly patriarchs to fill that vacuum. There was always a deep-rooted sadness that Burns, as an adult who eschewed navel-gazing and avoided self-reflection, was loath to even acknowledge. "I don't think he was ever a happy man," reflects Diane, who was his closest sibling. "From the day my dad died, there's been a gap in there so big, so big, that was never filled by anyone else—not men friends, not women, and there were a lot of women. He just had this big, big hole that never got filled. That affected all his relationships. He never learned how to be a father because he never really had one."

Louise received some insurance money and a widow's pension, but the family faced hardship. Three of her children—Sonny, Lillian and Phyllis—were working at Imperial Tobacco in Montreal, and Violet, soon to be married, at a plant that manufactured Aspirin. None of Alfred's offspring would receive a postsecondary education, all of them entering the work force right out of high school. When Alfred's brother-in-law evicted the family from the garage-cum-house, Louise faced a crisis. Younger children in tow, she returned to St. Henri, renting a small ground-floor apartment on St. Antoine Street. She got a job at a clothing shop. Then Louise was offered, and accepted, a job from her brother, who owned a restaurant in Pointe-au-Chine, not far from Hawkesbury, Ontario. Louise became the cook, and Phyllis also toiled in the restaurant for a year until she married her boyfriend and moved away. Four-year-old Pat was still attached to his mom's apron string, but Diane, then eleven, was sent to dwell temporarily with her maternal grandparents in Calumet. The family had been dispersed widely. "My mother was just trying to cope," says Diane.

Within a few years, widowed Louise, with Diane and Pat, relocated the shrinking family to Gatineau. Violet was living there then, and Louise wanted to be closer to her daughter and good-natured son-in-law, Bill Hickey. Another tiny apartment was rented for the three meandering

Burnses. This was not an unpleasant phase in the Burns family annals. The Christmas Pat was six, Louise had set aside money to buy him—at an employee discount because Diane was a salesgirl at the store, Handy Andy's—a complete set of Canadiens-logo hockey equipment. Dickie Moore was Pat's idol, the Hab he pretended to be while playing on frozen ponds and at the local rink.

"He would put on his skates at home, on Oak Street, and walk five blocks to the rink, which was next to our parish church, St. Aloysius. He would play there for hours and hours, sometimes by himself, just a boy with his stick and his puck. He'd stay so long that my mother would have to call the priest and say, 'Please send Patrick home.' And the priest would say, 'Oh, that's all right. I've already brought him in and given him dinner.' Later on, she'd call again and say, 'Father, really, tell Patrick to come home now.' When he walked in the house, he'd be so bush-tired, he could hardly stand on his skates. My mother would take his skates off and put his feet in the oven to warm them up."

Interestingly, in his own recollections, Burns would often transpose these events, resituating them in St. Henri, maintaining the fiction that his childhood was spent largely there, within walking distance of the Forum. But there may have been psychological reasons for editing history.

While closeness to Violet was probably a factor in Louise's decision to move to Gatineau, that particular event seems also to have been prompted by romance. Louise had by then met the man who would become her second husband. Her children were never certain exactly when or how Louise came to encounter Harvey Barbeau, a widower with a grown son, but it may have been as early as the family's tenancy in Châteauguay. What they all agree on is ruing the day he became their stepfather.

"He was a filing clerk for Veterans Affairs," says Diane, "and he was an alcoholic. Mum didn't know it at first because he never drank in front of her. I really think at this point our mother was eager to get her own home, her own house, which she'd never had. So they got married." To Diane and Pat, their mother's new husband was always Harvey, never

Dad. He worked in Ottawa, but Louise insisted on living in Gatineau, which is where Pat came of age.

"It was not a good union," says Diane of Louise's lengthy second marriage. "Harvey stayed in her life for thirty-five years. He wasn't physically abusive or anything, not to me and not to Pat. But my mother was a fighter. So, if he'd come home drunk, she'd fight. Pat and I would go in the bedroom, kind of hide. We didn't want to be there when the fighting was going on, so the two of us would stay in the bedroom, with the door closed.

"Harvey had a good job with the government and got a good pension, on top of his army pension, so Mom eventually had a bit of money. Oh my God, she did the best she could, a very courageous woman. But this all had a terrible impact on Pat. Harvey was not a good father to Pat. It was actually Violet's husband, Bill Hickey, who treated us more like he was our father. Pat got very close to Bill Hickey when he was young. Bill took us to the beach, took us driving, did a lot of things with us. Whenever Harvey would have a big blowout, Bill would come and get us, take us to my sister's house. It was all very scarring—more so for Pat, I think. Pat grew up with a chip on his shoulder, and I can't blame him. He was only three when our father died, so, whenever we talked about Dad, to him it was like a stranger. I could remember our father, but Pat never really knew him. Then my mother gets remarried to Harvey, who's an alcoholic and no father figure for Pat. Our family is scattered all over and here's Pat, hiding under the bed."

He found his comfort elsewhere. As an adolescent, Burns became deeply engrossed in music, teaching himself to play guitar. Like motorcycles, expensive guitars would later become his adult toys of choice. By age twelve, he had put together his own little garage band, and a year afterwards, when Diane married, that band played at her wedding reception.

Though boastful occasionally about adolescent misbehaviour, the usual scrapes and snarls that accompany the ripening of boys, Pat was in fact no trouble as a teenager. He had lots of friends and was somewhat protected from temptations within the bubble of sleepy Gatineau. He was a poor student, his worst marks in math; had zero interest or scholarly aptitude to pursue college; never even got his high school diploma, so impatient was he to get on with growing up and earning his own livelihood. Burns attended St. Aloysius until Grade 9, endured Grade 10 at St. Patrick's High School, and then quit. He continued playing organized hockey as a decent winger—a bruising type, with a bum knee, never rising very high in junior, undrafted, realizing early that there would be no NHL for him, although allegedly invited to attend the St. Louis Blues' training camp as a walk-on, which he declined.

For a year, he'd been a member of the Governor General's Foot Guards and studied welding at Ottawa Technical School. Then, shocking everyone in his family—and lying about his age—the seventeen-year-old joined the Ottawa police force. Louise wasn't having any of that. She marched off to the office of the Gatineau police chief—a man she'd never met before—and demanded that her son be hired on the local force, if the teen insisted on becoming a cop. Louise Burns Barbeau in mother-hen dudgeon was a formidable, irresistible force. "If she wanted something, she'd get it," says Diane. "Harvey used to call her the mayor of Gatineau."

For his part, Burns would say that it was the Gatineau chief who'd lured him into law enforcement as a career. "I said something like, 'What, are you crazy?' Then he said, 'You know, we've got motorcycles.' And that was it. I was sold." In fact, that wasn't it, and the Gatineau police didn't have motorcycles. But to an unskilled, unschooled teenager, policing offered a preferable alternative to working in the local paper mill, the town's major employer. "There weren't a lot of choices open to me," said Burns. So he was dispatched to the police academy in Aylmer. When he formally earned his cop chops and took up duties in Gatineau, in 1970, Burns was making a whopping $39 a week. "What do I do?" Burns asked of his police chief when he started on the job. And he was told: "Here's the hat, here's the whistle, here's the gun. Just follow the older guys. And point the gun away from you. It you want it to work, you pull that trigger."

He was given twenty-four uniform shirts and wondered, why so many? First shift on the job, working 8 p.m. to 4 a.m., police were called to break up a fight at a hotel. "I just knew half my friends would be in this place," Burns recounted to a Boston reporter years later. "Sure enough, I walk in and it's a bunch of my friends. I tell 'em to break it up, and they just laugh and say, 'Bleep you.' All of a sudden, I get stung, hit by a good punch on the side of the head. I'm covered in blood and my shirt gets torn off. Right there, I said, 'Hey, that's why they gave me twenty-four shirts.'"

It was around this time that a "gorgeous" young woman, Suzanne Francoeur, entered the picture. All his life, Burns would draw some of the prettiest ladies in the room, enticed by his sexy manliness, charmed by his personality, then inevitably crazed by his inability to stay put on the porch. Not long after they met, Suzanne discovered she was pregnant. That floored Burns. He was nineteen.

"I remember him coming home and telling my mother that Suzanne was pregnant, and Mom telling him that he had to marry her," says Diane. "It was a shotgun wedding. Suzanne wanted to marry him, but Pat was forced into it. He'd just started on the Gatineau police force at the time and he didn't want to cause a scandal. So he just gave in and got married. But he always knew this would be a short-term marriage."

Eleven months was all it lasted, just long enough to see Suzanne through the birth of their daughter, Maureen. The couple was not compatible and had issues thornier than their youthfulness, their palpable unpreparedness for matrimony. Suzanne, whisper relatives, was "a drinker," alcohol perhaps consolation for a rapidly disintegrating marriage. In one mortifying incident just before the couple separated, Burns responded to a police call about a drunken woman who needed assistance.

"Pat and I are in the squad car, he's driving," recalls a fellow Gatineau officer. "So, we show up at this address, and guess who it is on the street? Yup, Suzanne. They were going through stressful times as a couple. When she saw Pat, she took a fit. She was screaming, 'Get away from me! Get away from me!' I tried to calm her down, then she started giving it to me, too. Finally, I managed to cool her down and an ambulance showed up, took her away. That was tough for Pat. He was upset and embarrassed."

More frequently, it was his inebriated stepfather that Burns was called upon to scoop off the street. The army vet Harvey Barbeau was a habitué of the Legion hall. "Other cops would call Pat and say, 'Go get your stepfather and take him home,'" says Diane. "That would embarrass him no end, but he'd do it. And he'd give Harvey shit, but nothing changed."

Separated and then divorced from Suzanne, Burns became a fading presence in his young daughter's life, though he did try, clumsily, to fulfill his responsibilities as a daddy. "He'd go by once in a while and bring Suzanne back to my mother's place," says Diane, who was godmother to the child. "Of course, Mom would end up babysitting Maureen more than anything else. Pat did and paid what he could, but there was no formal child-support arrangement." It was a parental abandonment for which Burns would attempt to atone many years later.

There would be other women in Gatineau, a slew of them. And why not? Burns was young, handsome, beguiling. "A ladies' man, definitely," says John Janusz, who had two lengthy stints as his detective partner. "But it's not like he did the chasing. The women were more often chasing him. And maybe the uniform. The ladies have something for the uniform. Not only did Pat have the uniform, he had the looks and everything else to go with it. He was cool, man. I always wanted to me like him." Janusz laughs. "Actually, I wanted to *be* him."

His next serious relationship was with another beauty, Danielle Sauvé, who worked in the Gatineau library. Living together for five mostly happy years, though never wed, the couple had one child, a son, Jason. Burns would be a somewhat more attentive dad with Jason, even after departing Gatineau. The relationship with Danielle ended crushingly, each accusing the other of infidelity. Betrayal wounded Burns deeply. They tried to work it out, partly for Jason's sake but also because they did love one another, despite everything, but the relationship never recovered.

Single again, with two young children and absolutely no desire to procreate further, distrustful now of women who might manoeuvre him into marriage or a parallel commitment, Burns, still in his twenties, got a vasectomy. There would be no more pregnancies, planned or otherwise. "I like families," Burns told a girlfriend a decade later. "I like watching parents with their kids. I just don't want to be that family."

Given his domestic history, a family mutilated by the loss of its patriarch and repeatedly shifting domiciles thereafter, it's understandable that Burns, rather than seeking out constancy and hard covenants of mutual faith in his relationships, would have gone in the opposite direction, resisting deep attachments. What's more surprising is that, for someone raised almost entirely by females—a mother and four older sisters—Burns had precious little insight into women. He was the overweening, cosseted son of a domineering mother, and maybe that relationship influenced every adult liaison upon which he ventured.

"He didn't have the knowledge of what a man could be or do for a woman," suggests Diane. "I don't think he had that, because he never saw that. My mother was a very dominating person. Whether he was afraid of that or not, I don't know. Perhaps it affected him, thinking, 'If I get involved with these women, they're going to start ruling me too, and I don't want that.' I think it made him more standoffish. He certainly was attractive to beautiful women, and they were attracted to him. There was never a time when he wasn't with a woman, but it's like he wasn't looking for a genuine partner in life. He liked being taken care of. He always needed someone there and looked to women to fulfill a traditional role, doing things for him, which was strange, because our mother was definitely not a submissive person."

When Burns did remarry, at age forty-nine, taking the plunge was largely dictated by the logistics of immigration. His girlfriend was Canadian and he was by then coaching in Boston. She could not reside with him permanently unless they married, though Burns had first proposed before the Bruins job was offered.

Louise Burns lived to an indomitable ninety-two, continuing to dye her hair blond throughout her eighties, always impeccably groomed, stylishly dressed and with complete make-up, even when resettled in a senior citizens' home in Aylmer that had once been a monastery, threatening at one point to marry a fellow octogenarian resident, which sent her son into conniptions. Burns remained devoted to Louise, no matter how outrageous her behaviour, showering the woman with anything she coveted, including "the Cadillac of walkers." When there was an item Louise fancied, she'd call Diane and say, "If Pat wants to buy me something, here's what I want."

Endlessly, over the years, Louise would phone her son to correct anything he'd done or said that provoked her disapproval. "Pat was a dandy. He got that from Mom," says Diane. "But if she didn't like what he was wearing when she saw him on TV, she'd let him know. Or when she spotted him smoking a cigar during an interview, she told him to stop that. Then he started chewing tobacco, and she phoned, said, 'Stop that. It doesn't look good.' And he listened to her."

To the end, Louise basked in the reflected glory of her youngest child's extraordinary success, as chuffed with his celebrity as any of the arm-candy dames he squired. "From the time he first became an NHL coach, anytime we went anywhere—shopping, things like that—she would say who she was," Diane remembers fondly. "She'd say, 'You know who I am? I'm the mother of Pat Burns.'"

Chapter Two
Detective Story

"Once a cop, always a cop."

IT COULD HAVE BEEN a scene from a James Cagney gangster movie, with boilerplate dialogue. In the defendant's box, a young man committed to stand trial for murdering a priest turns to the detective who arrested him and snarls, "You're going to die, you dirty dog."

Pat Burns was that detective. He and his partner had solved one of the most sensational murder cases in Hull's history—the ghastly slaying of a Catholic priest who'd sadly gone trolling for a male prostitute. Father Roger Rinfret was found by a maid, lying in a pool of blood in his room at the Ritz Motel in Gatineau. He'd been stabbed nine times in the chest, twice in the back and twice in the throat. There were also cuts on the inside of his left hand and on his arms, suggesting the victim had struggled with his assailant.

Gay sex, murder, a priest—it had all the elements of lewd scandal. Burns told reporters early in the investigation that the police had no suspects and no motive, but he actually did have a clue for both in what had transpired the night of March 30, 1980. The detectives at first followed a lead emanating from another suspect—a vicious and violent local felon and Millhaven Penitentiary prisoner who'd escaped from custody in midtown Ottawa while being transported by two officers, after holding a knife to their throats. Burns thought that knife might have been used to kill Rinfret. But that trail fizzled out, so Burns and his partner turned their attention elsewhere, learning early from interviews conducted with lowbrow characters that Rinfret was a closeted homosexual—what other kind could there be in the Catholic clergy?—who occasionally sought to satisfy his compulsions on the seamy side of the street. Burns, then twenty-eight and assigned to his first homicide, had spent weeks undercover with his partner at Major's Hill Park, then a notorious gay haunt—a stakeout that led them to Alain McMurtie and another man, identified in court records only as Mr. X.

The forty-nine-year-old Rinfret had been a priest for twenty-four years, seven of them spent as pastor at St. Matthieu's Church in Gatineau before moving on to L'Ange Gardien Church in Masson, a Hull suburb. On the Sunday evening he was so brutally butchered, Rinfret had dinner with friends in Aylmer, then left alone to check into a motel, ostensibly so he could catch up on his sleep—overnight retreats away from the pressures of the parish were not uncommon. As would become known at the preliminary inquiry, Rinfret had encountered his killer while sitting in a car outside the posh Château Laurier hotel in Ottawa.

McMurtie and a friend had spent that evening smoking hash, gulping Valium and drinking beer. He suggested, "Let's go and roll one," meaning mug somebody. McMurtie, twenty years old, had been a prostitute at Major's Hill Park since the age of thirteen. Rinfret, as fate would have it, was the priest who'd buried his father. Outside the Château, around 10 p.m., McMurtie and his friend propositioned the target, wondered if he was interested in "a party for three." The man agreed and drove them to the Ritz Motel. Once inside the room, the client asked for a kiss. And McMurtie stabbed him, over and over again, knifing Rinfret with such ferocity that he severed an artery in the priest's left forearm.

The previous evening, McMurtie had picked up another client with a secret sex life. This was Mr. X, a prominent citizen who was desperate to keep his homosexuality hidden from family and his trolling expeditions hidden from the public. Mr. X brought McMurtie home. There, unprovoked, McMurtie began slicing at Mr. X with the butcher knife he would later use on Rinfret. But this victim fended off the onslaught, saving his life by promising to keep quiet about the attack.

At the preliminary hearing, Burns took the stand, providing investigative evidence against the accused deemed sufficient to send the case to trial. But it was the threatened testimony of Mr. X that convinced McMurtie to plead guilty—even as a mistrial seemed to be within his grasp—to second-degree murder in the killing of Rinfret, a crime described by the judge as committed "with savagery and sadistic fury." McMurtie was sentenced to life in prison at Laval Penitentiary, with the possibility of parole after ten years served.

In yet another twist of fate, Burns had known McMurtie well before the young man murdered the priest—he'd been his minor hockey coach. "He was a little brat, but he didn't show any violent streaks," Burns told *Ottawa Citizen* reporter Bob Marleau. "I remember warning him that he was going to get into a lot of trouble if he didn't smarten up."

Burns toiled sixteen years as a full-time cop, half his adult life, and that profession shaped his persona, his view of the world and the world's view of him, just as much as the other half spent coaching in the NHL. "Pat worked morality, alcohol, drugs, undercover," recalls John Janusz, who had two long hitches as Burns's detective partner in Gatineau, including their co-investigation of the stunning Rinfret murder. "You can imagine— priest in a motel room, gay sex. A good six months we worked on that case, got introduced to some of the people in the gay community through the Ottawa police, managed to resolve it. But it was intense . . . intense. And then, in the witness box, that guy threatens to eliminate him. You couldn't intimidate Pat, though, not with his Irish character."

The priest murder would be the highlight of Burns's policing career. Most cases were nowhere as dramatic, though oftentimes equally colourful or just plain goofy, as if plucked from old *Barney Miller* scripts. There was the Gatineau alderman who had his house broken into, three masked men aiming a shotgun in his face, robbing him of $14,700 in cash and jewellery.

Though the culprits wore stocking masks, the alderman, Claude Bérard, would later recognize one of them in a Masson bar. Bérard pretended to befriend the man, invited him home, then forced the guy to apologize to his wife for the horror the gang had put them through, before calling police. Burns took that call-out, recounting at a bail hearing his bemusement when he arrived at the scene and was handed a contrite suspect. He elicited enough information from the fellow to fly to Edmonton and arrest two others in connection with the robbery, catching a couple of Oilers games while he was at it.

Another memorable investigation had Burns undercover at a massage parlour operating as a bordello. A team of four cops put the Minou Noir under surveillance, scooping up a dozen of its clients for interrogation. One of them, apparently miffed about the "unsatisfactory" rub-a-dub he'd received, told investigators the masseuse had offered to take off her top for a further five dollars or masturbate him for twenty. Burns and his colleagues moved in for the raid, charging the owner and his wife with keeping a common bawdy house. At trial, Burns denied having threatened to charge the customers as found-ins if they didn't cooperate. But it was a touchy case that made enemies for Burns in high places: the parlour owner was an ex–Ottawa police sergeant.

Then there was the time he got clobbered by a woman wielding a frozen turkey when he tried to break up a domestic scuffle. Knocked Burns out cold, that wallop, though the story clearly got embellished over the many years of retelling. "Knocked out by a turkey. I had the cranberry sauce running down my neck. I had the stuffing in my ears. I was out. My partner had to subdue the woman and the man."

And the drunk driver he'd arrested, who later returned to the station brandishing a gun, which sent everybody ducking for cover, though Burns was out having lunch and missed the excitement. A sardonic sense of humour helped him cope with the crazies and the more common boring stretches of law enforcement. Once, the squad took into custody a strong suspect in a string of assaults who was refusing to cooperate. As it happened, their property room was full of costumes recovered from a truck robbery.

Burns proposed getting into a full Easter Bunny suit, his face covered by the floppy-eared mask, then entering the suspect's cell and beating the guy with his big felt-padded paws "until he talked." That suggestion was declined.

Hull's police force would become amalgamated with Gatineau's while Burns wore the uniform. For a long time previously, the two towns had spun in different orbits, though both were a late-night booze option for Ottawa tipplers. "Gatineau bars closed at 3," Burns remembered. "We'd sit in the cruiser and watch the cars come over the bridge. It was like watching an invasion of drunks."

Oh, how Burns loved to tell those cop stories after it was all safely behind him, feet up on the desk in his office, surrounded by an appreciative audience of reporters. When in the mood for gabbing, no one in the game was more entertaining a raconteur. Whether the tales were always true was irrelevant, though they had the ring of authenticity. After a reporter in Montreal published some of those accounts, Burns feigned indignation: "Listen, I put away a lot of bad guys. Some of them can even read."

When Pat joined the force in Gatineau, new recruits pulled the swing shift, 8 p.m. to 4 a.m., then worked their way to a squad car and eventually an investigative team. He and Janusz, who arrived a couple of years later, were the only English speakers in the department in the mid-'70s, so were drawn to each other even before being partnered as patrolmen and, afterwards, detectives. "His name was Burns and mine was Janusz," notes Janusz of their non-francophone commonality. "We both spoke English, we both came from Montreal." Both had also lost their fathers young. "We clicked."

Burns drew approval from the senior management ranks by his willingness to learn French after someone pointed out the fleur-de-lis on his uniform shoulder. It was a language he'd always understood growing up but had never learned to speak properly, mastering only snatches of the slangy *joual* version—eloquent Québécois street French. The issue would take on political significance when Burns got the coaching job in Montreal and had to deal daily with an aggressive francophone media that sneered at his pronunciation and accent. But as a newbie cop, he strove to improve his communication skills by taking French courses and submitting reports in both languages. "He didn't speak the best French, but it was colourful," smiles Janusz.

Burns went from traffic patrolman with a radar gun—though Gatineau did finally get those falsely advertised motorcycles—to walking a beat, to his own scout car, to unmarked vehicles, huge black Chevrolets immediately clocked by the bad guys. With the amalgamation of five regional police forces, management broke the Gatineau detachment down into three investigative teams. "We wore civilian clothes, drove unmarked vehicles," says Janusz. "We'd patrol and do surveillance, try to get information or find people for the sergeants that were in that criminal investigation branch. Pat and I were constables, but we ended up in criminal investigations together. They gave us the title *agent enquêteur,* which was basically a fancy way of saying an investigator or detective."

From the start, Burns had a knack for eliciting dope from contacts and snitches, slipping smoothly into the riffraff strata, the underbelly of urban crime. It was a peculiar talent, an intuitive instinct, but tailor-made for an ambitious cop. "He could talk to anybody," says Janusz. "To get information, you've got to have an approach, be able to speak to people in their milieu. He worked that. He could adapt. If he needed to be hard-nosed, he would be hard-nosed. And if he needed to be cool, he was cool."

Working undercover was the coolest cool of all. Burns tackled that challenge enthusiastically, growing his hair long—for a while, he actually sported a salon-perm Afro—cultivating goatee, sideburns and moustache, outlaw biker–style. He was fascinated by the desperado creed, felt at ease within that anti-establishment ethos. On many occasions later in life, Burns would admit that, had he not become a police officer, he might very well have gone the other way, seduced into vice. To a large extent, as a civilian, he would reproduce a quasi biker gang among friends similarly piggish about hogs, choppers, Harleys—the "Red Dogs," they'd call themselves—setting off on long *vroom-vroom* rides across Canada and the

U.S., rarely missing the annual motorcycle rally in Laconia, New Hampshire. His fondness for that culture—and some of the genuine biker gang kingpins held him in affection, too, probably too close an arm-around—would land him in hot water two decades later, when Burns's name came up in intercepts captured during a police investigation of Montreal's motorcycle mob.

"There was a pool room on the main drag in Gatineau, and all the bikers hung out there," remembers Janusz. "They had their patches and their shaved heads. They were called the Popeyes, out of Quebec, and then they became the Hells. They were involved with drugs, fencing stolen goods. Pat would go there and talk to them. He used to call them scumbags. But he could talk to them and feel comfortable with them, go the whole nine yards. He didn't fear them. Was he respected by the scumbags? Yeah, I really think he was."

In one of his own versions of those undercover days, the exaggerating Burns would claim to have actually *joined* the Outlaws, at a time when that gang was in full-out war with the rival Hells Angels, Hull affiliate. "Had my hair in a ponytail, drove a big Harley-Davidson. That wasn't a bad assignment. Drink beer all day and watch the girls dance in the topless bars."

Burns would never shake off the street-savvy cop reputation in his reincarnation as a coach—indeed, his law-enforcement background is precisely what captivated prospective GMs—but sixteen years on the force, deeply immersed in the funk of criminality, tainted him forever as well, skewed his view of the world and fostered a deep-rooted distrust of humanity. "Once a cop, always a cop," says Janusz. "People who are in our business, you get to see everything that's wrong in the world because nobody calls police when things are going great, only when something is wrong. You see that stuff and you learn; it stays with you always. It's hard for us to trust anybody. We might come to trust you, but it ain't gonna be on the first date."

It's easy to forget how much time Burns put in as a cop. But all the while, he kept up his interest in, and participation with, sports. He continued playing on a Junior B team in Hull, then a senior team, despite bad knees. "It was all fights, rough *Slap Shot* hockey, with people throwing rocks at the bus when we left town," he recalled. He joined the police force's softball team and immersed himself in coaching kids, from mosquitos through peewee, bantam and midget. One of his midget teams, the Hull Kiwanis, featured a shy kid from a rural Quebec town by the name of Stéphane Richer. A midget team he took over lost a tournament to the Ville-Émard Hurricanes when an elegant fourteen-year-old named Mario Lemieux scored an overtime goal. As time allowed, Burns attended local coaching clinics, thirsty for Xs-and-Os insight.

"He played a lot of sports, and was damn good at them, but he loved hockey," says Janusz. "At that time, when we were in criminal investigations, on Friday, towards the end of the afternoon when things were slowing down, everybody getting ready for the weekend, we'd all be sitting there and Pat would be talking about hockey. Like, if there were any big games coming up on the weekend, Pat would preview the game. And when we came back on Monday morning, sitting around drinking coffee and getting our files together, Pat would review the game. He'd give us his opinions as to the players, the coach, nah-nah-nah-nah-nah. He'd say, 'That idiot coach did this or did that, I would have done this and that.' He was essentially analyzing the game and telling us what he would have done as coach, the decisions he would have made. Where did that hockey smarts come from? You've got me. It's not like he'd had anybody mentoring him.

"I always said, 'Pat, one day we're going to see you on the screen analyzing hockey.' I'd joke, 'Pat, you're going to be the next Don Cherry.' Because he had . . . not necessarily the same attitude as Cherry, but Pat could be funny and also get to the point. Programs you see now on TV where they're talking about hockey, guys on a panel, we had that with Pat then. He was doing this long before he became an NHL coach, analyzing and assessing. He saw things the rest of us couldn't see. We were fans, but it was as if he was *investigating* the games."

Burns was coaching a Midget AAA team, roped into the gig by an ailing friend and taking it all the way to a championship, the Daoust Cup. At the buzzer, he looked up and motioned to Janusz to come and celebrate with them on the ice at the Robert Guertin Arena in Hull. "So I go down there, never imagining what he'd become one day. There's Pat with this trophy. It was a small trophy, but it meant so much. After that, things kind of started opening up for him in hockey. He got his opportunities."

Balancing those midgets and his day job was a time-juggling strain. The manager of the midget team was himself a Gatineau police inspector who cut Burns some slack on the roll call. More often, it was Janusz covering for him. "The scheduling was, we worked two weeks of days and one week of nights, Monday to Friday. There were weeks where we worked nights, starting at three in the afternoon and going to midnight. Plenty of nights, Pat had hockey games to coach. He'd say, 'Fuck, John, I have to go, gotta go, gotta go, you're going to cover for me, right?' I'd say, 'Okay, but if the shit hits the fan, a homicide or something else really big, you're gonna have to get your butt out of the arena and back over here.' To be honest, I was kind of nervous about it. I mean, he's kind of cheating the company a bit. But it's hockey, right? So I did it and I'm comfortable admitting that today. That was my little contribution to his career. But did I ever think this would all lead to him becoming an NHL coach? Nope. At most, I thought maybe he might coach in juniors or the minor leagues, maybe as an assistant coach in the NHL. But head coach? Coaching three of the Original Six clubs? Coach of the year three times? The Stanley Cup? Noooo, I would never have bet any money on that."

While with the midget team, Burns did a bit of scouting on the side for the Hull Olympiques (now the Gatineau Olympiques) of the Quebec Major Junior Hockey League. Meanwhile, they'd been scouting *him*. He was offered, and eagerly seized, the job as Hull's assistant coach in 1983, while continuing full-time employment as a police officer. "It was crazy, eh," he recalled. "I was a detective-sergeant by then, working days with the fraud unit, seven to three, mostly writing reports. I'd go straight from the station to the rink. Practice was from four to six. Games. Road trips. I worked a deal where I took my vacation time in hours instead of days. I'd work until noon and then get on the bus and go to the game. Crazy."

The next season, after finishing second-last and missing the playoffs for the fourth time in eleven years, head coach Michel Morin returned to teaching and the gig went to Burns. But mountains had to be moved to make it so.

Sniffing around the team at that time was a veteran hockey hand by the name of Charlie Henry, with his quarter-century of experience in the minors and junior ranks. Henry was, and remains, an avuncular aide-de-camp to none other than Wayne Gretzky. "I was working for Wayne then. I still work for Wayne now." The Great One had just sold his 46.5 per cent ownership stake in the Belleville Bulls of the Ontario Hockey League. "He said, 'Why don't we buy another team?' and I said fine. Lo and behold, the Hull team looked available." In fact, the sad-sack Olympiques, then owned by the city, had just declared bankruptcy. "Once they found out that Wayne was looking to buy the team, they were on their knees to sell, right?"

Burns, as assistant coach, would have been part of the package, but Gretzky and Henry, who became general manager, knew they wanted him as top boss behind the bench. "We were looking to change the attitude of the team," says Henry, who'd clandestinely observed some of the practices that Burns ran. "And we didn't have to look very far. I'd investigated other possibilities when we were buying the team. I looked all over, change this and change that, but we had the coach we wanted right there. It was a matter of 'This is who we want.' I talked to Pat and he jumped right in."

It was Gretzky who made the come-hither call. Burns was at home when the phone rang. "Pat, it's for you," said his girlfriend. Yeah, who is it? "They say it's from Edmonton, person-to-person," she said. "They say it's Wayne Gretzky." Burns thought it was a prank, but took the phone. The voice on the other end said, "Hi Pat, this is Wayne Gretzky." Burns, still convinced his cop pals at the station were having fun at his expense, growled: "Yeah, quit [bleeping] around." Caller: "No, really, it's me." Finally, Gretzky was able to convince the suspicious Burns that he was legitimate. He wanted Burns to stay on the job as Hull head coach. "Look,

I appreciate it," said Burns. "But I'm a police officer, not a hockey coach. I've had no time off and you don't understand, I've gone through hell the last year."

But the next day he was on a plane to Edmonton, at Gretzky's expense, and a deal was struck. Obvious logistical issues remained. "He still had a full-time job with the police department at that time," recalls Gretzky. "But we really believed he was going to be an NHL coach one day and that, if we got him, his tenure with the Olympiques probably wouldn't last that long. I said to Charlie, if we're going to pursue him, we'd have to catch him when we could, dive right in. There was a potential of us losing him rapidly. We thought we might be able to keep him for a year before an NHL team came calling."

No way though that Burns could maintain the manic pace of two jobs, each requiring his full attention. Gretzky personally made a call to the Gatineau chief. Henry followed up. "I went to see the mayor," says Henry. "I said, if we want to make a coach out of this young man, because he's got the capability, I need a [year's leave] of absence for him. That had never been done before. But I knew the mayor and he agreed. He said, 'Okay, I'll give you a year, but that's it.'" As Gretzky remembers it, denying with typical modesty that his participation in the plot carried any significant persuasive effect on Hizzoner: "They were very obliging. They knew that this was somebody who was going to be an NHL coach someday. I'm not sure anything I did was responsible for pushing it over the edge. Maybe I nudged them a bit. The people up there understood this was Pat's destiny and the NHL wasn't going to be very far down the road. Pat had such a good hockey mind, a strong presence, and he was a very hard worker."

Convinced that having a cop on staff who simultaneously coached for a Gretzky-owned team was an ambassadorial coup for the community, the police chief made the necessary arrangements, granting the leave of absence. Burns was doubly delighted because he received a good salary to coach the Olympiques while keeping his accumulated police force seniority and benefits. At that point, he and partner Janusz essentially parted professional company, though they remained friends till the end of Burns's life. Eventually, Janusz would become chief of police in Gatineau. Today, he's Director General, Security Services—deputy sergeant-at-arms—for the House of Commons. For a couple of scruffs from Montreal, each made good.

What Gretzky and Henry most liked about Burns were the obvious assets he brought: his hockey savvy—self-taught—and the hard-nosed cop reputation that preceded him. "He was disciplined, no-nonsense and firm in his decisions," says Henry. "When you talked to the players, they liked him, but they were scared of him. Oh yeah, he was tough. He could be a real P-R-I-C-K. I don't know if he could coach today, to be honest, because the type of discipline that he brought . . . a lot of times there was a lot of fear. Players were scared of Pat, and that was true when he got to the NHL, too." Adds Gretzky: "These were young guys he was coaching, sixteen to twenty years of age. He would be sharp with them, whether they liked it or not. He was always extremely honest with all of his players, sometimes even if they didn't want to hear it."

Henry would become yet another in the long line of substitute dads for Burns. "He could have been looking for a father figure." And the weathered hockey guru was careful not to put the team's well-being ahead of the "beautiful man" he came to love. While confident this novice would ultimately land in the NHL, he prudently attempted to craft a Plan B, lest that didn't happen. Known widely in the Ottawa region, where he'd been a fireman, and with a slew of contacts in all manner of business enterprises, Henry one day suggested to Burns that, well, if things didn't work out hockeywise, he could probably arrange for Burns to be hired as head of security at A.J. Freiman's, the capital's largest department store. He was taken aback by Burns's explosive reaction. "He got insulted! What I'd meant was, he didn't have to worry about ending up unemployed if he didn't go back to the police force, that he could go the department store and be the man in charge. Pat was, 'Jesus Christ, you think all I'm good for is security!'"

In any event, when that year's leave of absence was over—the Olympiques had shot up to second place in their division and fifth overall, losing the championship semifinals in five games—Henry was not about to let his coaching gem return to pounding a beat, or even solving homicides. "When that year was over, Pat was told he wasn't getting another leave. So now I went back to the mayor in Hull and got him to come with me to see the police chief, the two of us together, to get Pat Burns another year leave of absence. Lo and behold, we got it again."

There would be no need for a third sabbatical. As a cop, Pat Burns was done.

He'd never once drawn his gun.

Chapter Three
Adventures in the "Q"

"Sure, I was a bit of a showman coach in junior hockey."

IT WAS THE DAY after a stinker of a night before. The Hull Olympiques had lost a big game—lost it bad. Players, geared up, were huddled in the dressing room prior to practice, nervously awaiting the thunderclap of Pat Burns, a coach who could peel the paint off the walls with his blistering tirades even when his team *won*. "The trainer tells us nobody goes on the ice until Pat comes in," recalls defenceman Cam Russell. "Of course, we're shaking in our skates, worried about getting skated until we threw up. And Pat finally walks in with the trainer and four cases of beer. So everybody sat around and drank. It was a different time, right?" Burns circulated around the room for two hours, talking to the players. "The running joke became, if we had a bad game, we were always hoping the next day would be a beer practice. That was Pat. He had a lot of tricks up his sleeve and he knew went to pull them out."

Burns as trickster—and devotee of silly slapstick pranks—would remain a calling card throughout his career. Much of his future style behind the bench was forged during the three eventful years Burns spent as coach of the Hull Olympiques in the fiercely hardscrabble Q—the Quebec Major Junior Hockey League. Never a keen technician, Burns's particular strengths quickly emerged as motivator and ingenious hockey alchemist, a guy who could draw every last ounce of potential out of his players. This skill would be the catalyst for the rapid improvement of all NHL teams he took over, especially in his first year with clubs, and it was what made him so alluring to GMs.

Every player who fell under the Burns spell in junior hockey would subsequently acknowledge how crucial he'd been in their evolution towards the NHL, a roster of comers that included the likes of Russell, Luc Robitaille and Benoît Brunet, all of whom passed through his hands in Hull, a team Burns took to the Memorial Cup in 1986. The past is a different country in the United States of Hockey—in it, Pat Burns was slim and sported a perm for a while—but Burns identified, recruited and enhanced raw talent, foster-coaching teenagers into young men who could step into an NHL lineup.

The Hull Olympiques (renamed Gatineau Olympiques in 2002, following municipal amalgamation) shared a junior hockey market and intense rivalry with the Ottawa 67's across the river. When Burns arrived as an assistant coach in 1983, club ownership was still held by the City of Hull. The previous season, the team had finished forty points behind their quarter-final opponents, Laval, though they would extend them to a seven-game playoff round. The city then relinquished ownership to a non-profit corporation.

As an assistant in the 1983–84 season, Burns didn't work from behind the bench because head coach Michel Morin preferred to act alone at ice level. Instead, Burns watched every game from the bleachers, taking notes. What he observed wasn't pretty; the Olympiques finished second to last in the Lebel Division, the fourth time in eleven years they had been excluded from the postseason, even with a very impressive left winger, Robitaille, drafted onto the squad and immediately saddled with the nickname "The Franchise."

Morin lasted only a year and returned to academia as the reins were handed to Burns, still shuttling between his policeman job and the rink. In '84–85, the Olympiques ranked second in their division, Robitaille acquitting himself as advertised, scoring 55 goals and 148 points. The team lost in five games against Verdun in the semifinals. Meanwhile, Gretzky formally assumed ownership, his press conference at the Hull convention centre attended by nearly 150 journalists from across North America. With Gretzky's éclat, the Olympiques would no longer fly below the radar. Prime Minister Brian Mulroney was in the stands at their season opener.

In Burns's second season in charge, the team was assembled to win, with Robitaille its flashiest star. "When I went to Hull the first year, Pat was an assistant coach-slash-cop," says Robitaille. "He would do most of the games at home and, when he could, he would travel with us. The next year, he took over as coach. The year before, we'd made the playoffs and got out in the first round, but we had a very good team coming up. That's why Pat kept his job when Wayne came in: because they knew he was doing something pretty special already."

"Demanding" is the first word that comes to mind when Robitaille reflects on the Burns tenure. "Yet he was also a great communicator. He was so emotional and you never forgot that he was the coach. But there were still times where he would hang out with us and have fun, and that made it special. If we won a game, he'd come into the back of the bus, sit down and joke with us for, like, three hours. That wouldn't happen if we lost, but we knew he'd be our buddy again when he won. Every guy who played for Pat loved Pat. If you were honest with Pat, he became your friend off the ice. But he had a way of translating that onto the ice, a coach you could both like and respect. He was one of the few coaches I've seen who was able to do that."

The impish part of Burns delighted in "screwing around" with his players, says Robitaille, getting inside their heads, but usually with a tactical purpose. There was a kid on the team, local boy, whom Burns adored because he played with ferocious emotion. "One time Pat came on the bus when we were travelling to another city. He was talking real loud. Then he winked at me and said that the centre on the team we were going to face was a real tough guy and that we might be making a trade to get him. It wasn't true, but Pat was trying to get that Hull kid all revved up. And of course, when the game started, he went right after that hotshot as soon as the puck dropped. Pat did whatever he had to do to get the best out of you and help us win."

The Burns Rules were simple. "You have to perform, bottom line," continues Robitaille. "If he said we had a curfew, everybody respected it. But he was a disciplinarian in the way that made sense. He wanted you to be a better hockey player. He wanted you to be respectful of the organization and the city that we played in, but he let you be a human being. He knew it was a game and had to be fun." Then, adding with a chuckle: "Of course, it was more fun for him when we won. But he helped me become a better player in the sense of understanding the sacrifices you have to make in order to win. And that's everything, as far as a player is concerned."

Although Burns, in his second season with Hull, told reporters he was giving himself two years to make the NHL—and met that self-imposed deadline—he never gave his junior players the impression of just passing through, eyeing a finer prize up ahead. "We didn't think that way, not even him," says Robitaille, who would make the leap directly out of junior and play nineteen seasons in the NHL, sixteen of them during three separate stints as a Los Angeles King, where he's now president of business operations. "He and I kind of started together, but whatever we were doing at the time, we thought that was the greatest. He loved being a coach in junior. Then he went to the AHL and he loved that. I don't think when Pat went to the AHL he thought, 'Okay, I'm going to be two years in the minors and then I'm going to the National Hockey League.' He went to the AHL and just thought, 'I want to win here.' He looked at the team and thought, 'I'm going to do the best that I can here.' When he turned to the NHL, he didn't think, 'I'm going to coach in this league for ten years.' I know he thought, 'What can I do for this team to be the best team it can be today?' And he grinded that into us in juniors, too.

"That's probably why he was only in one city three or four years at a time, because he did so much about *that* day—what was important *that* day." Which, frankly, is a euphemistic way of saying Burns could also exhaust his players by being so remorselessly demanding, paying the penalty when players—or a cabal of them—ultimately revolted years later, in the NHL. "He never protected his own angle," notes Robitaille. "It was never, 'Okay, if I make this decision I'll be here longer.'"

Few players had a more complicated relationship with Burns than Stéphane Richer, the quixotic French-Canadian luminary, heir apparent in Montreal to the reverence bestowed on The Flower, Guy Lafleur. He possessed a similar flair and flourish, if not the emotional equilibrium necessary to withstand the pressure unique to being a Canadien. Richer's tendency towards depression, mental brittleness, is a subject he's opened up about only in recent years; at the time, he was pigeonholed as a flake, even a diva, and he certainly tested Burns's patience.

Richer was only a child when their paths first crossed, fatefully so. "He's the one who saved my life. I always say, if not for him, I'm sure I would never have become a professional hockey player. He picked me out from this little town in Quebec, brought me to play for his midget team in Hull. Pat knew I was a lonely kid from up north who was supposed to be good, I guess. He was still a cop at the time, but he knew people around who were watching young players. Pat called my dad and asked if I was willing to leave my hometown to go to Hull. That was a big step for me. My dad said, 'Well, it's up to you, kid. Do you want to go there? Then you call Pat. We're not doing it for you. You be a man.'

"Here I was, a fourteen-year-old kid thinking of leaving home. But Pat said, 'I believe you can do something right in your life.'"

The adjustment was difficult. "Scared? Oh man. When you play minor hockey with all your buddies and suddenly you're playing in a big city like Hull—full equipment, new pants. I was like, 'Wow, what just happened here?'" He was also the smallest player, only five foot three and 135 pounds. Burns put him on the fourth line. Then he shot up to five foot ten by the end of the season.

Hull Kiwanis, Burns's midget team, was a culture shock for the yokel Richer. "For Midget AA, they were pretty good. All the guys were older than me. We were supposed to win everything, and we almost did. It was funny, though. Pat used to put his policeman's stuff on the table, put on the hockey gear for a couple of hours, then change back into his policeman clothes, get in his car and go back to work."

After enticing the young Richer to Hull, Burns showed him no favour, cut him no slack for his rawness, his disorientation. "It was always, 'Do you realize how lucky you are?' A lot of times, I was the one who had to pay the price for everyone else. Trust me, he was tough. We were all scared of him. Pat was a good hockey man, but he forgot that we were only fourteen and fifteen years old."

Richer would be drafted onto a Midget AAA team but would be reunited with Burns, with considerable misery for both, several years later in Montreal, after playing his junior hockey in Granby and Chicoutimi. "In juniors, I wasn't dreaming about the NHL. I was just trying to survive, pretty much; never thought about the next level, whatever it might be. But I knew if I wanted to do something great in my life—like Pat had told me—I had to take care of myself, accept the discipline. When you're away from your family, it's easy to go astray. Pat understood that and kept a very close eye on me."

The life skills Burns imparted, in tough-love mode, came with the job as a junior coach, even though in his personal life he was, in those days, a distant and only sporadically involved dad. Burns was ushering his protégés towards maturity while teaching them how to tap into depths of potential most didn't quite realize they possessed.

Yet there were surprisingly few technical tutorials at a level of organized hockey—both midget and juniors—where instruction is a primary component. "He was never a technical coach," says Richer. "Pat didn't know anything about technique, to be honest. I don't think he even knew that word at the time."

Cam Russell, who landed with the Hull Olympiques as a sixteen-year-old, shares that assessment. "He was a motivator all the way. There wasn't a lot of technical coaching in him: one defenceman in the corner, one defenceman in front of the net, forecheck hard, backcheck hard and make sure you give 100 per cent every shift—and if you didn't, you'd hear it from him. The biggest thing with Pat was accountability, and it didn't matter who you were. Our best players were our hardest-working players, and that's a great credit to your coach when you can get your skill guys to be your hardest-working guys."

When Russell arrived, Gretzky was the team's owner, the clincher in his opting for the QMJHL. As a teen from the Maritimes, Russell—from Cole Harbour, Nova Scotia—could have chosen from any of the three junior leagues in Canada: Quebec, Ontario or the Western League. "Wayne would sometimes come on the ice and practise with us—and this was Wayne Gretzky in his heyday. It's pretty amazing when the greatest player in the world is even mentioning your name, much less skating with you."

Where Gretzky inspired awe, there was, typically for his new young charges, outright terror where Burns was concerned. "Oh, he was an intimidating person, and not just for the players. He was also feared by opposing coaches," says Russell. "You never knew if he was going to come over the glass after you if you were the other team's coach. And that rubbed off on us. We felt like we had an extra man on the ice because we had Pat behind us. He was the big brother." In one particularly violent game, Burns actually did come over the glass, squaring off at centre ice with his opposite, Ron Lapointe, a fight neither would admit to losing, even years later. That notorious incident would carry into NHL bitterness when Burns was coaching Montreal and Lapointe took over behind the Quebec Nordiques bench. They *hated* each other and it was real, not staged, animus. Burns simply looked more the part, with his chronic scowl, glowering. His rare smiles, in-game, were sneers.

"At my first training camp in Hull, I was standing outside the rink one day and this guy rides by on a motorcycle, all decked out in leather, with a beard," remembers Russell. "One of our players waved to him. I said, 'Who's that?' He said, 'That's Pat.' And this was a month after I'd started practising with the team. I didn't even recognize him. He was a big, imposing figure, intimidating, intense. But he was an intelligent guy, a great motivator and the kind of coach who always found a way to get the best out of you."

The youthful Russell, wet behind the ears though pegged early as a skill player, was agog, eyes like saucers, upon arrival in Hull. "This was my first time being coached by a professional. I didn't really have anyone to compare him to. It wasn't until later, when I'd played for some other guys, that I realized what a great coach he was."

Russell's first night at training camp, all the players were anxious, many pining for home. Burns joined the teens, sat down with them and cracked jokes, told stories for the next two hours. "He made us laugh, and that kind of broke the ice. Of course, the next day when the puck dropped, it was all business and Pat cracked the whip. But you respected that and you followed along because you knew that there was a fair side to him as well. Pat was the kind of guy, even though he had a tough exterior and looked like a big tough biker, he knew the right time to sit you down for a one-on-one talk. At that time, Hull was bringing in a lot of Maritimers and Americans, guys a long way from home. Pat had the gruff exterior but knew when you needed to have a good heart-to-heart. I had a tough time my first two years after leaving home, and he really helped me get through that."

Through three years up and down in the minors, and then a decade-long NHL career spent almost entirely with Chicago, Russell played for some of the hardest-nosed coaches in hockey, including Mike Keenan and Darryl Sutter. Burns had provided a primer for dealing with that type of individual. But it wasn't until much later on that Russell, eventually coach and now GM of the Halifax Mooseheads, would stop to consider where Burns had learned the tactics and psychology he applied. Unlike Russell, Burns had no significant mentors in the game, hadn't been exposed to elite coaching, and learned only by one-step-removed osmosis. Yet he thirsted for hockey knowledge and was alert to shifts in the style of the game as it was being played in the NHL. From close access to Gretzky, he adopted drills then almost exclusive to Edmonton Oilers practices, incorporating the long breakout in Hull, for all that he remained obsessed with defence-first hockey.

He was essentially self-taught about hockey, about handling athletes. Like others who came into his orbit, Russell suggests Burns's people instincts grew out of his policing years. "Being an officer, handling things like domestic disputes, he became someone who could read people, knowing what to say at the right time. That must have carried through into hockey. Hockey players, their psyches are delicate. Yet he just always seemed to say the right thing. It's like people who are successful in businesses without having a great education—he learned things quickly. He'd look at Cam Russell and think, 'What does Cam Russell need to make it to the next level?' He just knew. And those were the things that he worked on, the areas he made you better in. Growing up, I would usually win the most-sportsmanlike player awards. Pat taught me another level of intensity. He taught me how to show up every night and how to be consistent. Those are the things he really harped on me about."

Burns could browbeat, but he could also inspire. "Even as a young man, he commanded respect," says Pat Brisson, who played two seasons for Burns in Hull and would eventually become one of hockey's most powerful player agents. "You knew he wasn't there just for fun. He was there to get us to the next level, no messing around. It was written on his forehead."

Brisson had all but given up on a hockey career in the mid-'80s. At age twenty, having played junior all over the place, he enrolled at Ottawa University. One night, he ran into Burns. Almost offhandedly, Brisson wondered if Burns had any interest in securing his playing rights, which were held by Drummondville. To Brisson's surprise, Burns was receptive. "It took about three weeks, but Pat managed to get my rights traded to Hull." Looking back, Brisson remembers his remarkably cocky former self sashaying into Burns's office to push for more money before he'd even played one game as an Olympique. "I go in saying I want this and I want that. Pat said, 'Christ, I've been working on your frigging release and you're going to ask for another $100?' I thought I was gonna die or he was gonna kill me, cut me right there." Instead, Brisson's audacity was rewarded. "He ended up listening to me when I said, 'Man, I'm giving up university for this.' He gave me what I was looking for. Pat was intimidating, but if you had something to say that made sense, he'd listen. That was my first lesson in the art of negotiation. Pat was a tremendous influence on my life. There were no grey areas with Pat. It was his way or the highway, but he was no fake. Get on or get off."

Nor could Burns be conned by the creative excuses his players often invented when rationalizing a poor performance or simply being caught breaking curfew. "Hey, it's the same if you're an NHLer or a kid in juniors with $20 in your pocket," says Brisson. "You want to go out and have some fun. But Pat had a spiderweb of sources. This was Hull, and he was linked up everywhere, knew everything. If he confronted you, he knew the truth, he knew the story. If you tried lying to him, you were in trouble. The only thing he might forgive is if you were covering up for a roommate. He embraced that whole togetherness thing. But if you otherwise lied to him, he'd trade you or scratch you. Pat couldn't live with being lied to. It just bugged him too much." To that end, Burns vested responsibility in his older guys for seeing that players kept their noses clean. "He made sure the veterans were guiding us in the right direction. He loved those guys. Maybe the younger guys didn't quite feel the love as much as the older ones."

Many a time, none would feel the love; quite the contrary, Burns was already infamous for his spectacular eruptions of temper. One such incendiary episode remains burned into Brisson's memory. The team had just had a poor period when Burns strode into the dressing room. Inside the room was a bin used for collecting and recycling pop cans. "He starts kicking that bin, and his foot gets stuck in there. He tried kicking it across the room but he tripped and fell. You could tell he was embarrassed. It was funny, but none of us dared laugh. You could hear a pin drop."

Laughing at Burns could be fatal. "One player we had, an enforcement type, made some comment at practice when Pat was playing with us, just a joke. Pat couldn't take that. When you hit Pat's pride, you went to the wrong place. So Pat chased him right into the locker room. He didn't physically strike him, but he sure scared the hell out of him. Another time, we were losing something like 5–0 and he brought a guy right into the middle of the locker room to scream at him. With Pat, there was a time to have fun, but also a time to pay the price."

This was the squad, with eighteen players from the previous season, that Burns would take—or they would take him—to the Memorial Cup in 1986. The following year, Brisson had a tryout, unsuccessfully, with the Montreal Canadiens. He concluded there was no NHL in his future and was anxious to move on with his life, in a different direction. First, though, he had to explain his choice to Burns. "It was October 10—I remember the date exactly. I went to Pat's office and told him, 'I think I've made a decision to leave hockey. I just don't have it, I'm not going to make it to the NHL.'" Brisson had formulated a plan to move to Los Angeles, live with Luc Robitaille, start teaching hockey in California and see what opportunities arose. "Pat was, 'Are you sure? Because I can be more patient if you need more time.' Then he wished me good luck. But even that conversation, I was nervous having with him."

Junior hockey, with its long bus rides and pro aspirations, tends to cut the wheat from the chaff. Not all have realistic ambitions of making it to the NHL; some intuitively grasp this is as good as it gets, and rare are the examples of late-draft picks who will persevere and earn jobs in the big league. Benoît Brunet went unclaimed for Midget AAA, but was drafted by Hull in the sixth round from Midget AA and, to his surprise, stuck. He is among those who credit Burns for eventual matriculation to the NHL. Brunet has an alternate view of Burns's technical proficiency, or lack thereof. "He was the guy who made the difference to me in my career. A lot of people thought he was just a motivator, somebody who tried to intimidate his players. But I thought he was a good technical guy. It was just overshadowed by his personality, his character. I'd had good coaches in minor league, but he taught me how to play. We had a great team [in 1985–86], but we had a tough start and he took the time to go over the technical part of what we were doing wrong on the ice."

Brunet, who would go on to play for Montreal—he's now an analyst for Canadiens games on RDS—looks back and divides those Hull prospects into two camps: those who *got* Burns and those who didn't. "Pat would push and push and push. Some guys didn't understand that it was about trying to make us better. The guys who didn't understand what he was trying to teach didn't make it to the pros. If you understood that he was doing it for the right reasons, good reasons, that it would make you a better player in the long run, then you got Pat Burns." And Burns was prescient too about talent. "He gave the chance to some guys that people didn't expect to make the NHL. He saw something in players that others didn't see, who weren't key, and he put trust in us, pushed the right buttons. That was his best quality. If it wasn't for him, I wouldn't have turned pro, I'm pretty sure of it."

Late in the 1985–86 season, with the Olympiques already runaway leaders in their division, Burns made trades to add more muscle in preparation for the postseason, seeking to ensure the team had enough strength and stamina for a gruelling stab at the national championships. They won the President's Cup, the QMJHL championship trophy, for the first time in franchise history, with fifteen straight victories in the playoffs. It was on to the Memorial Cup in Portland, Oregon.

Their opponents were the Guelph Platers from the Ontario Hockey League, a team coached by Jacques Martin—in his first season in the OHL—with his signature style of sound discipline, backbone character and a tenacious forecheck. The Platers also had better goaltending and were rested from a four-day layoff. Martin broke down the first period of the deciding game into four five-minute segments, "and our objective was not to get beat in any of those segments." The Olympiques were weary. Their semifinal, a 9–3 victory on the Friday night over the Kamloops Blazers of the Western Hockey League, had ended at 11 p.m. Because of TV .commitments, the final started at eleven o'clock Saturday morning. Guelph right winger Luciano Fagioli scored goals eleven seconds apart in the opening period, and the Platers got another brace within thirteen seconds in the second period, en route to a 6–2 triumph. Hull got goals from Brunet and Robitaille. Robitaille and prolific scorer Guy Rouleau combined for fifteen goals in the tournament, but a Guelph defenceman, the late Steve

Chiasson, was selected as MVP for his solid play and leadership. Robitaille was designated Canadian major junior player of the year. Yet Burns was devastated. "There's no reason to be tired when you're winning," he grumped. "Guelph worked harder than we did." With Burns, that was the ultimate felony.

Burns's final season in Hull was a rebuilding year, focusing on youth. Lots of Americans were recruited. The Olympiques would finish fourth in their division and lose in the first round of the playoffs. Far more memorable, and scandalizing, in the annals of Pat Burns was his alleged complicity in the disaster that was the world junior championship that winter—when the lights went out in Piestany on January 4, 1987. Selected as an assistant coach to Bert Templeton for the squad deployed overseas, Burns was fingered by some in the media as an agent provocateur in the stunning bench-clearing brawl during the gold medal game against the Soviets, which resulted in a disgraceful exit by Canada from the tournament in Czechoslovakia and a three-year international ban hanging over the players' heads, a roster that included such future stars as Brendan Shanahan, Theoren Fleury and Pierre Turgeon.

It hadn't been Burns throwing haymakers on the ice in Piestany or exhorting his players to bolt the bench in a frenzy. Young Soviet Evgeny Davydov was identified as the first culprit to hop the boards. It hadn't been Burns who made the loopy decision to turn off the lights in the arena as television coverage faded to black, with disembodied commentary, Canada up 4–2 and assured of at least a bronze medal, though needing to defeat the Soviets by five or more goals to cop gold.

But Burns had admittedly seeded the ill will. Suspicious that Soviet coach Vladimir Vasiliev would try to bait the inexperienced referee, Burns lobbed a provocative shot across the bow, telling reporter Jim Cressman beforehand that he was planning to "stir things up." He added, "I'm not going to do anything stupid, but just try to keep his concentration off the game as much as I can." What this meant in practice was never specified, except that Burns was his usual glowering and yammering self behind the bench, hurling abuse at Vasiliev, who didn't need a Russian-English dictionary to grasp the menacing Canadian's words. But the assault was merely verbal.

Mayhem broke out early in the third period, a bloodying war that would have been unforgettable to anybody who saw it, except few actually could make out what was happening on the ice, including the combatants. Norwegian referee Hans Rønning and his two linesmen actually fled the scene, seeking shelter in the officials' room.

"A big-mouthed yo-yo who can't wait to agitate the opposition into yet another rumble," *Toronto Star* columnist John Robertson wrote of Burns in the next day's paper, from half a world away. It was a panic-stricken apparatchik from the International Ice Hockey Federation who gave the lights-out order in a vain attempt to douse the melee. Soviets and Canadians paired up, apparently intent on killing each other. It was the most wretched episode ever in international hockey, blackening the eye for country, coach and assistant coach, with heaps of I-told-you-so flung back home, Canadian hockey officials excoriated for putting a couple of known "hotheads"— Templeton and Burns—in charge of combustible youths. Yet future Montreal Canadiens captain Mike Keane, who'd gone *mano a mano* in an epic battle with future Olympic and NHL winger Valeri Zelepukin, insists nobody would have been capable of halting what ensued. "Pat and Bert were concerned with the five players on the ice. Something had to be done in a split second. As someone who was on the ice at that moment, I'm glad they did. The last time I looked, we were playing in a gold medal game, so the coaches must have done something right."

The game was never finished. Both teams were tossed out of the tournament, and Canada was tossed out of the country, players surrounded by soldiers when they emerged from the dressing room and proceeded to their bus, a military escort accompanying the vehicle to the border. Within weeks, a report submitted to the IIHF disciplinary committee recommended that all coaches and players (except for one goalie from each country because they hadn't participated in the donnybrook) be disqualified from international hockey for terms of up to three years. (Those suspensions would be lifted for the players six months later.) Canada had to forfeit the bronze medal they had been assured of before the gold medal game began. The coaches' suspensions held until December 31, 1989.

It was a scandal Burns rarely spoke about in later years, though he remained bitter. "What happened in Czechoslovakia was a spontaneous flare-up and it was blown out of proportion," he insisted. "It was amazing how many people who hadn't seen the game knew all about it and who was to blame." And the players, for the most part, remained unrepentant. "Looking back, it hurts," says Keane. "But it isn't a significant part of my life, that somebody didn't sacrifice a gold medal instead of their players. If we'd won the game, would it have been okay, then?"

Templeton would wear that disgrace until the day he died, but Burns's reputation and blossoming career did not suffer. On June 8, he was introduced as new head coach of the Sherbrooke Canadiens of the American Hockey League, one step away from the NHL.

Chapter Four

A Year on Serge's Farm

"Pat taught players how to play.
And if you didn't do it, you wouldn't play."

PAT BURNS could count on the fingers of one hand the people he trusted. His mother, Louise, was the thumb. In the summer of 1987, when he drove to Montreal to be interviewed by Serge Savard for the coaching job with the Sherbrooke Canadiens, Louise came along riding shotgun. Burns was thirty-five years old, a father, a divorced husband and already a veteran ex-cop, yet he still clung anxiously to maternal apron strings on matters of importance, fretful of his own galumphing gaucheness in the bigger world beyond hinterland Gatineau. "He needed her for emotional support," says sister Diane.

Sherbrooke was just a small city in the Eastern Townships, perhaps a little more culturally polished than Hull. But as Montreal's American League farm team, these Canadiens were umbilically tied to *those* Canadiens, although the affiliate had a hobo history, shunting around locales and shuffling place names: Montreal Voyageurs, Nova Scotia Voyageurs, later Fredericton Canadiens, Quebec Citadelles and currently reconstituted as the Hamilton Bulldogs. In 1985, they'd won the Calder Cup behind the goaltending of a young netminder named Patrick Roy.

Montreal GM Savard, hard-fisted Habs defenceman of an earlier era and known as "The Senator," his name engraved on no fewer than eight Stanley Cups, was the distant franchise field marshal. Burns wanted desperately to impress, a subaltern at the ready. This was the opportunity he'd longed for, the door into the NHL he intended to kick open, if he could make his bones in the AHL. Pierre Creamer had accepted the head coaching job with the Pittsburgh Penguins a week earlier, leaving Sherbrooke with a vacancy behind the bench.

Preoccupied with the parent club, Savard had little firsthand knowledge of the applicant. "Certainly, I'm not the one who followed him or knew much about him. I guess his background was fairly good as a coach in junior, where he'd had some success." At yearly state-of-the-union sessions with his amateur scouting staff, led by redoubtable talent sniffer André Boudrias, Savard would pose the same question: Who's the best coach around in the Quebec League? "For the last few years, André always came up with the name Pat Burns. So when it came time to hire a guy in Sherbrooke, it was a very easy decision for me. He was young, and when we hired a guy for the farm club, I was always thinking he might coach the big club as a backup."

Boudrias, director of scouting for Montreal, had been tracking the ripening of Burns in junior hockey. "Not knowing him personally," he says, "what brought Pat to my attention was watching him work behind the bench, his attitude, a guy that was always active and emotional, someone who reacted towards his players. If the game was not going his way, he showed it." The Hull squad, Boudrias observed, was one of the most robust organizations in juniors, and he was convinced their coach had a lot to do with that. "It was obvious he had an ability to develop players. He always seemed to get a very good team spirit out of them. His teams could score goals, but they were also in his image, very aggressive out there, very much alive. That's what first attracted me to him. He was a guy that you could fear. He didn't waste any time to help his team, whatever was needed. If he didn't like the calls a referee was making, he jumped at him. At the time, in those years, the teams that were winning in hockey were teams that were coached with emotion. It was still the time of the wars, you know? The teams that seemed able to get through had to have that second life, that extra little bit. Pat was able to show me that he could reach down into the second level of his players."

The opening was in Sherbrooke, but Boudrias was already looking ahead, making longer-term calculations. "There's no doubt when you hire a guy to coach in your system, you always want that guy to be able to move up the ladder. Pat was in the prime of his life. And his background as an ex-cop also entered the equation. It was an addition."

Boudrias talked to Burns first, then championed the cause with Savard. It was late May, and Burns was scheduled to go on vacation. Boudrias told Savard, "He's leaving so, if you want to talk to him, we need to do it right away." Burns was summoned for his audition with Savard. "Serge said to me after, 'He looks okay. It's your call, André. You want him, you decide.' So we went ahead."

In fact, Burns had just re-signed a contract with Charlie Henry in Hull. But when Savard called to ask for permission to speak with his coach, Henry said fine. "I told Serge that someday Pat would be coaching in the NHL, whether with Montreal or another club." It was Henry who gave Burns the news that Montreal was interested for the Sherbrooke position and to get his ass up there for an interview. "Well, Pat calls me from Montreal one night, about two o'clock in the morning, and he says, 'Guess what? They've offered me a contract!' I said, 'That's terrific.' Then he turns around and says, 'What's the matter? You don't want me to stay and coach your team no more?' He took it the wrong way."

Burns wasn't joking; typically, he would look through the wrong end of the telescope, searching for the negative, an implied criticism. "He said, 'Jesus Christ, I just signed a contract with the junior team and you want to get rid of me?' I said, 'Pat, I don't want to lose you, but this is your opportunity knocking.' But he was nervous, very nervous. I'm sure if I'd said, 'Don't go, you're working for Wayne here' and all that, he wouldn't have gone. I more or less kicked him out the door by saying, 'You can't refuse Montreal.' And he called me back a few hours later, around 6 a.m. He said, 'Okay, I've signed and I'm on my way home now. We having breakfast?'"

Burns had consulted with his ex-wife, Suzanne, on the offer because they'd remained friends. She thought he should go for it. That contract with Sherbrooke would pay Burns $35,000 for one year. A metamorphosing dandy, he immediately bought new suits.

The AHL was more than a feeder league for its NHL masters. It was barrelhousing hockey with a distinct identity, devoid of coddling of players—some of whom were on their way up, others on their way down, career paths that often transected and clashed. Elbows were sharp, noses frequently out of joint and grudges stoked. Coaches, with no on-ice canvas to paint a hockey portfolio, carved out personality niches to get noticed, because nobody wants to be stuck in the minors forever. Restraint was a rarity.

"I had no idea who Pat Burns was," says Mike Milbury, recalling the salad days of a coaching rivalry that would later assume epic proportions in the NHL. A New Englander by birth, a former Bruins defenceman and future Boston skipper before turning GM on Long Island, Milbury entered the AHL coaching ranks the same year as Burns, making his debut with the Maine Mariners, Boston's affiliate, and winning coach-of-the-year honours his first season. "All I knew was he was coaching a team in the organization that I had grown to hate. It was the American Hockey League, but it was still Montreal versus Boston on a minor scale. Pat was formerly a cop, and you didn't really need to know him personally to get that he didn't have a funny, smiley disposition. He was a very serious and very intense guy. In that first year, I had a very good team. He had a good team, but not good as mine. We had some serious battles. He was ready for it and I was ready for it."

They came to their coaching labours from opposite ends of the spectrum. Says Milbury: "I'd been thirteen years playing in the NHL and now I'm back in the American League level and piling on a bus to go to Sherbrooke." Milbury and Burns would never cultivate much of a relationship away from the rink; though the latter would eventually follow in the former's footsteps, plying his coaching trade for Harry Sinden in Beantown, each seared by the experience. "It was a time when you didn't really converse much with the other coach," says Milbury. "There weren't a lot of coaches' conventions. It was just, 'How do I beat the crap out of this guy's team?' Both of us were vocal, but I think it resulted in some pretty good hockey.

"We yapped at each other plenty of times. The smallest slight on the ice could be reflected in the coach, and neither one of us would let it pass. It was a way to keep your team alert and awake—'Look, this guy's out of line and you've got to take care of him.' We never got into it physically, but it set the stage for a couple of memorable Boston-Montreal playoffs in the late '80s. I came to know Pat as a guy whose strengths really were in making sure his team was ready to play, which I think is the art form of coaching. You can get guys in shape and you can teach them how to be in position, but there was not much doubt that Pat was able to manage people in a way to get the most out of them on most nights. The games were *personal* almost, and I think that's the way it's supposed to be."

What Burns had in spades, even in those AHL days, says Milbury, was *presence*, a force of personality. "All good coaches need to have command of the room so that people will pay attention to what you say. It comes from commitment, from knowledge, from a lot of things. I'm sure in Pat's case and in my case it came from different areas, but it was the ability, I think, to walk into a dressing room and grab the players' attention, make them listen and make them aware of accountability issues. There was a single-mindedness of coaching and a real resentment, almost, at the possibility of a loss."

Milbury waves off the broad perception that Burns then lacked, and perhaps would never hone, a technical hockey syllabus. "No coach worth his salt wants to be known as just a technician. What Pat had going for him, and what made him ultimately the terrific coach that he was, is that, yes, he scared the shit out of people. He walked into the room, and there's this ex-cop who looked like somebody had burnt his toast, and he was pissed coming in. If you don't have a little fear of that, then there's something wrong with you. But on the other hand, as with all young coaches, as time goes by, the harshness of it and the familiarity with the experience of being a coach starts to soften the edges. Really, the bully tool of a coach is to steal ice time, and that's always an insult to a player. It's communication that matters, and that takes different forms—whether it's throwing a stick at somebody or explaining to him in a quiet moment. As coaches go through their careers, they find the ability to try different methods of reaching players, because there's never just one type of player in the room and there's never just one way to get at it."

The gaining of coaching wisdom does indeed take time. But Burns, with no repository of NHL playing experience to draw upon, had to make it up as he went along in his AHL mad scientist's lab, concocting a team ethos out of bluster.

Life in the minors could be a dead end for players—those rebuffed by the big league after the proverbial cup of coffee, now playing out the string and resentful of young teammates on the opposite trajectory, one ding-a-ling away from a call-up. Burns, providentially, inherited a squad with a dozen emerging players who would make that NHL leap, several of them known quantities as ex-Olympiques or members of the Canadian junior squad chased from Prague. The 1987–88 roster included Mike Keane, Sylvain Lefebvre, Stéphane Richer, Stéphane Lebeau, Brent Gilchrist, Éric Desjardins and, in time for playoffs, Mathieu Schneider. In short order, they would become an extension of their coach's persona, each taking a piece of that into their NHL lives.

"I think we understood the game together, Pat and I," says Mike Keane, who came out of juniors in the Western League to play for Burns in Sherbrooke, both of them arriving the same year and known to each other from the world juniors. (Upon his return from overseas, Keane had a tattoo of Garfield the Cat waving a Canadian flag tattooed on his chest. "Actually, I was going to get it on my bum, but we had a game that night and you can't sweat on it, and I couldn't have a patch on my bum," he explained to a reporter.)

Burns saw in Keane the embodiment of those qualities he most admired: grit and heart, sand and soul, assets that would later make him a natural, if controversially anglophone, captain in Montreal. As well, Keane just plain tickled Burns's fancy, though he could damn him with faint praise for it.

"If we didn't have him on the buses, things would have been a lot quieter," Burns once harrumphed. "He's nuts. The guy never sleeps and he's talking all the time."

Keane: "I was lucky enough to have Pat at a very young age. Young players now, I think they're missing the part where a coach says, 'You know what, you're not the best player anymore and you're not the most important player on the team.' You might get a firm talking to, and that's your wake-up call. There's life and there's playing the game on and off the ice, representing your team, your teammates, and you have to respect what that involves. Pat Burns taught me that. My first year as a pro, in Sherbrooke, I learned so much from him."

That team finished third in its division and was eliminated by Fredericton in the first round of the Calder Cup playoffs. As Keane notes, the parent club in Montreal was "always taking our best players," leaving Burns with huge roster holes to fill, ad-libbing with the lineup and demanding instant allegiance to the system he imposed. "Pat taught players how to play," says Keane. "And if you didn't do it, you wouldn't play. He'd be very clear—do you understand it? If you signed off, saying, 'Yes I do' and then you didn't show it, well, that would be your fault for being so dumb. He'd say, 'But you told me you knew what you were doing!' He was lenient enough, but if you kept on making the same mistakes, not helping yourself or the team, then you weren't going to play and he was going to figure out some other way. The way he coached, it wasn't like nowadays, when you get three or four or five chances. You got yelled at. Right or wrong, I understand the game has changed. I understand the game evolves every year. But when you have someone harping on you, yelling down your throat, an intimidating man who just wants the best for the team and for you, it gets through pretty quickly."

It didn't matter to Keane that Burns had never played in the NHL. "Just because you didn't play the game doesn't mean you don't know the game. Scotty Bowman never played, either, and he wasn't too bad. Pat was a student of the game. He was very good at his systems. I find it funny that some people didn't like his coaching style. Look at his NHL career, which speaks for itself. Everywhere Pat went, he was successful right away."

Keane put his faith in Burns, and that fealty was mutual. He slotted Keane onto his first line with centre Brent Gilchrist, another prototypical "Burns guy," and both later advanced to Montreal with him. "We were two twenty-year-olds, first-year pro, and Pat was great for us," says Gilchrist. "He put us on the top line in Sherbrooke and expected a lot from us, but showed us a lot of trust too. If we stepped out of line or did things that he really disagreed with, there's no question we heard about it. But he helped us tremendously by teaching us how to be pros, how to put our work hats on every day."

Gilchrist, who would go on to play fifteen years in the NHL and is now coaching a midget team in Kelowna, has thought about where Burns learned his insights into the game and offers a theory. "The work ethic of a player is very similar to the work ethic in life. Pat was able to somehow transfer what he'd learned about life to what a player is going through, what a player is faced with. There aren't many guys who haven't played hockey at a high level who can transcend that and coach at a high level, but he was one of them.

"He taught me a great deal about playing the game in my zone. As a centreman, throughout my amateur career, it was goals, goals, goals. That's what I did, I scored. When I got to Sherbrooke, for sure to get to the next level, I had to learn how to play in my own end, learn about the defensive side of the game. Pat understood that. One thing Pat taught me in Sherbrooke, and continued to teach me my first few years in Montreal, was the whole repertoire of skills you need in the NHL. Montreal was always deep in centres—certainly, in those days they were—so Pat put me on the wing. From there, I learned to play all three forward positions, offensive roles, defensive roles. I look back on my long career in the NHL and I know it was possible because of the versatility I learned under Pat. That started in Sherbrooke."

In that single minor-league season, Burns speedily developed a reputation for outrageous behind-the-bench antics and opera-tenor emoting. "Sure, I was a bit of a showman coach in junior hockey," he would acknowledge later. "But we had to do everything possible to get attention, attract fans and pay the bills."

Cunningly or naturally, there was never an off-switch for Burns emotionally, not even a dimmer dial. "Pat just couldn't hide what he was feeling," Gilchrist recalls fondly. "It came out of his pores."

His volatility extended to his players, but there were redemptive features. "I remember him having all-out yelling matches, going one on one with players, and hard things were said. The thing is, he didn't mind if you came right back at him. Fifteen minutes later, it would all be forgotten anyway. It was emotional, heat-of-the-moment stuff, everybody got what they had to say off their chest and Pat wouldn't hold a grudge. That's where you get the trust of players. You could unleash on him with your own emotions when it's raw and right in front of you. Afterwards, it was just, 'Okay, let's move on.'"

Burns's closest friend, Kevin Dixon—they met in Sherbrooke, where Dixon was working in real estate and the incoming coach was looking for a property to rent—reveals that Burns detested having tête-à-têtes with his players off the ice. He did not do avuncular or confidant very well; it was a strain. "Pat hated sitting in his office, on the other side of the coach's desk, with his players." If so, he kept this aversion well concealed. "There's no doubt his door was always open," counters Gilchrist. "But did it even need to be? Because there was nothing hiding behind that door, nothing that you needed to talk about in private. Pat was a communicator, so you always knew where you stood. Sometimes, that wasn't a good place to be, but it was always in the open. He wasn't playing a bunch of head games with you. If he was upset, you knew it. If you said you didn't know why he was upset, you were lying."

Defenceman Sylvain Lefebvre had also landed in Sherbrooke that season, after playing junior for the Laval Titan, and he concedes Burns was a shock to the equilibrium for many of the younger guys who'd never before been exposed to so fiery a temperament. "Everybody knows now how passionate Pat was about the game and coaching. I think he was probably even more showing his passion down in the minors, where there wasn't the media around like he had later in Montreal and Toronto. A screamer, definitely, in the minors and in the NHL. Hey, you don't change spots on a leopard."

Lefebvre recalls with amusement—although it wasn't so ha-ha at the time—Burns's colossal clashes with opposing coaches, particularly Milbury in Maine and Rick Bowness in Moncton before the latter's promotion to the Winnipeg Jets. "Oh man, those were good rivalries, unbelievably intense." Everything in Burnsie World was intense, though, including practices. "We learned very quickly that he wanted us to work hard, to have good practice habits," says Lefebvre, now an assistant coach with the Colorado Avalanche and still practising what Burns preached a quarter-century ago. "His favourite line was: 'You play like you practice.' That was his trademark, and he instilled it in all of us. He was really tough, not just on the young players, but tough on everyone, so at least he was fair about it. And he was very direct, which sometimes hurt. Some of the younger guys who could not adjust or who could not take criticism had problems with that kind of hardcore coaching. But if you realized he was being tough because he wanted you to succeed, to get better, then everything was fine."

At the time, Lefebvre was fixated on his own career and didn't spend much time mulling over whether Burns was NHL-bound. "I couldn't have said that his destiny was to coach in the NHL. He was just coming out of junior himself, working his way up. But, yeah, you knew there was something special there."

The Montreal Canadiens saw it too. And at the conclusion of the 1987–88 season, that scandalously carousing NHL club was in need of what a Pat Burns could deliver. Enter the homicide dick.

Chapter Five

Under the Montreal Microscope

"The pressure is unreal and the spotlight is always there."

AT THE 1988 MEMORIAL CUP tournament in Chicoutimi, Serge Savard was besieged by reporters with the scent of blood in their nostrils, all clamouring for confirmation of rumours that Jean Perron had stepped down as coach of the Montreal Canadiens. The GM denied denied denied. "He's on holidays somewhere on a beach," Savard extemporized, by way of explaining why Perron was not in attendance at the junior championship, where hockey people annually congregate to take the measure of young comers.

Everybody knew that Perron's status was tenuous. Montreal had been eliminated by Boston in the second round, four games to one, their first playoff series loss to the Bruins in forty-five years, and fans were incandescent with rage. That the club had racked up 103 points, its best record in six years, was promptly forgotten. Ousted by detested Boston was an indignity that traumatized. Perron, cold and autocratic, was the perfect villain. More detrimental to his health as bench boss were ongoing dispatches from inside the dressing room of a player revolt. Savard had been inundated with complaints about Perron all season from Larry Robinson, Chris Nilan, Chris Chelios, Claude Lemieux and others. Some spoke out publicly, others from behind closed doors and under cover of anonymity. They whinged that Perron, a brilliant strategist but icy technocrat with an academic background, never talked to them, never spent time with them, didn't understand them.

As a rookie coach three years earlier, Perron had steered the team to its twenty-third Stanley Cup. The bloom was off that rose by the spring of 1988. The trifecta of one Cup, one division title and one regular-season crown was deemed insufficient, and Perron's coaching style was seized upon as root of the problem: the team's talent was not being directed properly on the ice. Full-out insubordination was afoot, with Perron perceived as too distant, too stiff-necked and utterly incapable of imposing discipline on a rump group of playboy players who had earned an off-ice reputation as the Wild Bunch.

On-ice, they chafed under Perron's defensive strategy, although that approach had just resulted in the fewest goals allowed, 238, by any team in the NHL that season. The players felt oppressed by Perron, even as they continually undermined his authority, and the dissidents had the ear of those in the front office. President Ronald Corey had been displeased when, during the Boston series, Perron seemed to have lost his nut, threatening to have his players take Bruins mainstay Raymond Bourque out of action in retaliation for Stéphane Richer's fractured thumb—courtesy of a slash by defenceman Michael Thelven—which really did spell doom for the Canadiens, their fifty-goal scorer sidelined. Corey, however, felt the Canadiens' image had been debased by rhetoric more suitable to the World Wrestling Federation.

Mere days before he was announced as a coach-of-the-year finalist, Perron joined Mike Keenan and Jacques Martin among the ranks of sudden ex-coaches, resigning May 16 because of what were described as "philosophical differences" with Savard. Those "differences" were more in the nature of an impasse over the disciplining of several key players. It was, in actuality, a firing. And that set up a hiring. Replacement names bruited in the media included Michel Bergeron, Jacques Lemaire (again) and even captain Bob Gainey. Savard claimed no other candidates had been approached and that the job was offered to only one individual.

On June 8, 1988, Pat Burns was introduced as Montreal's eighteenth and youngest coach, the latest in a long list of hockey savants, with a subset of skippers—Lemaire, Claude Ruel, Toe Blake, Al MacNeil, Bernie Geoffrion—who'd ultimately stepped down, driven bonkers by the manifold pressures of coaching in a city where every move was scrutinized by reporters from five newspapers and several broadcast stations, not counting the 16,084 coaches in the stands every night.

Savard's coyness at the Memorial Cup notwithstanding, the contract had been signed weeks before it was disclosed, a period during which Burns was ordered to say nothing. The cone of silence caused Burns to sweat bullets. "It was weird," recalls his friend Kevin Dixon. "We kept teasing him—'Hey, did you really sign that thing? Aren't they ever going to announce it?' Pat was getting worried. He said, 'Maybe they found someone else.'"

When the deal was finally announced, Savard stated Burns would have "carte blanche" to do whatever he felt necessary to bring an oft-wayward team into line. "The first thing we looked at were people who are successful and why they are successful. Pat commanded respect from his players."

The first person to send a congratulatory telegram—this in the days before email—was Wayne Gretzky. It said: See you in the Stanley Cup final. "Wayne was the first to ever tell me I'd coach in the NHL," said Burns. "I said, 'Get out of here.' He said, 'No, I've watched you work for two years and you'll be in the NHL.'"

Burns was instantly propagandized as a "players' coach," an un-Perron, albeit one without a single day of NHL experience on his resumé. But it was his cop chops that were hyped in the media. As a former policeman, Burns knew from delinquents, and this assortment of Habs had more than its share. So went the reasoning, though Burns pushed back against the stereotype when addressing the media horde, insisting he would not be walking into the dressing room carrying a big stick.

"It's a dream come true to be able to come into the Forum and know I'm the coach of the Montreal Canadiens. But I'm coming here as a coach, not a policeman."

Back home in Gatineau, the Burns family was stunned. "We were totally, totally shocked," says sister Diane. "I couldn't believe my brother had made it as an NHL coach. I couldn't believe he would be coaching the Montreal Canadiens. And he became an instant sensation."

The Habs always preferred hiring from within the organization, and Burns had been no farther than their own backyard in Sherbrooke. "I wasn't going to put him in Montreal right away," recalls Savard. "It's just that we decided to make a switch, the job became available and we never thought for a moment to go somewhere else. It was a very, very easy decision for me to make." Then, a tad patronizingly: "I don't think there were many coaches available at that time."

Still, it's unlikely Burns would have been summoned so speedily had it not been for his cop background and swinging homicide-dick reputation. "To me, he wasn't a policeman, he was a coach," says Savard. "But in his first life, he was a policeman. That was his whole alter ego, Pat the Policeman. It really helped him because he had that reputation—that he could be very strict and people would listen to him. That's one quality that is very necessary for a coach, that the players respect him and listen to him. Jean Perron was a wonderful person, but he didn't have those abilities like Pat did, discipline-wise. It happens to a lot of coaches. Sometimes you lose the players and the players lose respect for you. It becomes very difficult to coach when you don't have good control of a team."

Bob Gainey, who'd been a buffer between Perron and the players, sizes up the key contrary qualities of the two coaches. "Jean came from more of an academic university background and Pat was from a traditional minor hockey, junior hockey grass roots. Their personalities were as different as their background. Jean was very analytical and Pat was a roll-up-your-sleeves type, raw and edgy, but passionate, with good intuition and good instincts."

The Habs were seen to be in need of behaviour correction after bar brawls and reckless conduct had made headlines. A quarter-century later and returned to the Canadiens as a consultant, Savard remembers it differently. "Wait a minute, wait a minute," he objects. "We didn't have any problems worse than other teams. If you have a group of twenty-five players, there's always two or three guys that would break the rules at some time, that would go to bars, that would have one drink too many at times. We'd won the Cup with those same guys, mostly, in 1986, so we had a good group there."

"We had a lot of character," concurs Patrick Roy, the dynastic goaltender who'd captured a Conn Smythe Trophy as playoff MVP on the '86 Stanley Cup team. "That's why we won in '86 and why we went as far as we did in '89. But I could understand why Serge thought he needed a coach with a better grip. Burnsie was a good fit for us. He was different from Jean Perron, more strict, tougher. He was very demanding on the players. He had his views, but I thought he was fair. If you didn't want to work hard for him, then you were going for a good ride."

Adds Savard: "When Pat arrived, it was like a breath of fresh air for a lot of players. As a group, players like discipline, even if they might complain."

Perhaps. But this was also a group that liked to party hard, frequently spotted in the watering holes on Crescent Street and, because of who they were, easily identifiable, occasionally attracting trouble. As boulevardiers about town, a few of the bachelors had become notorious. Not that rich young hockey players should be expected to drink their milk, eat their cookies and be in bed by eleven o'clock. This was cosmopolitan Montreal, after all, bright lights and big city. Predecessor bon vivant Habs such as Guy Lafleur, a self-admitted rogue, were hardly known as recluses, either. But there had been eyebrow-raising incidents, some initially concealed by the club and only belatedly erupting in the media. "Yeah, we had a few guys who made a lot of mistakes off the ice," acknowledges Stéphane Richer, who wasn't one of them—all his stumbles occurred under the hot lights.

During the playoff series with Boston earlier that year, three players— Chris Chelios, Shayne Corson and Petr Svoboda—had gone bar-hopping on the eve of game two. The carousing climaxed with a car crash (none of them were driving), their vehicle smashing into a lamppost and flipping over. Subsequent reports claimed Corson suffered damaged tendons, Chelios and Svoboda injured ankles. Corson denies any of them were hurt in the accident, though he did play in that series with cracked ribs. The three told no one about their misadventure. Savard only learned of it when two provincial officers presented themselves as game five was about to start. After winning the series opener, Montreal dropped four in a row. Ignominiously bounced from the 1988 postseason on home ice, the door to the dressing room was slammed shut behind Savard and Corey. All hell broke loose inside, with the three hangdog players blamed for Montreal's elimination. Warnings were issued that each would be on probation the next season.

This was the environment of immature truancy that Burns encountered, tasked with cleaning up.

"It was no secret that guys liked to go out," says Chelios. "It was just the fact that we had so much more media attention in Montreal. They made it more personal, more of an issue, when players got in trouble. Obviously, being in Montreal, there was nowhere to hide. Hockey players can't blend in when they go out. We were also falsely accused a lot of the time. But that team, I'd say, was no different from my Chicago team. It was a lot different when I got to Detroit because we had an older, veteran club. The young guys were more scared of the veterans. And things had changed by then. Times had changed."

It was, indeed, another era, far removed from the tamer atmosphere of the NHL circa 2012. "We're talking thirty years ago; the whole general culture was different at that time, and hockey players reflected it," says Gainey. "They were young and popular and temptation was only a glance left or right. I don't think that group of players was any more out of bounds than others before it and some after it. At some point in the last three decades, there has been a shift, and many things that were acceptable in the 1980s and '90s are no longer part of the culture of NHL players."

Burns, realistic about temptations and well versed in boys behaving badly, was no puritanical Victorian. He was not going to tolerate wretchedly excessive debauchery, however. He became Big Brother, in the Orwellian sense, eyes and ears everywhere, amassing a snitch network that included police contacts, bouncers and even exotic dancers from Montreal's famous peeler bar, Chez Paree. He would become the coach who went undercover. And sometimes, not so undercover. There was the time he received a late-night tip from an informer that some Canadiens were at Chez Paree, well oiled. Burns got dressed, went to the club and took a stool, didn't even glance towards his players. But they saw him and skedaddled.

Savard acknowledges the bird-dogging that Burns embraced but notes that unofficial guardians of Canadiens morality were already in place, even if he didn't assemble them. "We had a lot of information before Pat Burns got there, from friends, from police, about what was going on, things that we never made public." The eyes-on became more intense with Burns's arrival, though.

"Whenever we went out, Pat would get calls, Serge would get calls," chuckles Chelios. "Every morning, it seemed like the papers would have a story about us out in the bars, whether it was true or not. So that's what Pat was dealing with. With his police background, he would literally go to guys' houses at night and stake them out, waiting for them to come home. We had rules and curfews, and Pat loved to enforce them. What he really loved was to catch guys lying. And he was really good at it."

Brent Gilchrist, who came up to Montreal with Burns from Sherbrooke, recalls one eye-opening incident. "There were certain places in the city where we thought we were incognito because people didn't ask us for autographs or pay any attention to us. So, one night, some of the guys had been out to one of these places where we thought we were 'safe.' The next day, I walk into the Forum and Pat says, 'Did you have a good time last night?' And he named the place where we'd been. He said, 'Hey, I know *everything*. I don't even have to make phone calls. They call me.'

"Pat knew we were young and wanted to have some fun. He wasn't trying to take that away from twenty-one-year-old kids who have lots of time on their hands. But every once in a while, he'd mention something when he thought it was getting a little bit excessive, or if he didn't like the way we were practising, like maybe we were having a bit too much fun off the ice. He made just enough comment to keep you on the straight and narrow."

Twenty-year-old rookie Mike Keane drew Corson as a road roomie and was more than once enticed into bar frolics. "I'm not going to lie; we had fun," he says. "A couple of times, curfews were broken. Pat was open with us about it. He said, 'I know guys go out. Just don't let it affect your game.' He took that extra time to find out, 'What are you doing tonight? Where are you going?' He'd say, 'Kid, don't think I don't know what's going on. Just make sure you're back at a decent hour.' I don't think coaches do that with their young players these days. They assume players will be taken care of because they have their agents, they have so many people around them, but it doesn't always work out that way. I was lucky enough to have Pat looking over my shoulder."

Rookie camp opened on September 2, the scrubeenies reporting a week earlier than the rest of the squad. The most prominent rookie on the ice was Pat Burns. Actually, on the first day, Burns watched from the stands while assistants Jacques Laperrière and François Allaire conducted the workout. But this was the media's first opportunity to observe the thirty-five-year-old coach in quasi-action. They descended en masse, and Burns got a preview of what, by necessity, would become a daily routine: fielding questions in French and English from the inquisitors. "Some of the youngsters here today played for me at Sherbrooke last year, so things were very much at ease when I spoke to the players in the dressing room before we started," he noted.

This was bland material, though Burns swiftly livened up. "I know that being the coach of the Montreal Canadiens is one of the highest pressure jobs in North America. No doubt, I'm going to have to adapt to that. But when you accept a job in the NHL, you have to expect that."

Little did he know. Feeding the beast, Burns quickly realized, was part of the job, and he discovered a natural flair for it. Press scrums, as much as Burns would profess to loathe the ritual throughout his career, were usually animated affairs, if mostly depending on his mood. And Lordy, Burns could be moody. But he had a knack for the adroit quote. Grateful reporters would fill their notebooks.

His teams had always been noted for their robust style of play. Yet Burns told his rapt audience that he was more interested in good defence than brawling. His Habs would not be the second coming of the Broad Street Bullies. This was mildly disappointing in some quarters. Burns was rather more intent on asserting his authority straight out of the chute, over both youngsters and veterans. Captain Bob Gainey—who'd flirted with retirement over the summer, meeting with the Minnesota North Stars about that team's vacant GM position before deciding to continue his playing career with a sixteenth season in Montreal—was only two years younger; legendary Larry Robinson was a year older. Between them, they had enough Stanley Cup rings to decorate every finger on both hands. And they cast long shadows, which would prove awkward soon enough. But mostly it was a group of curious and eager-to-impress players that convened.

It didn't take long for Burns to demonstrate what he was about. One week into camp, he laid a tongue-lashing on defenceman Svoboda for showing up fifteen minutes late for practice. Then he broke his stick over the net in anger about what he considered lackadaisical practice habits. On another occasion, Burns stormed into the dressing room, in high dudgeon about the practice session. "He knocked over the Gatorade container, there were tables flying left and right," recalls Pierre Gervais, who'd been in Sherbrooke with Burns and remains to this day head equipment manager for the Habs. "So I go into his office after and he's sitting and he's *laughing*. He just wanted to show them right away what he was about. Pat could be rough at times, but not mean, just very moody. He never picked on players personally. If you pick on players in front of everyone else, they won't forget that." Burns and Gervais became good friends that first season "because he was new in Montreal and didn't know many people." Never a victim of Burns's wrath, Gervais certainly witnessed it over and over. "He'd get mad, throw garbage all over the place. And then I'd find him smiling. Once, during the intermission, he put on such a show that he split the seam in his pants. Three, four minutes before the second period, I was chasing after him, trying to sew up this crack in his pants, and he couldn't stop laughing."

The sight of Burns screaming his guts out at the players was wildly entertaining for those with the pencils and cameras documenting such scenes. His charges had to be brought to heel straight off, Burns knew; no more of this feckless nonsense and half-assed reaction to commands, or not being on the ice at the designated time. Hop to it, the coach bellowed. One incident at practice made it difficult for Burns to keep a frown on his face, though. He'd ordered the power play unit to jump over the boards. "Everybody stood up to get on the ice. I said, 'Where the hell are you guys going?'" Either they weren't listening or they'd all fancied themselves PP specialists. "Guys were used to doing whatever they wanted to do. I'm just trying to put the discipline back in," Burns said. "It's hard at the start, but it will pay off in the long run. I'm just talking about normal discipline—like when a coach talks, shut up and listen."

Whether by design or intuitively, this newbie coach was already buffing up the cult of Burns. He hollered, he cussed, he turned the air blue. And then, so different from the man he replaced, he'd hang out in the dressing room, joking with players. From those perceived as disciplinary problems, there was not a peep of protest. "He was really good at recognizing the difference among players, their character, and how to deal with them individually," says Chelios. "What he maybe lacked was structure. But that was just inexperience."

Some, particularly the younger crew, responded well to the drill-sergeant tactics. Burns was adept at moulding men out of boys because they scared most easily. He was also prepared to give youth opportunity on a club where nudging out veterans was not the done thing. Mike Keane, who fully expected to be returned to Sherbrooke or worse at the end of training camp, instead found himself breaking through to the NHL roster, and many observers were critical of that decision.

"I fought everyone and hit everyone and just did whatever I could at camp to try and make an impression," the future Canadiens captain would recall many years later. "At the end of camp, he called me into his office and I thought, 'Here it comes, I'm going back to Sherbrooke.' But Pat looked at me and said, 'Can you do what you did in camp for eighty games for me?' I told him yes, and he told me to find a place to live in Montreal."

Keane had arrived at camp as an undrafted player. Suddenly he was in The Show, to borrow a baseball term. "He gave me a chance. I was an English player, too, and they don't get many chances in Montreal. There were other players who were more talented than I was. Things were written—'What's this guy doing here? He's too small, he doesn't have enough skill.' But Pat believed in me and I never forgot that. I knew every day at practice, not only would I be under the microscope if not playing well, so would he."

A third-line guy to start, and barely that, Keane benefited from Burns's fondness for grinder types. "He was blue collar. He liked to work, he liked passion. He absolutely despised people who were talented but didn't work. Pat appreciated people who put the time in, who'd do the shitty job to have success for the team."

If what Burns had set out to accomplish—changing the culture of the club—irked some of those who considered themselves entitled, he refused to be rattled by it. From his cubicle in the dressing room, Keane watched quietly as adjustments were absorbed, not always placidly. "There were a lot of Type A's in that dressing room. So you needed someone who was very strong in his beliefs, someone who said, 'I'm coming in here with one goal and one voice, and it's mine.' I don't think anyone else could have taken over that team. You look back at Larry Robinson, Bob Gainey, Bobby Smith, Mats Naslund, Patrick Roy, Guy Carbonneau—these are Hall of Fame players. Some were playing a lot where maybe they shouldn't have. Pat had to figure out what was best for the team. Make no mistake, it didn't make everyone happy. Behind closed doors, Pat had some fires he had to put out. Someone who didn't have as strong a personality as Pat wouldn't have been able to do it."

There was resistance. There were furious arguments, a lot of which went over Keane's head. "When they got into these heated shouting matches, Pat and some of the guys, believe it or not, it would go from English to French. They'd have a good old-fashioned fuck-you match and it would turn into French. It was funny because even in the minors, with Pat, when he got really irate he'd start talking French. Any time he got into arguments with Steph [Richer] and Peppy [Lemieux]—Claude is very Type A, Steph is Type A—it would be in French."

In French or English, Montreal's eightieth NHL season opened on a sour note, the Canadiens losing 3–2 in Buffalo on October 6, a game that illustrated the team's offensive impotence, an area Burns was committed to addressing. A club that lately had been living and dying on defence needed to find its scoring mojo again. That was an irony, because defence was Burns's coaching forte—very much of the check-or-sit mentality— and Montreal was the franchise that had invented firewagon hockey. The power play had become uncharacteristically enfeebled, clicking at a rate of 15.9 per cent the previous season, ranked twentieth in the league, though their penalty-killing success rate was a muscular 83.8 per cent, third-best. Also atypically, the Canadiens had been ninth in goal production, despite a contribution of fifty from Richer, the first Hab since Lafleur to hit those heights.

Burns explained he was attempting to make the team more spontaneous in its attacking style, but there was precious little evidence of that in their play. When the Maple Leafs dumped Montreal 6–2, right in the Forum, giving the Canadiens a 2–4 record in their first half-dozen games, the hand-wringing began in earnest. As the team sank into last place in their division, with a record of 4–7–1, Savard's acumen in hiring an NHL-unproven coach was questioned. Tensions were thick in the dressing room as doubts took hold, especially among veterans. Robinson was so displeased with the team's direction, he threatened to bolt. The team was clearly struggling. Burns had messed with a winning formula by altering the system instilled under Perron. Maybe he was just a dumb cop after all. "I knew what to expect," said Burns, shrugging off the wailing and gnashing of teeth. After the loss to Toronto, "one paper had me gone by Christmas—a front-page headline."

None of the players were bitching to the media, however, perhaps mindful of their orchestration of Perron's unceremonious dismissal six months earlier. "We're still searching for our team's character this season," suggested Bobby Smith. "What I mean is, we still haven't found out what type of team we will be." Gainey expressed his frustration in a way that seemed to reflect poorly on Burns. "We don't have any consistent coordination yet. We haven't stabilized our lines. Perhaps in trial and error you can find the right chemistry."

Burns persisted in preaching on-ice discipline as the necessary foundation for success. "The players have to adjust more to me. I'm a bit closer to them than Jean Perron was. Maybe there's more communication. When I blow the whistle in practice for them to come to centre ice, I want them all to come there right away. I don't want a few players not coming there at once. I don't want guys throwing sticks." Though *he* threw a few.

In an interview during this troubling stretch, Burns said, "When the time comes to talk, we'll talk." Pointing out that the club was coming off a season in which it had finished second overall in the league, with 103 points, and thus carrying high expectations, he said: "I'm a guy coming into a difficult situation. I'm a new coach with a new system and different ideas. There is an adjustment period. Many new coaches have problems at the start."

It was a two-way adjustment, and an agonizing one for Burns. "I was out—fired, gone, goodbye. That's the way it is here: win or else. I didn't want to walk the streets at night. I figured somebody would run me over. One guy was coming to the games dressed as a chicken, with my name on his shirt. The pressure is unreal, and the spotlight is always there. I don't like it, and I wish I could put it on somebody else, but I can't. So I just have to deal with it."

In late October, it was time for that talk. Burns called a meeting. "The team seemed to be separated between the young players and the old. I told them to wash their dirty clothes together."

That comment gave short shrift to what, in actuality, was a severe rift cracking open between younger guys and older guys, between veterans and coach. Publicly, Burns always paid lip service to the wise counsel imparted by his elder statesmen. They were a fount of advice and the team's backbone. But they were also busting his balls. He vacillated between awe and what some of those veterans construed as scorn, with the upstart exhibiting insufficient regard for their input, failing to adequately consult. Of course, Burns was striving to assert his primacy over the club. Further, he was attempting to cultivate a second tier of more youthful leadership, fully aware the club would soon need to transition into a post-Gainey, post-Robinson era.

Russ Courtnall, traded to Montreal from Toronto on November 7, sensed this internal tension immediately upon entering his new dressing room. "There were definitely some issues with some of the older players and Pat. And one of them was definitely with Larry [Robinson]. When I got there, Larry was threatening to quit the team, he was so unhappy. Eventually, they figured it out. I don't know how, but within maybe a week it had been smoothed out. It all went away. Maybe Pat stopped challenging them or realized that these guys were assets he could use to help him become a better coach."

In the locker room, Courtnall's stall was next to Gainey's. "Before every game, Pat would walk over to him with a piece of paper and they'd talk in French," Courtnall recalls. "I couldn't understand what they were saying, but they'd point at all the players' names on this paper and they'd have maybe a two-minute conversation. Then Pat would walk away. I know Pat respected Bob and Larry, but I think he realized he had to show that in front of all the other players. Once that happened, everything was fine."

Had the Canadiens enjoyed a stronger start, there likely would not have been much conflict in the room, though it's difficult to say which propelled which. "There was some fitting together early on in the year and, not being one who stops and analyzes a lot, I didn't look at it as specifically towards me or the veterans," says Gainey. "The whole team was off kilter. We'd had a pretty good run of five or six years, and this was near the end of it. But as the year progressed, I think there was real harmony there. We found a rhythm that was inclusive with veterans and good young players and ultimately had a very smooth and enjoyable season." Gainey attributes that segue to a combination of factors. "Players finding their place, their specific responsibilities on the team, having them either defined to them or just coming to understand them. Having the right players to fulfill those kinds of slots—a very good offensive centre, a very good goalie, a power-play defenceman, and we had all of those. So much of it is about momentum. Once things start to rumble in a positive way, it feeds on itself. That was one of those teams in the late '80s that is often dismissed because of the lack of good players. But if you take a closer look at the lineup, you discover all these players [who] are in the Hall of Fame or who played on their national teams, in the U.S., in Europe, in Canada. You see older, very successful players from the generation before. You see younger players who went on to be successful in the following generation. It was a great combination."

Burns had to make it work or there was no going forward. The new coach needed to show he was heeding the sagacity of veterans. There was veneration among teammates towards Gainey and Robinson, the only players left from Montreal's four consecutive Stanley Cup teams, 1976 to 1979. "A big part of the group listened to those veterans, Gainey and Robinson," says Roy. "They had a lot of influence. I think Pat and Bob were not eye to eye. I think Pat wanted to push Bob aside. And I thought that was a mistake."

Gainey picks his words carefully. "I think Pat had an idea that he had to establish himself as the alpha male. If that was the case, where he was trying to push some of the veterans out, he probably instigated better play in those veterans by challenging them. With time, there was a balance there, where he understood what those players bring and maybe didn't feel that he had to be as . . . not demanding or controlling, but clearly and visually in charge, that he could let things play out a bit more."

The situation took some finessing by Burns, a bit of genuflecting that did not come easily to him. The scraping was acknowledged, wounded feelings appeased, and the players made a commitment to coalesce behind Burns rather than invite more disruption from above. Burns was smart enough to relent somewhat in return, ditching what had clearly not been working in the early stages of the season, abandoning an offence-first system that wasn't in his nature anyway. Montreal hadn't been effective playing that way, and now they swung back to a grinding style, abetted by a resurgence of strong goaltending.

In other conspicuous ways, though, Burns was unyielding, sticking to his guns as enforcer-in-chief. He banned beer on the team bus and brought in a Breathalyzer device to show players how little alcohol it takes to cause impairment. Speaking from experience, Burns told the players: "The police don't want to hear your story. All that's important to them is you've had too many and you've killed someone with your car." He restored devotion to curfew observation. Even charter flights were quieter than in recent years. Customarily, a coach sits in the front. Burns altered his perspective, sitting in the back of the plane, arms folded across his chest, eyes straight ahead. Players could feel that stare. It was a seating arrangement Burns would maintain throughout all his years in the NHL. "I just didn't like a couple of things that were going on early in the season. I didn't like the card games with the big money pots. Guys having a couple beers before a game, stuff you don't want to see."

His rules provoked no sedition. Apart from the new conduct regulations, players adjudged Burns to be less strict than Perron. Under the former coach, the athletes felt they were treated like adolescents and often responded like brats. "Pat gives the players a little bit more freedom and he doesn't treat us like a bunch of schoolchildren," said Robinson. "He has brought a lot of discipline to our club, something that was lacking in previous years. If you keep a dog chained up too long, it becomes a very angry dog, whereas, if you give your dog some freedom and still keep the leash tight, it becomes a different animal. Pat gives guys plenty of rope, lots of freedom, but if they don't handle it the right way, then he reels it in. He's established that he's the boss, but he doesn't flaunt it."

Picking up the canine metaphor, Savard observed: "Pat doesn't have a doghouse that players get in and then have trouble getting out of. He deals with problems on the spot and then forgets about them. That means the air is cleared around the team very quickly, which helps to make a good atmosphere."

From the outset, Burns demonstrated the firm hand expected of him. No eyebrows were raised when he didn't have Claude Lemieux in uniform after the player had turned in a tepid performance. Lemieux returned to the lineup and scored three goals in the next game. The coach benched Lemieux again for taking a bad penalty—actually a double minor and a game misconduct—and "putting on a floor show." That let everyone know Burns was, as Savard had promised, "the man in charge." And no one rushed to defend Svoboda when the young defenceman argued he didn't deserve a suspension resulting from a high-stick infraction that Burns called "very, very stupid."

In late October, Montreal ground out a 1–1 tie in Boston and, while not pretty, Burns saw glimmers of the team he hoped was emerging from its early torpor. "We'll get better," he vowed at his postgame press conference. "We had to eat some crow for a while. Now it's time for some turkey and chicken." A fortnight later, Burns dispatched Guy Carbonneau to the press box and Montreal beat the Canucks 3–1 in Vancouver. That, most observers agree, was the turning point. Scratching Carbonneau from the lineup took *cojones*. The Frank Selke Trophy winner the year before as the league's top defensive forward, Carbonneau had missed only seven games over the previous six seasons.

Upon Burns's hiring, Carbonneau had applauded the move. "These days you need a disciplinarian to handle the younger players. Many of them come out of junior spoiled and they need someone to put them straight." But he was no kid and certainly never anticipated falling victim to Burns's evil eye. The coach, however, wanted Carbonneau to aspire to greater things than being a premier checker. Burns told the defensive stalwart he was playing *too* defensively. In dramatic fashion, he was challenging Carbonneau to contribute more on the attack, and that was unprecedented.

"I said, 'Be on the puck more, and you'll get goals,'" Burns explained. "He said, 'No, I can't do that, I'm a defensive player.' I said, 'Well, sit on the bench, then.'"

Confronting Carbonneau was a gamble for Burns, already criticized in some quarters for favouring anglophones over francophones in distributing ice time. But the benching and spurring conversation lit a flame under Carbonneau, triggering a remarkable transformation. Indeed, Carbonneau would go on a tear, potting 24 goals that season, 10 of them game winners, while putting up a plus-34 rating. "From that moment, everything started coming together," he said.

The other event of metamorphosis was addition by subtraction—Burns ridding himself of brash, troublesome John Kordic in what would go down in hockey history as one of the most disastrous trades ever for Toronto. The twenty-three-year-old enforcer and Burns were, surprisingly, chalk and cheese—or, more accurately, tinder and match. Kordic, who pined to be more than a pair of fists on skates, had expected an increased workload when Burns got to town, but the opposite resulted as he dressed for only six of Montreal's first fifteen games. Kordic didn't hide his displeasure. "Burns makes no secret that he's got 'his boys' and he's going to play his boys. I thought I was one of his boys at the start, but obviously not. I told them if they weren't going to play me, I wanted out. I told them to get rid of me."

There had been an infamous incident early on that poisoned the relationship between Burns and Kordic, although it went unreported at the time. They'd almost come to blows. Burns recounted the episode to his old mentor Charlie Henry. "This guy's yakking off in the dressing room, this and that, how he's not playing enough. Then he comes right into my goddamn office. He's standing there mouthing off at me. I had a big glass ashtray on my desk. So I took the ashtray and I threw it at him. Just lucky I didn't hit him, hit the wall instead and it broke into pieces. Kordic put his hands up and says, 'You're fucking crazy!'" Burns responded menacingly:

"I *am* crazy. And if you're not happy, we'll go down in the street right now and there will be no linesman to stop me." Instead, Kordic ran into the dressing room, screaming, "The fucking coach is crazy!"

Kordic stormed out of the rink. Burns waited a few minutes, and then poked his head into the dressing room, inquiring, "Where is he?" The players said, "He's gone, Coach." To Henry afterwards, Burns fumed, "That nut could have jumped over the desk and killed me." What Burns told reporters much later, revisiting the scene, was: "I told him to come back when he got some manners."

Burns also embarrassed Kordic when, after finding him in the team's whirlpool tub, he made a crack about being sure to drain the water lest sexually transmitted diseases be spread to his teammates.

Something had to give. Kordic was already so disgruntled that he spent as little time as possible at the Forum, even putting aside his passion for working out in the weight room. Such was his stress that at one point he landed in hospital for a few days with chest pains. What was allegedly unknown at the time was Kordic's heavy drug use—cocaine addiction compounded with alcohol, double demons that would ultimately bring him to a sad end, death by cardiac arrest in a Quebec City hotel room, just twenty-seven years old.

Burns reported the ashtray incident to Savard, but the GM had already heard enough about the increasingly volatile Kordic. In young Toronto general manager Gord Stellick, he found a sucker—er, agreeable trading partner—with Leaf coach John Brophy enthusiastic about making the deal. In return, Montreal got Courtnall, the speedy sniper who'd been languishing on the pine under Brophy. As a Canadien, Courtnall would be reborn, his offensive creativity valued by Burns on a team that had dim scoring wattage.

"I couldn't believe how young he was," says Courtnall, recalling his introduction to Burns. "It was only about twelve games into the season, so not too many people knew much about Pat yet. He was a tough man, a tough coach. Sometimes we didn't understand what he was really wanting out of us. But he was good to play for because he really demanded the most out of you."

Brophy—who would be canned by late December, replaced by George Armstrong—had been a screamer, too. "But there was a difference," says Courtnall. "Pat had Jacques Laperrière as his assistant, and they ran good practices. Pat didn't say a lot unless we were not doing what he wanted us to do, and then we'd hear it." Laperrière, the Hall of Fame Habs defenceman, was a gentle yin to Burns's tempestuous yang. "They were a really good team together. Jacques was quiet, but he had played in the NHL. And Pat, when things needed to be sorted out, came down on us pretty hard."

Courtnall was impressed by the Canadiens' use of videotape for instruction, though Burns was no Roger Neilson disciple and often left those sessions largely to Lappy. Says Courtnall: "We watched video before every game. We studied other teams, dissecting their strengths and weaknesses. Pat's teams always understood before every game what the other team did really well and what they didn't do well."

Astutely, Burns moved Courtnall from centre to right wing, to exploit his speed and shooting ability. "At centre, you have a lot of defensive responsibilities," says Courtnall. "When I went to right wing, I had less on my plate to worry about and the game became a lot easier for me." It proved a brilliant move. Courtnall would finish the season with 22 goals in 64 games for Montreal.

In Toronto, Kordic was tattling to anybody who would listen about the purported dissension in Montreal's dressing room, with veterans and francophones disgruntled over ice time invested in anglos and young'uns, Burns favouring his "Sherbrooke" boys, Mike Keane and Brent Gilchrist. "Some of the older guys, some of the sharpshooters on the team, aren't too happy," Kordic blabbed. "In the last minute of a game, you don't see Bobby Smith and Mats Naslund on the ice. You see Keane and Gilchrist."

There was truth in his accusation. Burns's attachment to Keane and Gilchrist was noted, disapprovingly, by the French media, always quick to pounce on any perceived snub of francophone Habs. "Mike and I, we didn't read the French newspapers or listen to French radio and TV, which was probably an advantage," says Gilchrist. "But Pat spoke the language.

They accused him of not liking francophones, and Pat at first thought that was funny. He'd say, 'But I *am* French.' He played the players he wanted to play, the ones he believed in. Mike and I were criticized at times, but I think for the most part we proved ourselves and those days disappeared. Those first two or three months, though, there were some strong young French-Canadians playing in the American League—they eventually became Montreal Canadiens—but we got there first. And Pat stuck to his guns. He took a lot of heat. I think Pat knew if he was going to be successful, he couldn't cave in to the media telling him who to play. He said, 'I'm going to play the guys I think can help us win hockey games.' And we did."

Burns was simply glad to shed the pain in the neck Kordic had been. And Courtnall was thriving under his direction, pulling spectators out of their seats with his rushes. There was no fuzzy warmth between Courtnall and coach, however. Courtnall credits Burns with making him a top-notch professional hockey player, but allows that the gruff boss always remained something of an enigma.

"He just didn't want the players to get close to him. Every morning for four years, I'd walk by his office and stick my head in his door, say good morning. And not once would he say good morning back to me. Ever. One time I ended up having breakfast with him, by accident, near the Forum and it was *so* uncomfortable. He was a grumpy coach. He just didn't want his players to get too close to him.

"Once you left his team, went to play somewhere else, he was totally different, nice and jolly. In the Forum, at practice, he would jump up on the boards and talk to guys on other teams, laughing. There were guys he'd coached as juniors, and he was very friendly with them. We were always, like, 'I wish he was like that with us.' We didn't have the best of relationships, Pat and I. I think I was a player that kind of frustrated him at times. But I sure played hard for Pat. Everybody wants to get recognition for what they're doing well or their hard work. Pat just wasn't a guy who would too often pick you out of a lineup and say, 'Hey, good game tonight.'"

Abruptly, the good-game nights started coming as the team began putting together winning streaks. By November 25, the Canadiens had gone undefeated in eleven of their past dozen, if largely on the strength of superb goaltending from Roy, who was proving unbeatable at the Forum. Burns was suddenly coaching one of the hottest teams in the league. With a victory over Boston on December 12, Montreal had lost only two of their last twenty-two and led the Adams Division by twelve points, opening up a huge bulge over Boston that the Bruins would never bridge. At Christmas, the joke in Montreal was that, when the Canadiens began the season 4–7–1, Burns was a dopey cop. Now he was an Einstein coach, tacking 100 points onto his bench IQ. They went four-for-four on a swing through the Smythe Division and extended their win streak on the road to eight games, even absorbing, without alarm, the broken right foot that would shelve Gainey for six weeks.

Burns basked in his plumped celebrity as "new thinker" genius while always carefully commending his players. "The secret has been twenty-five good individuals who can pull together and who care about hockey and want to give their best to the game. It's funny, but three or four bleep-bleeps on a team can screw things up. Well, we don't have any of those."

Except that he did have an expletive deleted—and Burns used them all—in the exasperating enigma that was Stéphane Richer, fallen idol. Coming off a fifty-goal season, the quintessential Flying Frenchman had fallen to Earth with a crashing thud and nobody could fathom why, least of all Richer. The young superstar tortured himself like a hockey Hamlet, trying to regain his Midas touch and tattered self-confidence. Acutely sensitive and mentally fragile, Richer had become a haunted man, repeatedly subjected to upbraiding by his coach, Burns monumentally mistaken in the belief that harping would be helpful. He'd known the twenty-two-year-old for nearly a decade and should have realized that a boot in this particular butt would pay no dividends. He punished Richer by reducing his ice time, which only exacerbated the scoring funk. A ten-game suspension early in the season for clubbing the Islanders' Jeff Norton with a stick set the template for a season of woe. When Richer took himself out of a game, claiming the flu, Burns sat him for the next match. When the Richer melodrama appeared on the front page of a Montreal paper twice in one week, Burns went ballistic. "I'm fed up to here with Richer," he thundered.

At the Forum, cheers turned to jeers and Richer was stricken. "When I make a check, they laugh. It's like they're saying, 'Look at him; he finally hit someone.'" Reporters dined out on the purported breach between player and coach. The more Richer took his grievances to the media, the more Burns seethed. "I feel like I'm in a war," Richer told journalists, bewildered by the controversy that raged in the papers and his aimless season. Roommate Guy Carbonneau stood in as layman therapist, providing the emotional support that was not forthcoming from an unsympathetic coach. Never a patient man, Burns was galled by the whole soap opera. "All that we've accomplished as a team suddenly doesn't seem to matter," he harrumphed. "All everyone is talking about is Stéphane Richer. I coach the Canadiens, and what's important to me is the team. I can't be concerned with just one player. I've played him regularly and on the power play. I can't do any more. I can't go out and play for him and I can't stop the fans from yelling at him."

In fact, Burns would claim for years afterwards—even from his deathbed—that he loved Richer like a son. That may have been the problem. Burns was no doting dad. He didn't show the love. And Richer, who personified the term "flake," often appearing to inhabit another planet, drove him nuts. "Huh, he loved me so much he traded me," Richer says now, not without affection. "It doesn't make sense, but it makes sense."

That trade was still far in the future, though, during the season of 1988–89, a crucible year for Richer. In retrospect, he doesn't blame Burns, or the hounding media. He was susceptible to depression, mood disorders that would not be diagnosed until middle age. "I was struggling inside," he says. "I didn't even know why. If I knew why at the time, it would have been easier to talk about. At the time, I was young. You don't know what's happening, [you're] looking for answers and not finding any. I'd ask myself, 'Why am I struggling like this?' I didn't have any fun on the ice. With Pat, it's A or B, there's no in-between. I tried to talk to him. I said, 'Pat, I'm struggling with some things.' But Pat, he didn't want to be involved with this. He had enough coping with me while I was struggling on the ice."

While grappling with his personal demons and finding no solace in the game that had turned on him, Richer was also burdened with the guilt of disappointing a man who'd plucked him as a boy from a dead-end small town. "He brought me up. All my buddies were on drugs. How would I have survived if he hadn't done that? What would have become of me? I said to him, 'Come on, Pat, you've known me from when I was fourteen, you know my background, you're supposed to understand that I'm struggling.' But he wanted to win so bad. When I saw him dealing with all the issues some players were having off the ice, I was, like, it doesn't matter if I sit down and talk with him now, he'll never listen. I told him once, 'Pat, you don't see me in the bar at four o'clock in the morning, you don't see me drunk.' But it was like he was deaf.

"It didn't matter if I had a good game or not; he was always on my case. If I scored two, I should have scored three. He was always that way with me. From the moment I first pulled on a jersey in Hull, he was so tough on me, people have no idea."

The Richer riddle aside, Montreal was firing on all cylinders, overtaking Calgary for first place overall in the league—the two teams would play leapfrog for the rest of the season—and everything was well in Burns World, though he was constitutionally incapable of disbelieving that catastrophe lurked just around the corner. Courtnall describes him as "kind of a doomsayer." So he continued to push relentlessly. "He was afraid to give us a day off," says Roy. "If we had a day off and we sucked the next game, the next day he would go at us and say, 'That's the last time you guys are going to have a day off . . . it's payback now.'"

At the Forum, Roy never got a day off, and he flourished with the workload. In late March, he tied the unbeaten streak for goalies in their home barn—25, set by Bill Durnan in 1943–44—and did it on just four hours' sleep, his girlfriend having given birth at 3 a.m. to their first child, son Jonathan. Then he broke the record, undefeated at the Forum all year with a record of 25–0–4—twenty-nine wins in a row dating back to the previous season; overall, 33–5–6 on the year.

Through the final weeks, Burns spelled his veteran players, even sending Robinson to Florida for five days to rest up. Youngsters from Sherbrooke were called upon to fill the holes and get a taste of the NHL. Montreal won ten of its last fifteen games, a tad off their torrid pace, which cost them the Presidents' Trophy as top team in the league. They finished with 115 points—their highest since 1981–82—2 behind Calgary and a whopping 27 points ahead of Boston.

It was often said of the Canadiens that they owned the Stanley Cup and just sometimes rented it out. Burns & Company squared up for the playoffs, intent on bringing their heirloom home.

Chapter Six
So Close

"They raised the Cup in our rink, and that killed Pat."

CLAUDE LEMIEUX is writhing on the ice. He appears to be in agony. At the Montreal bench, trainer Gaëtan Lefebvre starts clambering over the boards to render first aid. Pat Burns grabs his sweater, pulling him back. "Let the SOB lie there."

It is game one of the 1989 Stanley Cup final in Calgary, and Lemieux is a lonely figure under the white glare of TV lights. No teammate has come to help. No penalty has been called against Jamie Macoun, who had done nothing more to cause this drop-dead pantomime than lightly tap Lemieux's leg with his stick. As it dawns on him that assistance isn't forthcoming, Lemieux stops thrashing, wobbles onto his knees, laboriously stands erect and skates to the bench. Not a word is uttered.

"I just remember lying there thinking, 'Where's the trainer?' There's twenty thousand people in the building, it's the playoffs, and nobody's coming. I was like, 'Are you friggin' kidding me?' And then I have to get back to the bench. It was very embarrassing."

One of hockey's most notorious pests and a hammy injury faker, Lemieux has wearied of revisiting this humiliating incident. The story changes constantly. Twenty-three years later, in his downtown Toronto office, Lemieux says he wasn't faking. Much. Entirely. But he's vague about the pre-existing ailment that Macoun's touch-wood activated. He'd had a sore ankle, he seems to recall. And there was definitely an abdominal problem, which took more than a year to properly diagnose. "I was hurt. I wasn't faking. I went down and I was in a lot of pain."

What pained and exasperated Burns was the chronic penalty baiting at which Lemieux excelled and which had become a very tired act by the spring of 1989. At the time, Lemieux certainly seemed to acknowledge he'd been emoting when queried by reporters. "I used to do it in '86 when we won the Cup, but it's not working this year," he said. "If the referee, Andy Van Hellemond, had called a spear and they'd got a five-minute major and we'd scored, I'd be a hero."

He was not his coach's idea of a hero. Burns hated phony theatrics and considered such bush-league antics unworthy of a Canadien. If genuinely injured, Lemieux was the bad boy who'd cried wolf once too often, though Burns had picked an odd moment to wise up his great pretender, with seven minutes left in a playoff final game that Calgary would win 3–2. "I told him it doesn't work anymore," growled Burns. "The referees aren't stupid." Even prior to the episode, before the series had opened, Lemieux's well-known diving habits were mocked in a Calgary newspaper cartoon. It depicted him convulsing on the ice and the caption read: "As far as injuries go, Gary Suter is out indefinitely. Mark Hunter is day-to-day and Claude Lemieux is listed as minute-to-minute."

What wounded Lemieux most deeply was that no other Hab had made even a pretence of helping him off the ice. "I can understand that," he says now. "If the coach holds the trainer back, I think the team is going to be hands-off. No teammate is going to run over." The silence on the bench was crushing. "I remember saying to the trainer, 'What the eff?' And then I knew. I was totally embarrassed and I was truly hurt. After that, I thought, there's no way I'm going to keep playing here for this guy. I knew I was going to ask for a trade."

Lemieux and Burns had been rubbing each other the wrong way all year, dating back to the player's unsportsmanlike penalty (for arguing with a referee) and game misconduct in Montreal's first home game of the season. Many times, they'd sparred verbally. Burns believed Lemieux was malingering when he complained about a sore groin that never much improved.

"I had this mysterious injury that couldn't be diagnosed. It was a stomach tear, but no doctors could see anything. Pat thought I was faking an injury, like I didn't want to play for him and this was my way of doing it. That was foolish, because if you're going to get traded, you've got to be healthy. So that wasn't a very good assessment."

He says Burns also mocked him for wearing a visor. "He thought guys who wore visors were cowards. He was always making comments from the bench to guys who wore visors. In the back of his mind, he felt that if you're going to play a tough game, you can't wear a visor. To me, wearing a visor was about protecting my eyes from all the stickwork that was happening. It had nothing to do with not being tough or not wanting to fight, because I fought a ton in junior hockey and I wore a visor back then. So we weren't in agreement, Pat and I."

Lemieux suggests an undercurrent of tension may have arisen simply from the fact they were so much alike—emotional and stubborn. When sent down to Sherbrooke four years earlier, Lemieux was so distressed that he took a stick and shattered all the windows of his car. Burns could relate to that kind of passion. But as coach and tempestuous player, uh-uh. "It was too much fire for both of us in a setting like Montreal, where everything is looked at under a microscope," says Lemieux. Away from the ice, Lemieux claims he and Burns got on surprisingly well. During those '89 playoffs, Lemieux had opted to doss down at a Montreal hotel because he had young kids at home and needed quiet. Burns was staying at the same place. "One night he said to me, 'Come sit down, we'll have a beer.' And we got along just great. But there was that blockage once we got to the rink."

There was constant aggravation over Lemieux's ice time, a recurring theme in media coverage. Burns clearly had a preference for the likes of Mike Keane and Shayne Corson, hard-nosed types. "Those were his boys and he loved them. I loved them too, as teammates. And I knew they were very important players on the team. But not at my expense. I had a career, I had a living to make. I didn't like the fact that Pat didn't believe in me as much as I thought he should. I thought I was a much better player than he thought I was. And it turned out, in hindsight, 20/20, that I was right and he was wrong."

All that *sturm und drang* that erupted after the Calgary game, says Lemieux, could have been averted if Burns had counselled him better, opened his eyes to the error of his feigning ways before it came to a head. "These things, most coaches don't tell you to do it, but it was part of my game early on. For me, I was trying to create an odd-man situation for our team, and it would work most of the time. I wish Pat would have come to me and said, 'I just don't want you to do that anymore.' But we didn't have that kind of communication, so I'd do it, and if it worked it was great and if not, well, he didn't appreciate it. He definitely taught me a lesson, but it would have been better if we'd talked in a private room."

Lemieux had been a rookie on the Montreal team that won the Cup over Calgary in 1986 and he contributed tremendously to that triumph, scoring ten goals in twenty games. He also bit the finger of Jim Peplinski during a postgame brawl. But he had just two goals and two assists to that point in these playoffs. When Burns put him on the Black Aces line at practice the next day, Lemieux knew he would not be in the starting lineup for game two—which Montreal, regrouping, won 4–2. That triggered another blast against purported anti-francophone bias, from one high-profile correspondent, Réjean Tremblay, then of *La Presse,* the Montreal daily. Tremblay accused Burns of making scapegoats out of the French-Canadian players. Snarled Burns: "I'm not anti-francophone. I'm anti-asshole." That *l'Affaire Lemieux* column got Tremblay booted off the Canadiens charter when the team flew back to Montreal.

"I thought Pat had done something a coach should not do," says Tremblay. "You just don't leave one of your players on the ice, even if you know he's acting. What I wrote is that he seemed to favour players who were tough guys, like Chelios and Corson. The way he talked about them, he'd use their nicknames, you know? A player like Stéphane Richer (for example) was too sensitive to be part of Pat's gang. Maybe this is the difference in sensitivity between French and English." Looking back, Tremblay is more sanguine now about what happened then, stressing that he and Burns resolved that disagreement; indeed, Tremblay would become a media conduit for Burns later on, columnist and coach exploiting each other with slyly planted stories and scoops. "He was not anti-francophone, I don't think; he was anti–soft players. And Claude . . . well, Claude had problems with his coaches everywhere after Pat."

Press rewind.

The Canadiens teed up that Cup final against Calgary, a replay of 1986, by acquitting themselves with ferocity and flair through three earlier rounds. Before the games started, Burns went out and bought himself a new set of suits, establishing a tradition he would maintain throughout his career. Come the playoffs, he'd replenish his wardrobe. He loved shopping, dropping between $900 and $1,200 per ready-to-wear suit, preferring Canadian designers to Europeans, a valued customer of Aquascutum in Montreal. His rule: No suit worn twice on any road trip. Apart from the thirty-five-or-so suits he'd amassed, there were literally hundreds of ties, selected to suit his mood. And he was in a marvellous mood.

The Canadiens wiped out Hartford in the Adams Division semifinal, W-W-W-W, Montreal displaying a powerful transition game and relentless in capitalizing on the opposition's mistakes. No surprise in the outcome; Montreal had a 7–1 record against the Whalers in '88–89, were thirty-six points better on the regular season and had ousted them two years in a row. "Everybody except some psychic in Edmonton picked us to lose," said Hartford captain Ron Francis. Lose they did, though three of the games were decided by one goal, two of them in overtime. The sweep gave Montreal an eight-day rest to deal with niggling injuries before meeting Boston.

Bruins were decided underdogs, 0–7–1 in the regular season versus Montreal and badly banged up. Burns tried mightily to present his team as the disadvantaged side and longer shot. Nobody was buying it. That perception was not eroded when the Canadiens churned out a 3–2 win in a soporific opener, Montreal asserting its signature defensive potency, nor by the 3–2 overtime result that followed in game two. "Destiny's Doormats" the Bruins were being called. Yet there were some Cassandra voices that warned Montreal was playing just well enough to win, and now was headed to the hostile environs of the Boston Garden.

In game three it was a plucky Boston team that battled back from a 3–0 deficit for 3–3 and 4–4 ties, only to succumb 5–4 on Russ Courtnall's breakaway with 6:08 left to play in regulation time. Now Montreal had a stranglehold on the series. But Boston drew on its own grit in game four. The Bruins struck first, but that lead was erased when a misplay by Michael Thelven handed Russ Courtnall a breakaway. The disgusted audience treated Thelven to a hail of loafers, dress shoes and sneakers to show their displeasure. Thelven atoned by unloading a hard drive in the second period that sailed past Brian Hayward in the Montreal net, Boston up 3–1. A heart-stopping too-many-men-on-the-ice penalty with just over five minutes left in the game, Bruins ahead 3–2, brought back nightmares of the infamous night ten years earlier that will follow Don Cherry to his grave. In the box seats, GM Harry Sinden and owner Jeremy Jacobs looked at each other. Admitted Sinden, "We both said the same thing—'1979.'" This time, the Bruins survived unscathed—holding Montreal to only sixteen shots and emerging with a 3–2 win—and the series returned to Montreal. "Believe me, we wanted to finish it in four," said Burns. "But instead, they lit a fire under themselves." The coach singled out Shayne Corson and the entire D crew for scorching. "Our defence spent almost the whole game on their butts. We've got to start winning the battles in the corners and along the boards." He demanded they be meaner and tougher and stingier.

Corson responded by scoring his first goal of the series in game five to break a 1–1 tie in what was eventually an altogether thrilling 3–2 series victory for Montreal. Stéphane Richer, who'd lit the goal light just once in the Adams Division final and had been justly accused of failing to answer the bell, notched the winner. Facing reporters afterwards, Burns got in a last word first. "Before you say we didn't play well in this series, give

Boston some credit. [Coach] Terry O'Reilly did a tremendous job with the talent he had. It was a slugfest." For the fifth time in six seasons, Montreal had vanquished the Bruins. This was not good enough for some. Along press row, a columnist absurdly suggested Burns had actually plotted the game four loss—with Hayward in the net instead of the invincible Roy—because he coveted a series win at home. It's just that kind of media town.

Roy's aura of invincibility ended a few nights later. Facing Philadelphia in the conference final, Roy was riding the crest of a gaudy 30–0–4 record at home. On a pair of shorthanded Flyers goals, *pffft*, the streak was kaput, the spell broken. On May Day, Philadelphia triumphed 3–1. "All good things come to an end," Roy shrugged. It had been extensively commented on, in that day's papers, that Roy had never defeated the Flyers in his career. Burns used that as a launching pad. "How'd you like it if the paper put on the front page that you've never written a good story?" he snapped at a reporter at his press conference. After practice the next morning, Burns was in a sour frame of mind. "We've been favoured since day one of the playoffs. I'm glad we're not for the next game, because they won the first game. We're in another category now, and if everyone isn't prepared to pay the price, we'll lose again. We'd have to be scared going to Philadelphia down two games. Now it's up to us to catch them."

It was just one game, one loss, for criminy's sake. In game two, Roy bounced back and Philly was blanked 3–0. Burns pulled out the clichés in continuing his woe-is-us rhetoric. "We played the way we always do when our backs are to the wall." The game was distinguished—or *un*distinguished— by a melee that broke out before the puck was dropped, during the warmup. Philadelphia had their nose out of joint over the elbow Chris Chelios had laid on Brian Propp in the previous game, which sent the Flyer to hospital. It all revived memories of the conference final between these two clubs two years earlier, in which a brawl erupted before the national anthems were sung, players from both teams returning from the dressing room to slug it out.

Montreal, by now a highly efficient team functioning at its best, poised and confident, tossed Philadelphia aside 5–1 in Game 3 at the Spectrum.

Burns had given his players a day off in the City of Brotherly Love in between, and a batch of them went to Atlantic City for a bit of gambling. Roy shut out the Flyers 3–0 again in game four, and Philadelphia assistant coach Mike Eaves marvelled: "They are all on the same wavelength, both mentally and physically. It's so unselfish, it's almost utopian. They are a chain without a weak link." Spectrum fans, less gracious, hurled beer cans at the Habs as they left the ice, scoring bull's-eyes on Burns and his assistant, Jacques Laperrière.

The Flyers avoided elimination in game five on the road, Dave Poulin settling matters 2–1 in overtime. "We didn't play our style," Burns fulminated. "We've been reading how great we are for three games, and all the flowers the Flyers were throwing at us, and we just gobbled it up. We thought it was going to be easy."

It wasn't that hard, in fact, as the Canadiens—playing methodical and conservative hockey—prevailed 4–2 in game six. The Flyers lost their marbles in the closing minutes, seeking vengeance if nothing else, with goaltender Ron Hextall leaving his net to take a wallop at Chelios, then throwing his blocker and mask at the Canadien for good measure. He received a five-minute match penalty for intent to injure. Only Roy stayed out of the donnybrook that ensued, though Burns kept the players who were on the bench off the ice. Chelios laughed off the mugging. He, and the Habs, were done with Philly, and that's all that counted.

Calgary awaited, having enjoyed a less trying route to the Stanley Cup finals. While the Flames had been stretched by Vancouver to seven games in the first round, they'd then dispatched Los Angeles in four and Chicago in five. They were home and cooled out. Unlike Montreal, they also had marquee stars, including a guy by the name of Doug Gilmour and recent rookie-of-the-year Joe Nieuwendyk. The Canadiens had no scorer who'd reached the thirty-five-goal threshold in the regular season and only eight who had nineteen or more. But they had ascended on a solid team concept, with Burns—who'd proved himself an excellent motivator and more than adequate tactician—insisting he was not the preeminent factor.

The Canadiens arrived in Cow Town toting cylinders of oxygen—Burns's idea. "This first game is going to be a hummer because of the altitude problem. I brought a junior team to the Memorial Cup in Portland in 1986, and we brought oxygen and it helped." For Montreal, a club that traced its heritage back to 1909, predating the NHL, it was a thirty-first appearance in the Cup final; Calgary, an expansion outfit transplanted from Atlanta, had been there only once before, losing to the Canadiens. "Calgary's built up a hell of a head of steam, it seems to me," Burns demurred.

Game one went 3–2 the Flames' way, Theoren Fleury's second-period goal standing up as the winner. In game two at the Saddledome, the Habs burst out of the gate, built up a 2–0 lead, then watched it dissolve as Calgary rebounded to tie. In the dressing room between the second and third periods, Chelios was on his feet, rallying his teammates. "He stood up in the room and said there was no way we were going to lose this game," said Burns. At 8:01, practising what he preached, Chelios silenced the crowd with a blazing forty-five-foot slapshot that handcuffed Mike Vernon. Russ Courtnall added insurance and, with a 4–2 result, the Canadiens earned a split, removing Calgary's home-ice advantage. "Pat was upset with us after the second period," said Chelios. "We had no flow and we didn't play with discipline. We needed a kick in the butt."

Game three at the Forum was a marathon. Tied 3–3 by Mats Naslund's lob with just forty-one seconds left in the third, Roy pulled for an extra attacker, the teams then battled through more than thirty-eight minutes of extra time before Ryan Walter sent the fan faithful celebrating into the night. He stuffed Richer's pass behind Mike Vernon, the netminder widely and prematurely perceived as Calgary's Achilles heel. To a crush of reporters, Walter struggled valiantly to express his feelings in both official languages: "J'étais numb!" About Larry Robinson wrapping him in a bear hug after the goal: "Larry Robinson squeezed moi!" Burns credited "all those tough practices they complain about." No one could know it would be Montreal's last hurrah.

Calgary knotted the series at two apiece in game four. Gilmour and Joe Mullen propelled the Flames to a 2–0 lead, and this time there was no gallant comeback, Montreal falling 4–2. The sense of inevitability, of Habs destiny, was dissipating. At the Saddledome for game five, the temperature at ice level hit thirty degrees Celsius, and it was Montreal in a nervous sweat after absorbing a 3–2 loss. "It's the game we had to win, no doubt about it," an exhausted Burns conceded. They'd not lost two games in a row since January. The Habs still had the Forum factor to inspire— Montreal had never lost a Cup at home.

Montreal was the more spent team, however. "We were a very tired team when the playoffs rolled around," says Roy. "We'd been on the ice practically every day." And in the final, Burns may have made a tactical error. "We were equally good, if not better than Calgary," says Russ Courtnall. "But we were tired. And the reason we were tired is that we'd flown back from Calgary after the first two games on a red-eye. We didn't sleep. After game four, we flew directly back to Calgary. Meanwhile, Calgary slept in Montreal and flew back the next day. After game five, again, we flew red-eye back to Montreal. Calgary didn't. We were exhausted. You can imagine, flying back and forth, three red-eyes in one week, and trying to play to the best of your abilities every night. Pat mentioned to Larry Robinson later that he just didn't know any better. He was a young coach and it was a rookie mistake and he would never make it again."

Bob Gainey is unconvinced that fatigue was a determining factor. "We'd got behind in the series, lost a game at home, and were playing catch-up. We can hand this over to the guys who work from ten till one in the morning on the panels, and they'll figure out something we should have done different. But honest to God, I don't think there was anything dramatic, tactically, to blame."

Interestingly, Lemieux suggests maybe the Canadiens had drifted away from their team concept when it mattered most. Several veterans knew they would likely not be back next season, and perhaps rifts that had seemed patched over began to rip open again. "There was a lot of friction building up. I could feel it between the younger and older players. I think people felt that in '86 the older guys kind of ran the show behind the scenes, to a certain extent. Then, in '89, Pat was making sure he was running the show. He wanted to make it his deal, and with good reason. As a coach, that's what you want. I knew in my mind I would be gone. Other guys, like Larry [Robinson], most likely felt the same way." The early-season schism, Lemieux says, had not genuinely been resolved. "It was put aside, maybe. But Pat would make comments like, 'We've got older guys here who think they can run the show, but I'm running the show, I'm the coach, blah-blah-blah.' He was a young coach on the biggest stage in the world, surrounded by Hall of Fame-to-be players. Whew, tough job."

Tough, excruciating, would be watching Calgary's interim captain Lanny McDonald skating around the Forum ice, holding the Stanley Cup aloft. The walrus-moustached veteran hadn't dressed for game five. But rookie coach Terry Crisp had an inkling and reached out for the stimulating jolt McDonald would undoubtedly bring to game six. His goal, giving the Flames a 2–1 lead in the second period, stood up as the winner, Calgary triumphing 4–1, Gilmour contributing a pair, including one into the empty net. Fans in Montreal had the courtesy to applaud the enemy with seconds ticking down on the '89 finals.

Some Montreal players wept as they looked on, crushed but still proud of what they'd accomplished. "We don't have to apologize to the Richard brothers or Jean Béliveau," said Bobby Smith. "We gave it all we had."

"They raised the Cup in our rink, and that killed Pat," says Shayne Corson. "I know it killed us as players."

Burns was gracious: "They deserve what they got. It was a lot like the regular season, where we came up just a little bit short."

"We were so close," says Lemieux, who scored that lone Montreal goal. "Thinking back, maybe Calgary should have beaten us in '86 and we should have beaten them in '89. I think we were better in '89 than they were, and they were probably better than us in '86. I watched Lanny McDonald with the Cup and I thought, 'Maybe things do happen for a reason.'" For captain Bob Gainey, there would be no more Cups as a player; he retired that summer. "It was my final year, and it's one that has a very satisfying, lingering taste."

Six weeks into that season for *Les Glorieux*, assailed on all sides and worried that he wouldn't last until Christmas, Burns had quipped: "I don't want to be coach of the year. I want to be coach for a year." On June 8, a year to the day after he was formally handed the whistle as Montreal's rookie bench boss, Burns won the Jack Adams Award as coach of the year.

Chapter Seven
Lost in Transition

"If I use the word 'rebuilding' here, they'll hang me."

HOCKEY IS RIFE with the sophomore jinx. This is particularly true for those who were streaking meteors the year before. From heady heights, many are pulled down by NHL gravity. Pucks don't go in, stats take a nosedive and reality bites hard. It's almost expected that phenom-rookie plus one equals backsliding, and nobody is surprised when it occurs, except maybe the bewildered player. But Pat Burns wasn't a player and, while few reckoned Montreal would unspool a dream season to match that of 1988–89, when just about everything went extraordinarily right, little slack would be afforded the second-year coach.

Montreal was a profoundly altered team, however. Bob Gainey had retired, gone off to France, of all places, to coach an obscure club outside Paris, and Larry Robinson had defected to Los Angeles as a free agent, unable to agree on terms with GM Serge Savard in a messy contract dispute. Sturdy defenceman Rick Green had hung 'em up as well.

Burns was given job security September 1 with a four-year contract, the longest guaranteed deal granted a Montreal coach in memory. The leadership void in the dressing room was filled by Guy Carbonneau and Chris Chelios, appointed co-captains when a vote among teammates came in tied 9–9, quite possibly dividing along English and French lines. "Now you C it, now you don't," was the joke in town, as Carbonneau and Chelios considered wearing the *C* on alternating nights. Chelios had won the Norris Trophy in June, Carbonneau his second straight Selke.

"I'm sure there are some guys who know they'll have to talk a little louder in the dressing room," Burns observed as the players assembled at training camp. "I don't have to pick them out. I don't think much building has to be done with this club. There's a good foundation. We've lost veterans, so some kids will have to come in and take their places. But I liked the image of the team last year. We just have to keep it up to the same standards."

To say their roster resembled the Sherbrooke Canadiens more than the parent club would be stretching it. But a complement of greenhorns and just-slightly-worn cohorts were going to be blessed with big playing minutes. "I have to spend more time with them," said Burns. "You just can't take a kid and say, 'You're going to be like Larry Robinson or Bob Gainey or Rick Green.' You have to be very patient."

Claude Lemieux was looking for a fresh start after a season of knocking heads with Burns, retreating from his request for a trade if their grudge match wasn't resolved, and allegedly chastened by his dying-Camille humiliation in the playoffs. "I'm sure Claude will think twice about diving again," said Brian Skrudland. "He's sorry about his little antics." Yet Lemieux reported to camp with some excess weight, played one game and reaggravated a groin injury, the existence of which was doubted by many observers. It was real. On November 1, Lemieux underwent surgery to repair a torn muscle in the abdominal wall, out for two months. Stéphane Richer just wanted to erase the previous season from memory, reporting fit and champing at the bit to atone. "Shape's not a problem. With me, it is always in my head."

When a false rumour about Richer being gay sucked him into another media vortex, his head almost exploded. The player had, for more than a year, shared a house with a male friend—hardly unusual, but those living arrangements, slyly skewed, provided oxygen for scandal. Richer took his frustration to Burns, who agreed it might be best to bring the innuendo out into the open, to confront the scuttlebutt head on. So Richer called *Le Journal de Montréal* and sought an interview to deny the gossip. He was, in fact, quite the ladies' man, as teammates could well attest. "I was sick and tired of hearing that crap," Richer told reporters. "It wasn't fair to me and my family. I wanted it to stop. Me, I'm going out with a lot of different girls, but who says I have to be married?"

Not long afterwards, Burns opined that an out-of-the-closet gay hockey player was unthinkable in the NHL. "An avowed homosexual, that would never be accepted in hockey—never." Everybody concurred. This was nearly a quarter-century ago, and no one could foresee that same-sex marriage would one day be legal in Canada—not that progressive attitudes would remove the stigma for professional athletes in macho sports.

It was typical of hockey in Montreal, though, that even the whispers should be shrill. The game exists in a heightened atmosphere there, a hothouse ecosystem of rumour and melodrama—and expectations. From the moment training camp opened, Burns tried to temper assumptions of a Stanley Cup final redux. He knew the recalibrated Canadiens weren't nearly as good as conventional wisdom might suggest.

There were bright spots, however, when the training bivouac opened. One was Stéphan Lebeau, coming off an MVP and AHL rookie-of-the-year season in Sherbrooke. Lebeau had been called up for a single game the previous spring and watched the playoffs from the stands as part of the club's taxi squad, dressed only for practice. He was small, and Burns hated small. That he was listed as five foot ten in the media guide was a dodge. "When they took the measurement, I put two hockey pucks under my feet," Lebeau chuckles. "I'm more like five foot eight and a half when I really stretch in the morning." But his offensive skills were no deception. "I was a scoring machine."

The twenty-one-year-old Lebeau made the roster out of camp, yet Burns remained skeptical and limited the centre's ice time, preferring the banging qualities of a Brent Gilchrist. "I was not physical," Lebeau admits. "I was often playing on Pat's first power play, but five-on-five, I had limitations. I was identified as a small hockey player that didn't like to go into traffic, which I don't think was the case. I put good numbers on the board for the amount of ice time that I had. But when you get that sticker put on you, it is very difficult to peel it off your skin. I just had a way of doing things differently, perhaps, more using my head than my physicality. That was not the best type of hockey player for Pat Burns."

Francophone reporters, especially, would harangue Burns all season for underutilizing Lebeau, yet again advancing the slag that the coach was cool to French players. It was useless for Burns to point out that he was born in Montreal to a French-Canadian mother and was bilingual. He was profiled as the Irishman, not the Frenchman. "The French media were really pushing in my favour, saying I was not treated properly," recalls Lebeau, a native of Saint-Jérôme, just north of Montreal. "Pat became a little sensitive about that because they were coming back and coming back. He'd say, 'I'm the one in charge, I'm the boss.'"

Rather deftly, Lebeau played both sides of the fence, tugging at his francophone forelock for French reporters when they came 'round, but never overtly criticizing his coach. He also understood that, in Montreal, youngsters had to wait their turn, no matter who they were.

"We had a funny relationship, me and Pat," says Lebeau. "He was a policeman in his previous life, and I think he was also a policeman as coach. He really behaved like the man of authority, to the point of intimidation. That's how I felt, especially as a rookie. But even veterans were often scared of him, of his reaction. At the same time, he was respected because, despite having that attitude, he was also *respectful,* which I think is how he ended up keeping his players around him."

At one fraught juncture, Burns took Lebeau for lunch across the street from the Forum. "He said he had nothing against me, it was just a coaching decision. He said he believed in me and he asked me to continue working hard. But Pat was not an easy person to deal with. In the dressing room, he could pass right in front of you for five days in a row without even looking at you. And then, on another morning, he could act like you were his best buddy—'How's your family doing?' So you'd say, 'Okay, now he's going to talk to me.' And the next day, he'd be back to walking by without looking at you again. He was tough to read."

Frequently dour and frightening to his players, Burns was also an unregenerate prankster, endlessly devising tricks to pull on the guys and good-humoured about those pulled on him. This was lowbrow, Three Stooges slapstick. "There was one really funny joke he pulled on Patrick Roy," recalls Sylvain Lefebvre, who was then in his rookie season, another Sherbrooke graduate. "He had some powder that police use for getting fingerprints. When it gets wet, it turns blue. He put some in Patrick's mask before practice. When Patrick started sweating, his face turned blue and he didn't even realize it. He took off his mask and all the guys were practically falling down laughing."

Lefebvre was the son of a Quebec police officer and so had some insight into what should be expected from the cop/coach when he arrived at camp. "Pat was tough but fair. Maybe there were some personality clashes, but Pat wanted to put his foot down early, make sure everybody was on board. Maybe he allowed a little more leeway with the veterans, but not that much, and that's what made him respected." Burns's squabbling partner could be Mats Naslund one night, Stéphane Richer the next; nobody was safe or coach's pet.

The extent to which these set-tos and perpetual ice-time disagreements were documented in the press reflected the media's favourites. Says Lefebvre: "I mean, if he didn't play me one night, you didn't hear about it."

A star Burns never crossed was Roy, largely because there was no reason. On a team that would be plagued by injuries all year—283 man-games lost due to ailments by the time playoffs rolled around, 126 more than the previous season—Roy was Burns's ace in the hole.

"Pat was very good to me," says Roy. "He would talk to me a lot. I felt he had confidence in myself, and that really helped. What I truly appreciated was he would explain everything and, when I was not playing, why." In Burns's first season, goaltending duties were generally split between Roy and Brian Hayward, the latter most often starting on the road. "The big change came the following year," says Roy. "I remember going into his office and he said, 'You know, you just won the Vezina and we lost in the finals.' I told him I was ready to take on more games; I wanted to see if he felt the same way. I was nervous because I wasn't sure how he would react, and I surely didn't want to change my relationship with him. Well, he didn't say much. But from then, he started giving me more games and more games and more games. He was the first to give me close to sixty games. He really gave me the net."

And never considered taking it back, even when Roy surrendered three goals in fifty-seven seconds—a pair through the wickets—against the Bruins in a 3–2 loss in November, unflustered that his ace might be overloaded with work. Of far more concern was the continuing spate of injuries, which didn't diminish expectations. "Because we wear the red-white-and-blue sweaters, they expect us to win," said Burns of both fans and the team's media entourage. But they beat Calgary in a Cup final rematch 3–2, reasserted Canadian proprietary rights over the game by defeating the Soviet Wings 2–1 in a January exhibition game at the Forum, and were 23–19–6 by the All-Star break, with Burns behind the Wales (Eastern) Conference bench. Nobody was remotely surprised when he padded out the ballot selection by naming three of his players to the roster: Richer, Chelios and Shayne Corson. For the actual game, his presence as coach was almost superfluous, simply opening the gate for superstar Mario Lemieux—fittingly, the spectacle was hosted by Pittsburgh—who scored three goals in the first period as the Wales Conference dumped the Campbell Conference 12–7.

More stimulating was a late-January match with the Division-leading Bruins, marked by a heated exchange of words with his opposite number, Mike Milbury, who'd taken the coaching reins in Boston. Standing atop the Montreal bench, Burns hollered and gestured towards Milbury, who was just as vocal in return. The harsh words prompted the two coaches to move menacingly towards each other, but the officiating crew—and police— held them back and order was eventually restored. Boston squeaked out a 2–1 victory.

Burns reminded anyone who asked—and they all asked—that Montreal was rebuilding, a word he was antsy about using. "We can't call it rebuilding," he told a media scrum in mock horror. "We have to call it a transition. If I use the word 'rebuilding' here, they'll hang me." When a package arrived for him at the Forum, he gave it a leery shake, pretending to be worried about a bomb. "It's the greatest job in hockey, but it comes with a curse. The curse is, you've got to win. I'm trying to make everybody understand that we won't get 115 points this year and we might not get to the Stanley Cup final."

There was no jovial bantering a month later, when co-captain Guy Carbonneau and defenceman Craig Ludwig were scratched for a game—suspended—after disobeying a Burns order not to leave their hotel following a crushing 5–3 loss in Boston and sneaking off to a bar. Carbonneau sucked up the punishment as just. "Even if I'm captain, the rules are there for everybody."

The injured started trickling back, but Burns was still forced to lean heavily on his "brats," especially on the blue line, Lefebvre and Mathieu Schneider stepping up when Chelios was felled by a stretched cruciate ligament in his left knee, for which he went under the knife in late March. Without "Cheli," it would be a prohibitive task to catch Buffalo for second place in the Adams Division—they didn't—much less make another run at reaching the finals. A nightmare season of injuries had taken Carbonneau, Lemieux, Bobby Smith and Brian Skrudland out of the lineup for more than a month at a time.

Back-to-back ties closed out the season, giving them 93 points overall and third place in the Adams Division, the Sabres their first-round opponent. Buffalo had twice defeated Montreal since February, when their hold on second was threatened, and were 3–0–1 against the Canadiens in the cozy confines of the Memorial Auditorium, where the series would open.

A classic Buffalo blizzard raged outside the rink on April 5 as the teams lined up for game one. Inside, the Sabres whipped up an ice storm of their own, freezing out the visitors 4–1. High-tempo, fast-paced and bone-crunching, Buffalo punished the Habs' battered bodies with goalie Daren Puppa prolonging his mastery of Montreal. In the trainer's room, Chelios continued his frantic rehab regimen.

The Sabres, unwisely, crowed about their win, some speaking prematurely about a Stanley Cup final for the franchise. Montreal's players were indignant to learn Buffalo had a cardboard Cup cut-out in the dressing room. For game two, the Aud was festooned with "Pump it up for the Stanley Cup" banners. Carbonneau sniffed: "You could see all those banners. They made the mistake of being overconfident. You have to know how to stay humble."

Montreal humbled the Sabres, surviving an early two-man disadvantage, their confidence growing from there to surface with a 3–0 win. "Playoff hockey has a lot to do with luck, with who gets the breaks," Burns said afterwards. "It was our turn." It was more than merely luck. While Burns had sometimes been damned with faint praise as a coach big on motivational genius but wanting on Xs-and-Os tactics, it was his sharp penalty-killing strategy that kept Buffalo off the score sheet: setting up a passive box that frustrated Buffalo's penchant for making pretty cross-ice passes, Burns ordered his players not to rush the puck carrier or challenge aggressively against the point. The Sabres were thrown off stride by this passive-aggressive technique.

On the morning of game three in Montreal, Burns woke up sniffing OT in the air. "We're due for an overtime game," he predicted, correctly. "I can smell it." Montreal prevailed in the ultra-conservative encounter that unfolded, Brian Skrudland squeezing the winner past Puppa and the left post at 12:35 of the extra frame. Two nights later, Buffalo evened the series on Montreal ice, Pierre Turgeon notching a pair in the 4–2 victory. It was their last hurrah. Montreal edged the Sabres 3–2 in Buffalo—Burns double-shifting Richer, who scored his fifth and sixth of the playoffs—and the coach was anxious to end it back at the Forum in game six. "We don't want to come back here for a seventh game." Actually, neither home nor away ice seemed to please Burns, who found reason to fret over playing in front of a keyed-up Montreal audience. "Playing at home, guys get more nervous. The fans get impatient. They want a goal right away. By doing that, the players tend to lose the team concept and start playing as individuals. Players start doing things that aren't them. Then mistakes happen and the other team scores." He tried to quell the rah-rah. "We can't win a game in the first five minutes or even the first period."

And Montreal did start sluggishly, but there was no real doubt about the outcome from then on, as the home side emerged 5–2 victors, taking the first round in six. Montreal had proved too opportunistic, too experienced and too quick for the Sabres to handle. The grinding goaltenders' duel was not particularly entertaining hockey, and Burns made no apologies for that, though Claude Lemieux did. "I know sometimes we're not a pretty team to watch. I know people pay good money to see us put on a show, but we're not here to do that—we're here to win."

Inside their dressing room, the Habs celebrated in reserved fashion. They'd been the underdogs against Buffalo—Burns's preferred status— because the Sabres had the better season. But few truly expected the Queen City to emerge triumphant when tossed into the playoff bell jar against a club with Montreal's history. For the seventh consecutive season, Buffalo had lost in the first round.

In New England, Boston had weathered seven-game fits with Hartford en route to what was expected to be yet another titanic showdown with historical nemesis Montreal in the Adams Division final. There was no time to savour the triumph. Said first-year coach Mike Milbury following his team's game seven thriller: "A series win over Hartford deserves more than a Budweiser, a baloney sandwich and five hours of sleep." Burns professed to have preferred Boston as a playoff dance partner over Hartford: "Montreal versus Boston is the series all of Canada wants to see. I would have been a bit worried if we'd played Hartford. I know the guys will have no trouble getting up for Boston—the feeling is completely different in the dressing room when we play the Bruins." That history gave Boston GM Harry Sinden agita. "I'm tired of losing to them every spring." Montreal, of course, had eliminated the Bs in five of the last six seasons and were 21–3 overall in playoff series against them. Despite their edge in season play, the Bruins were yet again staring down a playoff barrel, seeing red-white-and-blue jerseys stampeding their way.

Montreal got an emotional—and lineup—boost when Chris Chelios, who'd missed the final twenty-one regular-season games and the Buffalo series, was pronounced fit to resume his hockey labours. Didn't make a lick of difference as the Bruins outdefended the defence-first Canadiens with a crisp, pristine, 1–0 win behind Andy Moog's stellar goaltending. For game two, sniper Stéphane Richer also returned from a twisted ankle and scored two. But in the oppressive heat of the Boston Garden, the Bruins rallied from four one-goal deficits, Cam Neely's second of the night with 1:49 left in regulation time sending it into overtime and Garry Galley scoring the 5–4 winner. Suddenly, the Bruins had a stunning 2–0 lead in the series. When the Canadiens were then rudely smacked around 6–3 back at the Forum, Patrick Roy chased from the net, they found themselves in the mortifying position of becoming the first Montreal squad in thirty-eight years to bow out in a straight set. Fans had emptied the Forum with seven minutes left. "It was hard, very hard, but he understood," said Burns of yanking Roy. "I can tell you right now, Patrick Roy is going back in."

The Montreal machine was unravelling like a ball of string, and tempers were fraying. Burns tried to strike a reasonable tone at first, pointing out Boston had finished eight points ahead of Montreal in the regular season and the Habs had been hard pressed to get past the Sabres. "People didn't give us a chance in hell of beating Buffalo. And when we did, everyone gave us the Cup. We know that's not true."

Reporters, retroactively, studied the entrails of the season, seeking indicators for this precipitous downfall. The obvious chink was Montreal's pitiful power play, but that was too banal an explanation for many. There were rumours of dissension in the ranks, a tendency towards cliques cool to each other, in defiance of Burns's all-for-one doctrine. Some traced the friction all the way back to the split-vote over the captaincy. One loss away from elimination, Burns was clearly in a state of shock, looking and behaving like a man carrying the woes of the world on his shoulders, his voice strained by inflamed tonsils. In the crisis, he became once more the focus of attention, with answers demanded. At practice, Burns and Lemieux got into a heated exchange within earshot of reporters, and cameras caught the red-faced coach brandishing a stick right under his insolent player's chin. Lemieux grumbled: "I know what's wrong with our power play, and I'm not a genius."

"BOSTON BROOMS!" shrieked gleeful headlines in Beantown, anticipating the sweep, which no B-team had ever accomplished in a seven-game series with Montreal. In desperation, and with no small amount of smirking from his French-Canadian critics in the media, Burns pulled Stéphan Lebeau out of street clothes for game four. The fan-favourite rookie, with fifteen goals on the season, hadn't played in three weeks, and Burns had heard an earful, though the insertion had more to do with an ankle injury that sidelined Richer.

Lebeau's playoff debut was memorable. In fairy-tale fashion, he broke a 1–1 third-period tie with his first NHL postseason goal, finishing off a play he'd started, and then stuffing a wraparound past Moog for his second of the night, giving Montreal the only two-goal lead it had enjoyed in the series. Coupled with a tough-as-rawhide effort from Carbonneau, who contributed two goals, the Canadiens staved off elimination 4–1. Montreal played with an intensity bordering on anger.

"Lebeau made a big difference," said Burns. "With the injuries we've had all year, we've had to look for different people to step up and help us find a way to win. And tonight we found Stéphan just in time."

The kid was over the moon. "I've tried to keep a positive attitude. I didn't play much at the end of the regular season, but I kept ready in practice just in case there was an injury and I would be needed. And tonight was the night. I was on the puck all night long and it kept coming to me. I felt good in the warmup and confident that I could help. We're still in this thing, and anything can happen."

A reporter approached Milbury afterwards, wondering why the Bruins always lost to Montreal when it counted. Smiling warmly, Milbury responded, "Fuck you."

Before the game, Lebeau had warned that he was no saviour. But a French paper the next day trumpeted his impact as "LEBEAU: LE SAUVEUR!" The team was already in Boston by then, where Burns vainly tried to justify his scarce use of Lebeau by claiming he'd simply hoped to nurture him slowly. "I'm sure this morning in Montreal I look like a dummy."

Lebeau had almost singlehandedly averted the sweep. "How sweep it wasn't," mourned a Boston columnist. And in game five, Lebeau looked primed to do it again, notching the 1–1 equalizer with thirty-three seconds remaining in the second period. But there'd be no miracle. Boston pulled ahead, and a Cam Neely empty-netter sealed Montreal's fate, 3–1. Bounced in five.

If the guillotine were still in use, Forum faithful would have been screaming for heads to roll. In fact, the Canadiens had been in over their heads, Boston too strong an opponent, palpably the better team. Montreal finished the series 1-for-22 on the power play, 2-for-51 in the playoffs; that was the main problem. Carbonneau, it was revealed, had been playing with a cracked bone in his wrist. And Chelios would go under the scalpel again for a hernia operation. As a coach, Burns had shrunk to mortal dimensions, but the failures were not laid primarily at his doorstep—not yet.

Of course, this being Montreal, there was no real off-season. GM Savard, who'd taken intense heat from local media for not making late-season trades to strengthen his team as the playoffs approached, said the organization would "take a long, serious look at our hockey club," indicating changes would be made.

Chelios was among those hoping there would be no shakeup. Then he became, dramatically, the first big name to depart. He learned about his trade to Chicago in a one-minute phone call from Savard, who was at the AHL meetings in Bermuda. The swap for native Montrealer Denis Savard—hometown boys trading places—had been in the works, allegedly, for about a week when announced in early July. But it seemed more than coincidence that Savard pulled the trigger within twenty-four hours of discovering that Chelios and close buddy Gary Suter had been arrested following a punch-up outside a bar in Madison, Wisconsin.

According to the criminal complaint, the players had fought with two police officers, Chelios struggling with the cops when they tried to arrest him for urinating in public. Chelios was charged with resisting arrest and disorderly conduct, a misdemeanour. It was not his first brush with law enforcement in the state where he lived during the off-season. In 1984, Chelios was convicted of escaping from police who were taking him to a Madison hospital for an alcohol test after he'd been arrested for driving under the influence. He pleaded no contest to the escape and paid a fine, but was never charged with drunk driving. The policemen involved in the new incident sued both players, claiming to having been "assaulted, battered, abused and ridiculed." At his arraignment, Chelios entered a not guilty plea.

In any event, Serge Savard had reached the end of his rope with Chelios. And the player professed to be pleased with the trade. "I'm really happy that I'm coming home. It was so unexpected." All these years on, Chelios admits the abrupt exit from Montreal shook him severely. "It hit me out of nowhere when I was traded, to be honest." But his biggest regret was not having been a better captain for Burns. "You're supposed to be the go-between guy with the coach and the players. I had a really tough time and struggled with that. I still think to this day that I failed as a captain in Montreal. I wasn't ready for the role. And I think Pat, being a young coach in the NHL at that time, didn't know how to handle that, either—what my role was, what my relationship with him should be. I'll be the first to admit that I didn't understand. I'd had guys like Bob Gainey who showed me, taught me, what it took to be a team guy. You needed a captain like Gainey, who was level-headed, didn't get too up or too down. And that wasn't me at that point in my career, at my age. I didn't help the situation one bit when I was in Montreal. When I got traded, I thought I was just starting to figure it out and was ready to accept the responsibility. But at that point, we'd lost, and someone had to pay and I was the guy that year." After the trade, Burns invited Chelios to his cottage in the Eastern Townships. "We spent a couple of days there and talked about everything, what I would have done differently. But it was too late . . ."

A month later, it was Claude Lemieux, the thorn in Burns's side, out the door, dispatched to New Jersey for Sylvain Turgeon after failing to join the team when it jetted off to training camp in distant Moscow, an ill-advised NHL goodwill experiment. Serge Savard had brought player and coach together for one final stab at resolving their conflict, but no joy. Recalls Lemieux: "I told Pat, 'I like you.' And he said, 'I like you too.' I said, 'But you don't play me.' He said, 'I play you as much as I think you should play.' I told Serge, 'You're going to have to trade me.' I know he didn't want to, but Serge promised me after that meeting he'd trade me by training camp. Serge was an honourable man. He was trying to do what was right for the team."

Burns maintained their spats had been exaggerated by the media and he was not the impetus behind the trade. "Claude didn't want to leave because of me. I talked to him and wished him luck."

He was being disingenuous, as Savard confirms. "He had a real tough time with Claude Lemieux. I had to get rid of Claude because those two could not reconcile. That's something Pat should have been able to do. But he was very stubborn. He would not change his mind. It was like he couldn't recover. As a manager, you have the choice to get rid of a player or the coach. Obviously, in this case it was the player who went. It turned out to be a terrible mistake for us, a very bad trade for us. Turgeon turned out to be a bad player.

"Claude was pretty tough with Pat, too. It came to a point where, you don't connect, you don't listen. Pat wanted no part of him. That's one side of Pat that could have improved, and did improve later. But Pat was a guy who was always right and you couldn't change his mind."

Chapter Eight

Rioting Russians, Milbury Mind Games

"If we get beat in Boston in April, I'm not going to blame Russia."

A RINGING PHONE in his hotel room woke Pat Burns in the middle of the night. Three of his players were in jail. Did he wish to bail them out?

The Canadiens had arrived in chilly Winnipeg two days early for a December game in 1990. Apart from practice, they had a lot of idle time on their hands. Most of the players went out on the first evening to a bar called the Marble Club. By closing time, only three remained: Shayne Corson, Mike Keane and Brian Skrudland. They were just leaving, had stepped through the door, when Corson noticed that a young woman was being smacked around by her male companion. With two sisters of his own, Corson was outraged by the spectacle of a female being abused. He told the man to knock it off. Harsh words were exchanged. Suddenly, someone else struck Corson over the head from behind with a cane. Keane made to grab this second man and was himself whipped across the forehead with the same cane. Skrudland, just emerging into the night air, saw both teammates covered in blood and thought for a moment they'd been shot. Coming to their defence, he too joined the fray, which had now turned into a full rumble. Police were called, and all the participants were handcuffed and thrown in the slammer.

"We spent the night together, in the same cell, wearing prison jumpsuits they gave us," Corson remembers. "Keaner and I were pretty young at the time. It was scary. And there were other guys in the cell too, pretty tough guys. We sat on a bench together, the three of us, side by side, and didn't speak. Skrudland kept saying, 'Don't speak, don't say a word, just sit and shut up.' We didn't want anybody to know who we were, but they recognized us and then they started talking to us, even asking for autographs. So that made us feel a little more comfortable, but we were still scared."

Someone—Corson thinks it was Skrudland—rang up Burns when police permitted the obligatory one phone call. "But he didn't come right away. He left us there till morning." News of the arrest had already broken, and Burns tried to sneak his wayward threesome out the back exit. "He wasn't happy," says Corson. "He gave us shit. Pat said, 'We'll talk about this later.'" That afternoon, after practice, Burns sat the three quasi-felons down for a stern chat. "Pat wanted to know what happened. We realized the best thing was to be honest, tell the truth. I explained about the girl getting beat up and that we hadn't started the fight. Pat said, 'Okay, did you learn something from this?' We said yeah, definitely. And that was it."

For Corson, this was neither the first nor the last time he'd have brushes with the law. More often, his shenanigans were harmless—on that same trip, Corson and Keane picked up a Christmas tree in the hotel lobby and dumped it in Chris Chelios's room. But on other occasions, fuelled by alcohol, things turned ugly. Eventually, when Burns was no longer there to watch his back, the bar brawls would get him tossed out of Montreal.

Life for a Montreal coach is always eventful and never predictable, no matter how precisely charted in a schedule that's released well in advance of every new season. In the late summer of 1990, that schedule sent the *bleu, blanc et rouge* across the Atlantic. The "Friendship Tour," a promotional brainwave of the NHL, had the Canadiens, their wives and their children boinging from Sweden to Latvia to the Soviet Union over a fortnight of exhibition games. Pat Burns loathed the whole undertaking.

"I don't think it's going to be the kind of training camp that a coach would like to conduct," he grumped prophetically as the travelling circus aboard Air Habs landed in Stockholm.

Perhaps, given his history at the junior worlds in Czechoslovakia, the league should have had a rethink. The NHL was, after all, at that very moment trying to soothe feathers ruffled by Sergei Fedorov's walking away from the Soviet national team to sign with Detroit. Burns didn't do unruffling very well.

The excursion had started mildly enough. It would conclude with an ugly brawl and empty vodka bottles hurled at the "dirty" Canadiens. Following an unremarkable match in Leningrad, the team had flown on to Moscow, worn out, sleep-deprived and grouchy. The culture shock had already knocked them for a loop, and now they were simply eager to go home. In the capital, Stéphan Lebeau had his clothes stolen, players complained about the food—until Patrick Roy discovered a just-opened Pizza Hut, placing a massive to-go order—and everyone was pretty much confined to their hotel, partly because of the language barrier and partly because there was nowhere to go, few Habs particularly interested in camera-clicking tourist jaunts to the onion domes of St. Basil's Cathedral or Lenin's Tomb. Burns claimed several wives had been accosted by Russian men who thought they were hookers, and so the women were afraid to venture outside the hotel.

It quickly became apparent that the Soviets were taking these games all too seriously. "To us, this is preseason hockey, it doesn't have too much importance," Burns objected. "But the Soviets have put a lot of emphasis on these games, too much emphasis sometimes." Yet it was Montreal that was criticized for playing too aggressively in the first Moscow encounter, a 4–1 loss to Dynamo. That was merely the aperitif. The next night, facing a keyed-up Central Red Army squad, was déjà vu for Burns, fingered as the culprit in yet another diplomatic fiasco. Fights had already twice stopped the game. In the third period, a couple of bottles smashed on the ice after being thrown towards the Canadiens' bench, and the glass had to be swept up before play could resume. Several Montreal players were hit with coins. A number of scuffles broke out simultaneously, Shayne Corson and Stéphane Richer jumping off the bench to join the fray, giving the Canadiens a two-man advantage on the fight card that ensued. Petr Svoboda was ejected for a deliberate attempt to injure. Peace was just being restored when fans began pelting the visitors with debris, so Burns ordered his team off the ice. "When that vodka bottle broke in front of the bench, Coach Burns said, 'Let's get out of here,'" said defenceman Mathieu Schneider. Burns insisted that Soviet hockey federation president Leonid Kravchenko get on the public address system and calm the unruly crowd. Having done so, Kravchenko pleaded with the Canadiens to finish the match, adding, as a bizarre pleasantry, his hopes that the visitors would leave the Soviet Union with good memories.

"It hasn't been much fun," Burns fumed later, after Red Army edged his team 3–2 in overtime. He justified his ten-minute timeout as a necessary precaution. He'd been worried about his players' safety. "When the president of the [federation] comes over and says how sorry he was and says his fans were hooligans to throw bottles and this and that, and then he comes back and says he wants our wives . . . to leave with good memories of Russia, you sort of look at him and say, 'What?' We've been stalled and we've been lied to and we've been almost shafted in every corner in nearly every place we've been."

Red Army coach Viktor Tikhonov blamed the Canadiens for the melee. "They started this fight and they had no right to leave the ice."

As the Canadiens bid their fare-thee-well to Mother Russia, legendary ex-goalie Vladislav Tretiak and others delivered parting shots at their guests, castigating Montreal for the third-period donnybrook. "Can you believe it, they felt insulted," he told the Tass news service. "They provoked a clash and were forced to leave the rink. Canadian players have always been clean sportsmen. But in this match they used the dirtiest moves—hitting players already down on the ice and jumping out from the bench to help their teammates in hand-to-hand fights." Soviet customs officers got the last laugh, confiscating dozens of jars of caviar at the airport, the Canadiens' flight delayed for three hours as a thorough search of the players' luggage was conducted. Montreal had arrived with $3,000 worth of medical supplies and equipment to donate to Soviet hockey. They left with a bill for fourteen rubles, accused of stealing two tiny, rough-textured towels from the Moscow visitors' dressing room.

When training camp reconvened as normal in Montreal, Burns tried to put the whole sorry affair behind him. "If we get beat in Boston in April, I'm not going to blame it on Russia. If I have a heart attack next year, I'm not going to blame it on Russia. But it will affect us at the start of the season. When we got back, we had to start training camp all over again."

Turns out, Burns was prescient about Boston.

The regular season came and went, bringing with it Burns's 100th NHL win and nasty jeering for Stéphane Richer—who scored 51 goals the previous year—on Fan Appreciation Day at the Forum, with his coach observing, "Here, you can go quickly from hero to zero." But the frustration of late-season slumps had been trained on the delicate flower that was Richer, the hockey public continuing its love-hate relationship with its star. Richer had done himself no favours by revealing he'd consulted with an astrologist about his scoring travails. "As a Gemini, it's all or nothing with me," Richer told snickering reporters. "I'm loved or I'm despised."

If the love was no longer quite as fervent for Burns either, he remained very much Montreal's celebrity coach, more ink-worthy than a tepid pool of player personalities, even Denis Savard—proving less than the spin-o-rama saviour advertised. The diet Burns put himself on in preparation for the postseason was closely documented: twenty pounds lost, smoking habit snapped. Canadiens finished second in the Adams Division, eleven points behind the Bruins, and thus drew Buffalo for a second straight playoff-opening opponent. What was expected to be a low-scoring wrangle between defensive-oriented squads was anything but: forty goals scored through the first four kooky games; each club taking two apiece on home ice; pucks going in off skates, shins and shoulders; Patrick Roy yanked during game four and then returned to the net for the next period. Montreal eked out a 4–3 overtime victory in game five and then ripped the Sabres 5–1 at the Memorial Auditorium to close it out with a bang.

That set the table for another *mano-a-mano* with bitter rival Boston. Francis Rosa wrote in the *Boston Globe*: "April has become official. Daylight Savings Time has come, as it does every year. The Red Sox have opened the season, as they do every April. The Marathon is upon us, as it is annually. And the Bruins and Montreal are matched again in the playoffs. All is well in our corner of the wonderful world of sports. The Bruins and the Canadiens for the 10th time in the last 15 years. Now, that makes spring official."

Boston had a firm regular-season edge over Montreal, with a 5–2–1 head-to-head record. Yet there was anxiety over the "Montreal Jinx," even though Boston had won two of their last three series and even after the Bruins tasted first blood, grinding out a 2–1 decision in the plodding, eye-glazing opener on Causeway Street. Burns had warned this would be a tight and emotional playoff set. "There was the jinx for years and years, how Boston couldn't beat Montreal. That's over now. They don't believe in the ghosts anymore. Anyone who's not motivated to play Boston shouldn't even put on skates. You see it when you go into the old Garden and they've won five Stanley Cups, and it's the same for them when they come into the Forum and see our twenty-three banners. This rivalry is good for everyone."

Mike Milbury scoffed at the Montreal jinx. "If you look back at the Montreal teams that beat Boston, they were probably mostly better teams. Now the talent has evened out a little bit. We don't have the sword of Damocles hanging over our head. It puts us more on an even footing psychologically."

Game one was an unusually polite, fight-free affair that had fans wondering what had become of the Flying Frenchmen and the Big, Bad Bruins. One wag suggested game two would be played with both sides wearing tuxedos. Asked why there wasn't more emotion, Burns was miffed: "I can't understand that question. Why do you ask it? Because we're not throwing the gloves and not fighting? Everyone's waiting for a brawl because it's Boston and Montreal. Well, it's not going to happen. We don't have the ammunition for that and I don't think Mike Milbury has either. It may not seem so upstairs, but it's rough hockey down on the ice level. It's tough but it's clean."

The ice-level excitement was considerably cranked in game two, Montreal staging a dramatic come-from-behind effort, Richer tying the score 3–3, beating Andy Moog with 8:30 remaining in the third period. "I was really surprised to be by myself in front of the net. In the Garden, it's so small that every time you get one shot off, you get pushed out of the way."

Burns rested Richer and his first-line mates for the rest of regulation time. He had a feeling, a hunch. When the horn sounded and the teams retired to their dressing rooms, Burns pulled his goal-scorer aside. "I told Richer, 'You're going to win the game for us in overtime.'" Twenty-seven seconds was all it took. Richer struck for his second goal of the night. "Am I a coach or a prophet?" Burns crowed.

Moog missed the Bruins team bus to the Forum for game three because he was watching golf on TV in his hotel room. He hitched a ride with some Boston media and slipped into the dressing room without Milbury noticing the tardy arrival. The goalie made the difference in the net with forty saves, holding off the Canadiens after Ken Hodge scored the 3–2 marker with just under a minute and a half remaining in regulation time. "We deserved to win, but Andy made saves like I've never seen," said Burns, tipping his hat. "I don't think he can have another game like this."

In game four he most assuredly didn't, Montreal storming back 6–2, Shayne Corson leading the way with two goals and two assists. Burns had called his tough winger out for particular criticism, his idea of motivation, and it was front-page fodder for the press. But the tactic worked. "That's one thing Burns was awesome at," says Corson, "knowing which players he could push hard and call out, and which he had to be a bit more delicate with. He knew he could kick me in the butt and get the best out of me." Corson came out of the chute in the fourth game like a man on fire. He completed his lively evening by picking up a five-minute major and game misconduct for high-sticking Dave Christian. "It was probably one of the best games I've seen him play since he first put on the uniform of the Montreal Canadiens," said Burns. Just a couple of months earlier, Montreal had almost traded Corson to Toronto for Wendel Clark, but backed off the deal, leery of the Leaf captain's injury stats: 159 games missed over the three previous seasons.

Milbury was apoplectic over his team's performance, deciding the series required drastic intervention. "I felt the momentum had completely shifted to Montreal," he recalls. His solution was to pluck the Bruins from their comfy beds at home and schlep them all to a one-star motel in the strip-mall boonies, sequestering them in low-rent surroundings the night before game five. "It was really a welfare motel. I can't describe it any better than that. It's still there. We went to a dumpy little rink where we held an intense practice, me mostly out of control. If somebody from the outside world had seen me, they would have had me put in a loonie bin. I screamed at the guys for about an hour. I knew I couldn't beat them up physically, but I needed to make a point. Pat's team had stormed back and was going to take control of the series. So I made them stay at this dump. We practised, had dinner, and then I sent them out bowling. But that's the kind of stuff you had to do in order to stay even with Pat, because his force of personality, his presence, was obvious. He had that ugly snarl about him, and his team played with that same ugly snarl, and you had to be ready to match that competitiveness or you weren't going to win."

Something worked. The Bruins smartened up and played their best hockey of the year in the fifth game, slamming Montreal 4–1. "We had guys that thought it was all over," Burns fumed, smoke coming out his ears. "We had guys who didn't have ten games' experience in the National Hockey League making big quotes to the media. We didn't respect the opposition; that's where we missed out. They outplayed us, outskated us, outhit us, out-everythinged us."

Facing elimination, Burns had to counter Milbury's extracurricular wang-dang-doodling. So he hijacked the team bus. While reporters waited for the Canadiens at their suburban practice rink, wondering what the heck had become of the no-show Habs, Burns had absconded with the players in full equipment, ordering the bus driver to take them all on a scenic tour of Montreal's seedier neighbourhoods. "Take a look," he told the players, directing their gaze at blue-collar life. These were the folks who lived and died by the Canadiens. The players owed *them* the best they had to give in game six. It was pretty hokey stuff. Burns didn't rant or rave; he was preternaturally calm. "He told us stories," says Corson. "He wanted us to remember how lucky we were, how fortunate we were to play a game that we loved to play and to make good money at it. That's what he tried to explain to us that day." And Burns reminded his charges they hadn't lost anything yet; the Adams Division final was still there for the taking. Then the bus returned to the Forum, where players changed back into street clothes and went out for a team meal.

Psyched up, the club matched Boston's intensity from game five in game six, Corson again providing the heroics. "It was warfare," he says. "At that point, I would have gone through a wall for Pat." The Bruins had a 2–1 lead with barely four minutes left in the third period when Corson chopped a rebound past Moog, who'd just made a sparkling save on Richer. In overtime, Patrick Roy needed to be at his awesome best, because Boston had the edge in play and scoring chances. At one point, he put his face in front of a shot. Then, practically carrying Craig Janney on his back, Corson swept in a pass from Brian Skrudland, falling down as he shovelled a shot that knocked in off the right post at 17:47 of OT, giving Montreal the 3–2 decision needed to send the series back to Boston for game seven.

Burns didn't have much personal experience of game sevens in hockey, but claimed to have been at the Forum in 1979 for the famous too-many-men-on-the-ice encounter with Boston. "My brother-in-law got me the ticket." When Yvon Lambert scored the winner, "I jumped up just like everybody else." Who knows if that was true? Burns was never beyond fabricating for a good anecdote.

At their Cambridge hotel, Burns cancelled the off-day practice, reasoning his players needed a rest for the final showdown more than they needed to skate. He'd pondered pulling another motivational trick, but was stumped. "I tried to think of something on the plane, but I couldn't. So I just let them be themselves. I asked them not to be lying around the lobby, but to maybe go out for a walk together." That's what he always did on a game day. "We'll have a team dinner and then a team meeting together, and that's about it. I asked them to be relaxed. I don't want anybody walking around in his hockey underwear in the lobby, but I want them to stay as loose as possible. We don't want anybody to be too tight. We want them to think about it, but we don't want them not to sleep about it."

One thing Burns had done was caution his players against putting too much faith in Montreal's historical knack for winning the big games. "I don't believe in history at all. I think the things that were done in the past are in the past and don't reflect on anything that's going to happen here. Hockey's different now. Teams are different."

In the Boston dressing room, Milbury tacked up a story written by a Montreal columnist, saying it was "mandatory reading" for his troops. The column ridiculed the Bruins, theorizing that they'd been put on earth for the express purpose of losing important games to the Canadiens. "He called us ugly and dumb. Ugly I can accept, but never dumb," said Milbury. "It gave my guys something to think about it. They were focused. The writer thought he was pretty clever, I guess, but he actually helped us." Then Milbury brought in Harry Sinden—winning coach in the '72 Canada-Soviet series, the pinnacle of hockey competition—to preach the Boston gospel.

Game seven would be a down-to-the-wire finish, Moog magnificent from start to end. Scoreless in the first period, Boston got on the board in the second and then made it 2–0 early in the third when Cam Neely converted on a power play. Moog's shutout was spoiled by Stéphan Lebeau's backhand with one minute remaining in regulation time, a controversial goal because Moog had knocked his net off its moorings during a goalmouth scramble. Officials determined it had been a deliberate ploy, and the goal stood.

Burns pulled Roy with 2:49 left on the clock. The final minute was mayhem and madness as Montreal desperately sought the equalizer. At the other end, four Boston shots at the gaping Canadiens' net were blocked by Montreal skaters, and several other shots went wide. Milbury couldn't believe his eyes. "For the life of me, I don't know how we didn't score." In fact, he thought it was Montreal that had scored on one of their surges. "There was a goalmouth scramble around the front of the net where Brian Skrudland and Shayne Corson were using their sticks like machetes on Ray Bourque," he recalls. "It was incredibly vicious."

"It was wild," an exhausted Moog said afterwards, savouring the hard-earned 2–1 victory and 4–3 series decision. "They just rushed the net and were right on top of us. The pucks just hit me." It was the first time Boston had ever defeated Montreal in a game seven.

Being bested by Boston stuck in the craw. But there was nothing to berate the Canadiens for in this series, or their coach. Burns was rightly proud of his team, players black and blue and bloodied as they readied for the flight home. In painful, poignant defeat, he was also classy. "I just wish Mike and the Bruins good luck. I hope they go all the way so we can say we went right down to the wire with them."

The Bruins were halted in the conference finals by Pittsburgh. But any Montreal ghosts that had been hanging around had been exorcized for Boston in a gut-check series that could so easily have gone the other way. Said Milbury, "The gods were with us." And then, because hockey gods are fickle, they weren't.

Chapter Nine

Hoedowns and Harleys

"I figured he had two completely different personalities."

IT WAS CALLED the Stogie Shack and it's where Pat Burns played—literally.

Eight fine guitars, electric and acoustic, nested in their stands, as lovingly tended as his Harley-Davidsons, strummed or plucked as the mood struck. While coaching in the NHL was a dream come wildly true, Burns had other fantasies—guitar picker, cowboy, Hells Angel—and often dressed the part.

In wrangler mode, Burns wore hand-tooled boots, bolo tie, soft lambskin vests and suede cattleman's hat fitted low over his brow. As motorcyclist, it was fingerless gloves and stompers. And as the Nashville crooner he fancied himself, there were flamboyantly embroidered shirts tucked into belts with ornate buckles. Country 'n' western was always on the radio in his pickup truck—his preferred vehicle. It was the music he rarely convinced players to blast in the dressing room. "With Pat, it had to be country and nothing else," recalls Pat Brisson, the hockey agent who played for Burns in Hull. That was but one of several notable passions for the blue-collar Renaissance man. In another life, if perhaps not the Harley outlaw who would always beguile, Burns might have taken to the honky-tonk stage. He possessed a velvety singing voice and was totally in his element in front of a crowd, requiring no coaxing to perform.

The kid with the garage band who'd entertained guests at his sister's wedding had grown up into an adult who could afford expensive toys: bikes, boats and Fenders. Frugal in other aspects, he'd spend top dollar on a custom-made axe, caressing its contours as if running his fingers along a woman's curves. Though he couldn't read a note, Burns had taught himself the basic chords and remembered all the lyrics to songs, including—off the hurtin' twang reservation—the complete Bob Dylan and Cat Stevens canons.

Who was Pat Burns when he wasn't being PAT BURNS, coach of the Montreal Canadiens? Even players who considered themselves close to their boss had no real clue, nor was there any reason to explore the personal side. These were professional relationships, forged on the ice and fortified under the hot lights of NHL rinks, inside dank dressing rooms, aboard planes, idling in hotel lobbies; motley groups of individuals, the game their only common denominator, who might spend up to ten months together, from training camp through playoffs, then scatter into the diaspora of the off-season, perhaps never to cross paths again except as opponents, formerly of the same crest. The intensity of a season burns furiously and is then abruptly extinguished. Hockey life is both unstable and relentlessly forward-thrusting. There's no standing still. Burns burned his candle at one end—as coach—but simmered down at the other end, unwound.

He found his traction, his equilibrium, in the Eastern Townships, surrounded by people who had no connection to hockey, a bucolic Neverland where he could relax, stop being Coach Burns, though his thoughts never truly strayed from the game. In the dog days of summer, he'd still be scribbling potential line combinations on bar napkins or considering players he coveted while sitting at the pilot wheel of his fishing boat. Fishing was for contemplating, entire days spent on the sun-dappled water, and Burns went through one particularly ardent angling phase, kitting himself out with the most sophisticated gear. But usually, he preferred boats with speed, towing water-skiers or just crashing across the lake's gentle waves.

The Stogie Shack was no more than a shed at the rear of a property he owned near Magog, the upscale resort town on the shores of Lake Memphremagog, close to the Vermont border. Burns had assembled an upright piano and drum set, with propane stove seeing service as another percussion instrument. Various friends sat in for jam sessions late at night, everybody often well oiled. If any of them picked up one of his guitars, Burns would growl: "Don't fuck with that. It's worth a lot of money."

He'd first found his Magog niche—Donald Sutherland was among the local residents—while coaching in Sherbrooke, and would thereafter keep it as his private base of operations, handy enough to Montreal—even, later, Boston and New Jersey—for quick getaways as well as long, languid summers, children Maureen and Jason spending weeks with him. Burns was eager to make up for all the years he hadn't been a hands-on dad, barely present, especially for Maureen. He relished giving them this tiny piece of paradise.

His buddies, high-spirited and idiotically silly—most of them sufficiently well-heeled to indulge in leisurely sabbaticals when Burns was *in situ,* one of them a senator's son and heir to the Daoust hockey equipment fortune—constituted a kind of jesters' court for the off-duty coach. The "Pat's Court" retinue was a familiar sight around the Forum during the season. "Fools and jesters," sniffed a thoroughly unimpressed Ronald Corey, team president. The Magog gang, which adopted the name Red Dogs—from a beer company mascot—were all motorcycle enthusiasts who every summer would embark on a lengthy road trip aboard their hogs, Burns and his posse rarely missing biker week in Laconia, New Hampshire, a vroom-vroom convention. The crew grew out of a friendship Burns had struck up with his next-door neighbour his first summer in Magog, a fellow known to all as Pecker. A narrow driveway separated the houses, and that's where long boozy nights had their genesis. "We were always there, drinking and being stupid, and then Pat joined in," recalls Kevin Dixon, a friend of Pecker's, who became Burns's closest amigo. "He didn't have any friends. Maybe some, from the police force in Gatineau, but he'd left that world behind."

Dixon, a jack of many trades, became Burns's go-to guy, multitasking as pseudo-agent, realtor, accountant, amanuensis and fellow goof. "Pat was so dedicated to hockey that he'd have a hard time taking care of paying his bills. At one point, he needed a notary to take care of his alimony. He got himself into a position where he had to trust somebody. I guess he trusted me. He knew I wasn't a crook." During the off-season, they were inseparable, to the point that some teased them about being lovers. Burns claimed Dixon wasn't his type. But it was very much a testosterone-infused band of fellow travellers, seriously stag, all coarse jokes and nonsense.

For a long time, there wasn't a lot of money. Burns continually deferred his salary. In Toronto, later, he was still cashing cheques cut by the Canadiens, and he was careful to stash as much as possible for the future, aware that this year's coach of the year could be next year's unemployed stiff. "All the big money that you think he was making, he didn't actually have it," Dixon reveals. "He was trying to cover himself for the future, not knowing what was going to happen." Apart from his big-ticket toys, including a boat he named the *Rum'n Dick*, Burns contentedly lived a frugal life. That came naturally to a fundamentally unpretentious man. It was not until his third season in Montreal that he actually bought his own house in Magog—a regular place, nothing gaudy—rather than rent.

Outgoing on the surface and certainly approachable by fans on the street, Burns was in fact a deeply private individual, even shy, quite distrusting, who let very few people into his inner circle. He was wary of hangers-on who wished to befriend him because of who he was, or as entrée to the hockey heights. Genuine intimates had to prove faithful and closed-mouthed, the farther removed from the hockey beehive the better.

Those who were in his company daily, "at work," were befuddled by the tales they heard of a laid-back Burns who never barked or scowled. Stéphan Lebeau had a summer home on the same lake and couldn't reconcile it. "We used to live very close, almost neighbours. I would hear all these stories about how funny he was, what a great person. I figured he had two completely different personalities." To his Magog cabal, Burns's meltdowns and patented histrionics behind the bench were the source of endless hilarity. "We'd watch him on TV taking a fit, and it would crack us up," says Dixon. "Away from the rink, he never showed that anger. Sometimes, we'd even mock him for that, like when some dopey boater came flying past, making wakes that would rock Pat while he was fishing, and he wouldn't yell, wouldn't say a word. He'd just laugh it off. He was never confrontational. I know there were times when he was steaming mad, but he never let it out."

Serge Savard, with whom Burns remained close in subsequent years, nevertheless felt like he was trespassing when he approached socially. "I have to say he was a little bit of a loner. If I was on the road when he was my coach, I would have a tough time to go and sit down with him after a game, say, 'Let's have a beer, Pat, and discuss it.' He'd rather be alone."

Not that he was entirely solitary. There were always significant others in the frame, women who nestled as close as they could and stayed until they decided to leave, Burns loath to do the breaking up, his body language and emotional isolation doing the talking for him. With girlfriends, Burns avoided messy encounters, had a low threshold of tolerance for sticky "let's talk" sessions. He was, as Dixon recounts, "a puppy dog where ladies were concerned," affectionate and nuzzling, more demonstrative than many men, a hand-holder. He could wine and dine, but recoiled when the whining began.

"He always needed someone there, not necessarily to marry or have children, just to be there," agrees Burns's sister Diane. "Some of these women were not genuine partners, in that sense, but they were definitely good for him and good to him. The truth is, he'd had a lot of problems with his early marriage and the children. It impacted all his future relationships with women. Growing up with sisters, being so close to me and my mom, you'd think he'd be more confident with women. But he just couldn't seem to hang on to a relationship."

By his late twenties, Burns had one brief marriage and one long-term union behind him, each producing a child. A woman he'd met in Gatineau,

Lynn Soucy, then accompanied him to Sherbrooke and Montreal. But the NHL apparently went to her head, according to those who were nearby at the time. "She was changing—the whole lifestyle, she went overboard," says someone who spent a lot of time with the couple. "Every time she went to a hockey game, she had to have a new outfit, get her hair done. She didn't work but she was spending all of Pat's money. Oh, did she love to spend. As much as he brought in, she put out. She was going in a direction that Pat didn't like."

Early on, Lynn had formed a tight friendship with Luc Robitaille's wife, Stacia, who'd been previously married to the son of actor Steve McQueen. (Robitaille's stepson, Steve McQueen, Jr., is an actor on the TV series *The Vampire Diaries*.) Lynn was thrilled by their celebrity-studded life in L.A. and would fly to the coast at the drop of a hat. "She would take trips out there just to get her hair cut, $400 a shot," marvels a friend, still amazed by such profligacy. "They'd hang out with that actress from *Dynasty*, Linda Evans. Pat didn't want any part of it."

Diane was also disapproving. "Lynn was a beautiful woman, always well dressed, but snobby. Whenever we went to visit them, she was not very friendly to us. She'd whisper in Patrick's ear, which I totally disliked. She enjoyed being a celebrity spouse, that's for sure. No, Lynn wasn't our favourite by any means."

The couple was obviously growing apart. In Burns's third Montreal season, Lynn mostly remained at the house he'd purchased in Magog, only coming into the city for games. In his fourth year, Burns moved into a Montreal house on Nun's Island that he shared with Expos manager Buck Rodgers, each in residence for their respective season and only briefly overlapping.

When the formal bust-up with Lynn inevitably occurred, it was not amicable. Burns, straining to disentangle himself, handed over the Magog house and all its contents to his ex, said, "Keep it." In the basement of that house, however, Burns had stored all the hockey memorabilia he'd been assiduously collecting for years. Not particularly sentimental about collectibles, he'd amassed it for son Jason. "He'd built this rec room, a little shrine, and he was so proud of it," says Dixon. "It was crammed with memorabilia: a sweater from Gretzky, hockey sticks signed to Jason, that kind of stuff. And what did Lynn do? She gave it all away, just to piss him off."

Observes Diane: "It was the act of a vengeful woman."

Burns did not speak ill of her. He would rarely mention Lynn at all in later years, as if she'd belonged to an alternate existence. But there was already another woman on the horizon and, clandestinely, in his bed; a married woman, at that, another beauty, who would eventually assume the "fiancée" designation, though no proposal had ever been made and no marriage would ever take place.

"Pat was a simple man," sighs Dixon. "But he was living a complicated life."

Chapter Ten
Last Tango in Montreal

"The message was not getting through anymore."

IN THE SUMMER OF 1991, Pat Burns was named assistant to Mike Keenan for the Canada Cup series. Team Canada would spend eight weeks together, from training camp in August through the finals—a two-game sweep over Team USA—in early September. Brian Sutter was also an assistant coach. The two became Laurel and Hardy, a brace of buffoons who brought lightheartedness to the occasion with their juvenile pranks, Sutter more often getting the best of Burns. He'd order a stack of pizzas to be delivered to Burns's door and place wake-up calls for three o'clock in the morning. He'd sneak into Burns's room, filling his suitcase with hotel towels and ashtrays. "I'd be carrying it to the airport thinking, 'Geez, this is heavy.'" After Canada copped the Cup—undefeated in the series with six wins and two ties—Burns and Sutter made off with the trophy during celebrations and paraded it in a golf cart driven through the hotel lobby, goalie Ed Belfour also stuffed in the back. In the wee hours, they stealthily deposited the Cup in Keenan's bed as he slept, *Godfather*-style. In retaliation, Keenan called hotel security to have it removed and stashed, announcing to reporters the next morning that it had been swiped.

Frivolities finished, it was back to serious business when the NHL season opened. The league was celebrating its seventy-fifth year of operation, and Montreal and Toronto wore vintage replica uniforms, coaches in cardigans and fedoras, when the teams faced off at the Forum for their opener, Canadiens winning 4–3. Notable for his absence was Stéphane Richer, who'd cleared out his locker on September 20, traded to the Devils, future captain Kirk Muller received in return. "I think Stéphane will be a better player in New Jersey because he's going to a place where there's less media attention," opined Burns, reflecting on the relentless spotlight that had been trained on Richer and how he withered under that stress. "A player has to be really strong to deal with it." That Montreal had lost a star who had twice put up fifty-goal seasons Burns dismissed as inconsequential. "The importance of fifty-goal scorers in this league is a lot of garbage," the coach said, unconvincingly and nonsensically. Later, he expounded on the Richer soap opera. "When I sat Richer out for even a shift, he would move down to the end of the bench where the French TV camera was set. He would sit there with this really sad, kicked-dog look on his face, knowing that the picture was going across the province with commentary about Richer being sat out by bad Burns again. One time, Richer had two French-Canadian rookies who weren't playing sitting with him, looking sad. I wanted to ask them which one heard no evil."

Of course, Burns was a gritty guy who was overly fond of grinding third-liners and often careless with the egos of genuine stars. That first week of 1991, he benched Denis Savard during a game in Detroit that Montreal won 4–1. Savard was piqued, and the French media took his side. Burns saw the blowback coming. "When you bench a guy on a French club, there's always a howl from the fans back home. It's hanging time for me tomorrow. My house is probably burning down right now. I love Denis Savard but he's got to learn to listen to me. He's got to get my message."

Was that when it began, the fatal fissure between coach and club, coach and media, in what would be Burns's swan song season in Montreal? At the end of the year, Sylvain Turgeon bitterly remarked, "He has the biggest ego on the team and if he's not the star of the show, he's not happy."

Nobody saw the alienation looming, certainly not during Montreal's fast start, 14–4–1, nor through the midpoint of the season, the Canadiens sitting atop the league on January 1, 1992, owning the best defensive record in the NHL, and doing it all without a single scorer in the top twenty-five. They weren't a flashy squad, but efficient and resilient as the team transitioned seamlessly through roster-rebuilding changes. "We don't need a hero," said Burns. "That's one thing I try to stress. I know fans like a Lafleur, a Béliveau, a Geoffrion. The press would like one. But I'm sorry to say we don't have one. They tried to put pressure on Stéphane Richer and he couldn't handle it. We'd like to have a different hero every night."

Melodrama actually occurred off the ice when a Montreal doctor announced at a press conference that a female patient who had died of AIDS two years earlier claimed to have had sex with about fifty NHL players. This stunning revelation came just days after NBA star Magic Johnson disclosed he'd been infected with HIV (human immunodeficiency virus). Suddenly the bed-hopping habits of professional athletes became a topic of conversation everyone was having. Burns, quite enlightened for the times, ordered that a condom machine be installed in the trainer's room. "I'm not distributing them myself. I'm not out there handing them out like candy. But in Montreal, the players are well known and recognized. They might have that macho thing about not wanting to go into a pharmacy and have everybody looking at them. So I told them, 'Boys, they're at your disposal. And don't use them for water balloons!'"

He defended athletes against the bad rap they were getting for promiscuity. "Being in the field as a police officer, I saw politicians getting involved with hookers and whatnots. Let's not pick on professional athletes. They are the most exposed because they're public figures, but you could find politicians or travelling salesmen looking for female companionship in any bar in any city." Burns revealed that 90 per cent of NHL players had been tested for AIDS already, either of their own volition or as part of the application process for life insurance. "But having a blood test is a personal thing. I can't take anybody by the hand and lead him up the hill to Montreal General Hospital."

———

On the ice, everything felt safe as houses. Burns's security had been assured with a contract renegotiated in December that made him the highest-paid coach in the NHL, among those not also functioning as general manager. The three-year deal reportedly paid Burns $350,000 a season. "There are probably twenty-one coaches giving me a standing ovation in their offices right now. The coaches have all been waiting for someone to do this."

Columnist Réjean Tremblay describes how he helped launch Burns's bid for a fat new deal. "One day, he was shaving in the dressing room as I passed by. He opened the conversation by saying, 'Do you think a coach like me plays a big role on the team?' I said, 'Pat, you're the heart of the team.'" At the time, Montreal had an enforcer by the name of Mario Roberge, a low-scoring winger with a limited role. Burns asked Tremblay, "Do you think I'm more important than a guy like Mario?" Tremblay replied, "No comparison." Burns: "So I should earn at least the average of what the players are making." In those years, that meant around $400,000.

"I understood the message," says Tremblay. "The next day, I wrote a big column saying a coach like Pat Burns should get a new contract. In those days, the relationship between the writers and management was very close. So I got a phone call from Serge Savard. He said, 'Reg, are you Pat's new agent?'" Burns got his plump raise with no apologies for it. "To be president of the United States is a lot different from being president in Zimbabwe, just like coaching in Montreal is different from other cities. Now watch, I'll get a pack of angry letters from people in Zimbabwe."

He was happy, not a care in the world beyond the usual day-to-day aggravations, his team seemingly serene. "I've said before I'd like to stay in Montreal my whole life, and this should make it a little longer." GM Savard was equally pleased with locking Burns into the franchise. "My wish now is never to have to make another coaching change in my career." Now *there* was a proclamation to tempt fate.

From January, the team started to lurch, sliding through the standings. Still, there was no immediate panic. When not using them to achieve his own ends, Burns continued squabbling with the media. Now, though, there was more of an edge to the thrust-and-parry. Burns increasingly showed his contempt for journalists, and the feeling was mutual. "I don't think he hated us personally, but he hated the way we were doing our job," says Tremblay. "Don't forget, before Pat Burns, we covered Jean Perron. Perron had a master's degree, so he was a new type of coach for us. Pat Burns was the former cop/tough guy. You could not intimidate Pat Burns. Personally, I thought he was a tough son of a bitch. But he could take it better than most guys. Maybe we were harder on him than we had been with other coaches. Nobody wants to destroy a man, but, when you believe a guy has the strength to take a hit, maybe you go a little bit further in your criticism."

From where Burns was standing, the writers went much too far. As the team stumbled, relations with the entourage that cover the Canadiens turned toxic. Not only were the Habs flattening out, they were playing boring hockey. And boring hockey, especially in Montreal, is only tolerated when it's also winning hockey. "Flying Frenchmen," went the joke, "only when they board a plane." Banging off the boards and chasing was not aesthetically satisfying for fans. "It wasn't dull for me," notes Sylvain Lefebvre, who did a lot of that banging. "At the same time, Pat wasn't telling our offensive-minded players they couldn't make plays. But there was a way that he wanted us to play in the neutral zone, between both blue lines. That's where he was very strict. He'd didn't want the team to create turnovers. He wanted us to win a certain way and not to lose a certain way."

Burns bristled when his defensive system was maligned. "Everybody talks about our defensive system," he said. "I laugh at that one, I really do laugh. There is no defensive system. This great system, you know what it is? If you lose the puck, you have to get it back. That's our system. Awesome, isn't it?"

Rekindled were the allusions to an anti-francophone bias. But now some reporters were openly mocking Burns's own French usage. "His French was very colourful," says Tremblay. "His accent was good. It was a French that you learn at home and in the streets." Other commentators were less kind. Burns recoiled from the sting, which he equated to class snobbery. In Quebec, vigilance about the French language and French culture is a social, political and journalistic pillar. Mike Keane, the western boy who was made Montreal captain in 1995, felt the wrath. "If it was a Tuesday when I got named, I was taking my French-language class on the Wednesday, respecting the fact this is part of the game and you have to do this when you're captain in Montreal. One of the reporters asked me, 'What do you guys speak in the dressing room?' I said most guys speak English. The next day in the papers, it was: 'Keane refuses to speak our language.' Things went sour from there. That's the reason I got traded out of Montreal." Keane's captaincy lasted four months. He was dealt to Colorado with Patrick Roy in the mega-swap triggered by Roy's rage over rookie coach Mario Tremblay hanging him out to dry in a mortifying loss to Detroit.

Keane is still trying to set the record straight. "I wouldn't know if Pat mangled his French. But we spoke mostly English in the dressing room. The French guys spoke French to each other. If someone didn't feel comfortable speaking in English, they wouldn't. I just find it all really strange. It's something that's never an issue in the dressing room—only outside."

Burns could empathize. When the Habs won, it was the work of Pat Burns, the French-Canadian. When they lost, it was because of "that damned Irishman."

One issue outside the dressing room in the winter of '92 actually took place *inside* a St. Laurent Boulevard saloon around 3 a.m. That's when police were called to the Zoo Bar to break up a brawl in which Shayne Corson had been a central punch-swinger. The bar manager said Corson, who had been downing shooters and tossing empty shot glasses around the premises, became incensed when a man approach his female companion. Corson was arrested, briefly suspended by the franchise, and afterwards, apologized profusely. On this occasion, there was no rescue-me call placed to the coach. "I wouldn't have gone this time," Burns said. He was furious, calling Corson "the Charles Barkley of hockey"—it wasn't a compliment—and, during an interview with a French TV station, using a deeply insulting slur: "*Qu'il mange de la merde,*" which translates roughly as "Corson can eat shit" but is much more venomous in French semantics. "It's probably the most vulgar thing you can say," explains Réjean Tremblay. "Really disgusting. And he said it about one of his favourite English players."

On another occasion, it was allegedly Burns blowing over the limit. Tremblay received a bizarre formal letter from a lawyer, ordering him to refrain from writing anything about Burns failing to pass a sobriety test when pulled over following a game in Montreal. This was strange because Tremblay had heard nothing about the incident and still remains doubtful any such thing happened. "There was not a cop in Montreal that would write up a report on Burns. I could find no record of it. So I wrote a column about the letter." He laughs. "It was the only time I received a warning from a lawyer to stop me from writing about something that I didn't know about." When the story was published, Burns growled, "You shit-disturber."

For the club, there was no soul-destroying collapse akin to the Leafs circa 2012, but things were clearly not right. As was commonly the case, a vexed Burns was an ornery Burns. He did not handle the team's fluctuations well; he worsened the anxious mood. Incessant screeching and hollering was bringing diminishing returns. Though the Canadiens did challenge for first overall through February and March, they stumbled to an 0–5–3 finish in the last two weeks of the campaign, and couldn't win a thing after the ten-day players' strike that interrupted the late season. "The second half of the season, we've been horrible," said Burns. "It's mind-boggling." Still, Montreal wound up first in the Adams Division, fifth overall, with 93 points. Once again, they'd open the playoffs against Hartford.

It was an arduous seven-game series that Montreal won by the skin of its teeth. In game five at Hartford, Burns had even been accused of using a stick to butt-end a fan heckling as the players departed the ice via the visiting team's exit, which had no protective canopy. Actually, Burns had slammed the stick against the wall. Police investigated the fan's complaint and closed the file. "A guy just spit on me, that's all," said Burns.

But the Canadiens were spent. Boston swept them out of the playoffs in the next round, Montreal cracking under the pressure of their inability to score—a feeble offence that produced just eight goals against Mike Milbury's Bruins. Not since 1952 had Montreal been swept in a seven-game series. And to Boston! The horror, the horror. In three consecutive years, they'd been dispatched by the Bruins. It was unendurable.

Rumbles trickled out from the dressing room. "During the playoffs, the climate was far from healthy," said Denis Savard. "I didn't see any arguments between players, but certain guys were visibly unhappy." If the players weren't arguing among themselves, who did that leave? Burns, obviously.

The writing was on the wall. But who was responsible for the graffiti? Was the impetus rebellious players or did the shove come from far above? Réjean Tremblay remembers running into a steady stream of players at the food court across from the team's hotel prior to the last game in Boston. "I spent the whole afternoon there, had coffee with maybe eight, ten players. It was not at all clear that they'd had enough of Burns. Instead, what they talked about was that big management was fed up with his swearing, his bad mouth behind the bench. At the time, Mr. Ronald Corey always had guests in the first row behind the bench at the Forum, very close. Many players told me, 'Pat will be in trouble, Pat will be in trouble, Pat will be in trouble.' I don't know, maybe it was all a pretext. But at least half of the players on this afternoon told me how management had had enough of the ways of Burns, his talking and reacting behind the bench. At the time, myself, I expected he would last at least one more year. He still seemed in control of the team."

Burns was aware of ownership disenchantment. He mentioned to friend Kevin Dixon, "[Ronald] Corey won't talk to me anymore, doesn't even say hello." If his pungent language behind the bench was mentioned, he disregarded the complaint. "Burns was always a guy who went his own way; he didn't care about management," says the team equipment majordomo, Pierre Gervais. "But I've never seen a better bench coach. He kept everybody on edge."

For all of his career, Burns would chafe under the sobriquet of being a three-year coach with a four-year contract. Incoming, he could grab a team by the throat and turn things around immediately—three coach-of-the-year laurels in his first season on three different teams. Outgoing, there was paranoia, disillusionment, regressing and a coach who, in the parlance, had lost his players.

"It's hard to be as strict as he was and maintain that success for a long time," observes Patrick Roy. "You can do it for one, two years, and then you have to find a way to adjust, to adapt to the group. Burnsie had only one way, and that was his way. He would not move one step from that."

Says Keane: "I think with the way Pat approached the game, that kind of coach has a shelf life of three or four years. With his demanding ways, players either tune out or it just doesn't work anymore. They start saying, 'Okay, enough's enough. We can't have the perfect game every night.' That push-push-push works for a while, and then players just shut down."

Stéphan Lebeau, who had more than his share of difficulties with Burns yet never lost respect for the man, remembers the gloominess in the dressing room during the Boston series. "Many players were unhappy, for sure. When you're losing and you come to the rink, you always have that heavy mood. Pat knew what he wanted, but perhaps, when things go your way all the time, you start believing that every decision you make is the right one. In reality, that's not the case. Hockey is a sport, and it should be fun. When it starts not being so much fun coming to the rink, then this is where, perhaps, some players in the dressing room threw in the towel, or threw it at the coach. That did happen, yes."

Shayne Corson forcefully disagrees. "Pat had not lost that room—never, never. He certainly didn't lose me. I never felt that, I never saw that." Within months, after another altercation at a Montreal bar—Corson just beginning to suffer the panic attacks that would curse him for years—Serge Savard would trade his problem child to Edmonton for Vincent Damphousse. "I wish Pat would have stayed. I think that was one of the reasons I got moved. He left, and I was gone that summer. I don't blame Serge, because he was a big part of my hockey career and my life. But he just threw up his arms and said, 'What can I do?'"

Russ Courtnall is reluctant to state that players no longer respected Burns. "Maybe he just didn't have the same influence on the players that they had brought in for him to coach that he once had. Being in Montreal was hard on Pat too, tougher on francophones than anglophones. He used to always say to us: 'You guys all get to go home after the season. We have to stay here for the whole summer and hear what we did wrong and why we didn't win.'"

Sylvain Lefebvre cuts to the chase. "We lost to Boston in the second round three years in a row. If you keep losing to Boston—not good."

Serge Savard took the pulse of his club during that series. He'd grown increasingly dismayed. "At the end of those playoffs, when we lost in straight games to Boston, I could see that Pat had lost his grip on his team. That doesn't mean that he wasn't a good coach. This happens to a lot of good coaches. When things start to go down and the coach cannot be himself and the players feel that . . . the message was not getting through anymore."

Burns would always insist he was not fired in Montreal. Technically, that's true. "I did not fire Pat," says Savard. But neither did Burns quit, exactly. It was a mutual parting of the ways, but the coach really had no choice. Savard invited Burns, just back from a week's vacation in Jamaica, to his office to discuss the situation. "We started there, and then went to a bar and then a restaurant and had dinner—talk-talk-talk. After a few drinks, we could speak more honestly with each other. I knew he had a five-hundred-pound weight on his shoulders. I knew I was not going to start the next season with Pat. And he knew he could not coach here anymore; he knew it. He knew and I knew that he could not continue."

Savard also knew something else: Rogie Vachon, the GM in Los Angeles, had serious interest in hiring Burns. So did Cliff Fletcher in Toronto. "These were the two options Pat had in front of him. And it was crystal clear to me that he was going to Toronto."

Before that meeting, there had been plenty of finessing behind the scenes, most of it orchestrated by powerful player agent Don Meehan. Burns and Meehan had spoken casually over a coffee earlier in the year. Recalls Meehan: "He told me things weren't going well. I said, 'If you ever have any issues or problems, give me a call and I'll try to help.'"

Burns had no agent to that point; he'd negotiated his contracts with Montreal on his own. Now he needed top-drawer representation. When he sensed the axe hovering, he contacted Meehan. The agent learned from Savard that the Canadiens were going to make a change. He informed Burns, who said, "I think it's coming," and Meehan confirmed it, yup. Burns admitted he didn't know how to handle the situation. Burns had three years remaining on his contract, and Meehan emphasized, "You have to be very careful in terms of how you're going to react." The agent formally took him on as a client and tried to calm Burns down. "This is where you're going to get my worth, because I'm going to negotiate a settlement. I know there's pressure to get you out of here. Let me use this as leverage with Savard, because I can do well for you, knowing what the circumstances are from the ownership point of view."

Then Meehan revealed to Burns that "I have something else in mind, too." Burns asked what that might be. What Meehan had in mind was the coaching job in Toronto. He knew, from discussions with Fletcher, that the Leafs wanted to replace the ineffective Tom Watt. "I told Pat, 'Toronto's going to be available.' He said, 'Are you kidding me?'"

So Meehan got to work on Fletcher. When he placed the initial call to the Leaf GM, Fletcher was on another line and asked if he could call back later. "I said, 'No, you better talk to me now. I think I have something for you here which isn't official, but I think it would meet your best interests. Montreal is going to terminate Pat Burns and I think he'd be terrific in Toronto. It would really make sense for you. You could make a real statement, getting a guy with real presence in the league. It's just what your team needs.'"

Fletcher was keen but needed to run the idea by his board of directors. Meehan urged him to do it quickly, because there was a press conference to make the announcement of Burns's termination scheduled for Montreal the next day. Coincidentally, Meehan had just been contacted by Jacques Demers, who wanted to get back into coaching, though he was making a mint as a TV commentator. So now Meehan had two new coach clients. He was frantically juggling balls in the air.

Meehan spoke again to Savard, who was seeing Burns that night. Then he got back to Fletcher. "Are you on?" Fletcher said yes, and they talked money. It was a done deal except for the signature on the contract. Burns was over the moon, if gobsmacked. On the blower with Meehan, he kept repeating, "Are you serious?" Meehan was clear: If you want this to happen, it will happen. "Coach the Toronto Maple Leafs? Oh yeah."

In Montreal the next day, the announcement of Burns's departure was made to a mostly shocked media horde. Burns, emotional, claimed reluctance to leave, insisted he wasn't running away—anybody in the room care to dispute that?—but admitted feeling overwhelming pressure to resign. "When you're criticized openly, in the way I have been, I don't care who's in the seat, it's really hard to take." The flower of Montreal journalism, caught napping, was thunderstruck. And they were still clueless as to what was about to unfold five hundred kilometres down Highway 401. Meehan had booked plane tickets for himself and Burns. They went directly from the Montreal presser to the airport. During the flight, Burns was bewildered. "I can't believe all this happening." Recalls Meehan: "He was in seventh heaven."

Landing in Toronto, Meehan and Burns went straight to Maple Leaf Gardens for a first face-to-face meeting with Fletcher and their second press conference of the day. Welcome the new Toronto coach: Pat Burns.

It was a win-win dénouement, or actually win-win-win, because Meehan placed Demers with the Canadiens. The agent was justifiably pleased with himself. "Montreal was happy to move Burns out, both sides got their settlement, Pat could say he hadn't been fired, and the Canadiens got a new coach who ended up taking them to the Stanley Cup. There was no bitterness. Everybody was happy."

Chapter Eleven

The Passion Returns

"We love you, Pat Burns!"

RULE NUMBER I: The Toronto Maple Leaf crest was never to touch the ground.

Symbols meant a lot to Pat Burns. His primary job in a city where the hapless hockey team was being mocked as the Maple Laughs was to regenerate respect—for the franchise, among the players, and definitely for the new coach. For starters, that meant no more tossing of the jersey on the grimy floor of the dressing room, like a used Kleenex. Veneration of club logos has since become a widespread practice across the NHL, where reporters can even be fined for stepping on the crest woven into carpeting. But in the fall of 1992, in a grungy Maple Leaf Gardens dressing room that had no broadloom underfoot, Burns was the first to initiate a statute against sacrilegious abuse of the trademark insignia.

"After a game, we used to just throw our sweaters into a laundry cart— it was really just a grocery cart—in the middle of the room," recalls Mike Foligno, one of the returning Leafs who'd been part of the team that had finished out of the playoffs in the spring. "Pat wanted to make sure that we held ourselves accountable for the fact we were playing in a hockey-hungry city like Toronto. I remember him specifically saying he was so proud to be able to coach one of the Original Six teams, and he wanted to impress upon us what that really meant. There was a hanger behind your stall. When you took off the sweater, you had to hang it up on the hanger and the trainer would pick it up later to do the laundry. You might not think those kinds of little things would make a difference, but they do when you're talking about the attention to detail that makes the difference from one organization to another. Even something as small as that, never letting the jersey drop on the floor, never letting the logo touch the ground, was about bringing back pride in the club."

Cliff Fletcher, president and general manager, had begun the process of rehabilitating the Leafs when he swung a blockbuster deal towards the end of the 1991–92 campaign, picking the pocket of his counterpart and former protégé in Calgary, Doug Risebrough. That ten-player swap remains the biggest trade ever in the NHL. Toronto gave up a fifty-goal scorer in Gary Leeman, with enforcer Craig Berube and other movable parts thrown into the package. But in return, the Leafs got Doug Gilmour—the club's mainstay for several years to come—along with Jamie Macoun, Ric Nattress, Kent Manderville and backup goalie Rick Wamsley. Then, for the first and only time in his long career, Fletcher hired a coach over the phone.

Toronto had been without a coach since May 4, when Tom Watt moved into the front office as director of player development. Fletcher was looking for a bench boss who would command instant esteem, who would grow with the team. "I did not want to sit at home and twiddle my thumbs," said Burns at his May 29 introductory press conference, explaining why he'd wasted not a minute jumping from Montreal to the Leafs. And Fletcher had made Burns an offer he couldn't refuse: two years that matched the $750,000 remaining on his contract with Montreal, and two more years with a salary hike after that—$1.7 million overall. That made Burns, the twenty-second man entrusted with the whistle in Toronto's history, one of the highest-paid coaches in the league. He became only the second man in the annals of the NHL to coach both storied franchises, Dick Irvin being the other. But Burns had switched from a perennial contender, with whom he'd posted a .609 winning percentage in four seasons—the best mark in the NHL during that span—to a franchise that hadn't finished over .500 since 1978–79. He had his hands full.

Asked what needed doing to transform a team that had missed the playoffs in three of the past four years, Burns said, "The players will have to learn what it takes to win, and I'll be there every night to remind them." Finally, after an absence of fifteen years and with the death of barmy owner Harold Ballard, there was a palpable sense of change in the air, something to fuel optimism. When a French-language reporter at the packed press conference asked Burns, "*Quelques mots en français?*" he retorted in faux exasperation: "I thought that was finished." The forty-year-old coach pulled on a Leaf jacket for photographs. "It's a funny feeling, but I like the feeling."

The local media horde was excited, and so was Burns. "Coming to another hockey Mecca like Toronto makes you a better coach. I want to have fun again. I want to make it fun for everybody, and it's fun when you win." The fun, he said, had gone out of his job in Montreal. "When you won, they didn't like the style you played. When you won, it was because the other team was no good. If you lost, it was because you had no system. If a player didn't score on certain nights, it was because you were holding him back. If he did score, you didn't play him enough. It was a no-win situation."

Compared to Montreal, Toronto's fans had modest expectations. Simply returning to postseason play would be grounds for hoopla. Burns tacitly let on that there had been interest in him from other organizations, though he didn't specifically mention the Los Angeles overture, saying only: "I wasn't interested in going to practice with sandals on. I want to wear some good boots and go to work. I wish we could start tomorrow." He also committed a blooper when admitting unfamiliarity with the Toronto players: "I don't know the players very well. There's Darryl Gilmour, and I've always been a Wendel Clark fan." Darryl Gilmour had been an obscure goaltender in the minors, and where Burns came up with that name is anybody's guess. The other Gilmour, Doug, was at a fast-food restaurant with daughter Maddison when he heard that Burns had been hired, and he was dumbstruck. "At first I said, 'Yeah, right, good one.' It came as a huge surprise, because nobody expected it." He cracked up over the new coach getting his first name wrong. "Tell George no problem." They met face to face shortly afterwards. "He took me to Filmores." That's one of Toronto's oldest strip joints. "We were there for half an hour, and then all of a sudden it went crazy with people congratulating him and asking for autographs, so we went on to a little pub. Right away, he told me, 'This is what I expect: you're one of our best players, and every day in practice you better work hard. I'm going to give you time off, but make sure, games and practices, you're the best player on the ice, and everybody will follow you.'" Burns added: "I just got here, you just got here. Let's do this together."

Burns talked seriously with Wendel Clark as well, delicately suggesting that improved conditioning might help keep the captain out of the medical room. Clark was unquestionably the most popular athlete in town—he and Todd Gill were the longest-tenured Leafs, survivors of the worst era in Toronto hockey history—but with only 187 games on his resumé over the previous five seasons, constantly felled by injuries, it was unclear where Clark fit into Burns's plans. The coach settled that matter quickly. "I believe in Wendel Clark. We want Wendel to be a prime-time player."

The addition of Burns, who kept Mike Murphy and Mike Kitchen as assistants, imbued the Leafs with instant cachet. He was the embodiment of Irish temper and Gallic pride, he was colourful after years of bland coaching in Toronto, and he was a proven winner even without a Stanley Cup ring. Not since Punch Imlach's first tour of duty in the '60s had Toronto boasted a coach with such presence. "I have never, ever missed the playoffs," he stressed. "I don't intend to start now." No slouches in the kaching-kaching department, the club's bean-counters immediately jacked up ticket prices to reflect the promise Burns represented. When the organization threw a party to reveal the team's new jersey for the upcoming season—the current, straight-edged Maple Leaf logo on a retro striped sweater—more than 7,500 fans showed up, delivering an outpouring of affection: "We love you, Pat Burns!" As caught up as anybody in optimism, Burns nevertheless tried to calm anticipations. "They're not a good team,

I don't hide the fact. And I'm not a saviour. I'm coming in here with a lot of help from guys like Cliff. If we make the playoffs, we'll be that much better. People talk Stanley Cup and I say, 'Just relax.' They haven't seen it in a long time here. I think they just want a hard-working hockey club, and I can give them that every night." Fletcher observed: "Pat Burns's hockey teams are notorious for giving a consistent effort every shift of every game. He won't tolerate anything less." He confidently predicted Toronto would make the playoffs. "Pat's teams have, in my opinion, always overachieved." When Glenn Anderson, notable space cadet, enthused that the Leafs would undoubtedly make the playoffs, even "definitely contend for the Stanley Cup this year," Burns called a timeout. "Let's not block off Yonge Street for the parade just yet."

Training camp in September opened with the proverbial clean slate, Burns warning his players he intended to run hard workouts, no goofing around. "I've been out in the work world myself with my lunch box, and I don't see anything wrong with asking for an all-out effort. We will try a variety of things to make the workouts interesting but, yes, they will be tough." He chose not to look at videotape of the team's games from the year before. "I don't want to hate some of the things I see before we get started."

The elder statesman on the team was Foligno, at age thirty-two. He was also the resident jokester, spiritual focal point and social convener. Once, years earlier during a preseason game in Kitchener that was held up by lighting problems, Foligno soothed the restless fans by crooning Italian love songs over the PA system. But he checked into camp on September 11, 1992, after months and months of painstakingly rehabbing a leg that had been shattered in two places below the knee just before the previous Christmas, unsure whether the limb would hold up to the rigours of a fourteenth NHL season. "Pat pulled me aside and said, 'Look, I want you to be part of this thing. You've worked your butt off to get back here. Just take whatever time you need and know that I want you on my team.' So that was a real boost of confidence for me."

Upwards of seventy players reported for day one of training camp, with only a few guaranteed jobs. "I remember the first meeting that we had," says Foligno. "Sometimes that first meeting is the one that sets the tone for the relationship between coach and players. We were all wondering about Pat's thought process, what his expectations were. So we had this meeting, the introductions made, and at the end he kicked everybody out except the guys who'd played on the team the year before. He told us we had jobs if we wanted them—that they were our jobs to earn, but also to lose. He said there were a lot of young players at camp, but he wasn't going to give a kid a job just for the sake of making a change. If we came in with the right attitude, the right work ethic and dedication, and showed leadership qualities and also the sportsmanship qualities that he wanted, he would give us the opportunity. After that meeting, we all said, 'You know what? This guy's genuine.' He wanted to move forward with a veteran team if he could, because that would be a more smooth transition for any coach."

On the second day of camp, Burns blew a gasket. Partway through the morning session, the coach decided he'd seen enough, storming down from his perch high in the stands and ordering a halt. He gave the twenty-two players on the ice a thirty-second tongue-lashing before returning to his seat. Burns hadn't liked the low tempo he'd just observed. "The attitude was, 'Let's get this over with and punch the clock.' I wasn't going to put up with that. I don't want to whip players, but I'll do it if I have to."

Sylvain Lefebvre, who'd signed with Toronto as a free agent over the summer, chuckled. This was the Burns he knew and mostly loved from Montreal. "If you don't work, it really ticks him off. He likes practices at a high tempo. You never stop. He doesn't keep you out there for two hours every day, but you learn to come to practice and work full out, not just float."

Veteran Leafs, some of whom had endured the screeching antics of John Brophy, another hothead coach, were unaccustomed to such a pace. "They've got to have it drilled into their minds that we want to be better every day," Burns explained. "Better tomorrow, better the next day, better the day after that." And by the way, how do you like me so far?

As per usual, reporters were lapping it up. When Burns actually laced up his skates and took to the ice with his players, he kept up a constant barrage of cussing yips and yelps during drills. "If you miss the net, I'll just [expletive deleted]. There's no excuse for missing the net." Addressing the goalies before a rapid-fire shooting drill: "If you [expletive deleted] up, it will be really scary." To all: "If you miss a pass in practice this season, it's going to be five or ten pushups. If you [expletive deleted] all season, your pipes [arms] will be out to here."

Go hard! he bellowed. As in Montreal, it drove Burns batty if players failed to assemble quickly in a circle when he blew the whistle for a tutorial. Last man into the scrum, if not hopping to it, was required to do two laps of the ice full out. Poor Martin Prochazka, a Czech forward, didn't understand English. Last to fall in, Burns sent him for laps. When it happened a second time—two more laps—Prochazka just stood there, staring blankly, not grasping why the coach was picking on him. Finally, another player spoke up, telling Burns Prochazka didn't speak the lingo. "Oh."

Toronto had a decent set of exhibition game results—3–2–2—which, of course, presage absolutely nothing. When the team headed to a Collingwood, Ontario, resort for a bit of preseason bonding, Burns expounded on the culture of losing that had become fatally ingrained with the club, as well as his aversion to laziness. "The work ethic is one area where guys were taking shortcuts and getting away with it. I've told these guys that taking shortcuts may save you some energy now, but you'll pay for it during the games. I'm talking about getting back in your own end quickly and cheating in drills by not following them to completion. If you do that, you'll cheat in a game, too, and that costs everybody."

In Toronto, at that time, the Leafs had also slipped behind the Blue Jays as the most adored local sports franchise. The Jays, drawing four million fans to the ballpark that season, were about to win their first World Series. It was baseball, baseball, baseball around town. The Leafs wisely moved the date of their season opener to avoid a direct conflict with a Blue Jays playoff game.

The race to respectability began October 6. "I think we'll be exciting," said Burns. "Our big concern will be goal scoring. But I think that's a concern for most coaches. I think we'll know more after ten games or so." Looking ahead, he mused: "There are going to be peaks and valleys in any season. But if we can come out of the gate strong and get a few wins, we can get through the valleys and not be biting our nails for a playoff spot at the end."

The Gardens was spruced up with a fresh coat of paint for opening night, cheerful banners hung from the ceiling in the corridors, new uniforms worn by the concession staff, a laser show—very '80s, but hip by franchise standards—heralding the season's onset. Blue Jays Joe Carter and Roberto Alomar, sitting in fourth-row golds, were greeted with even louder cheers than the players when starting-lineup introductions were made.

Burns's well-established preference for mind-numbing, check-to-a-standstill defensive hockey had elicited some sour notes in Toronto, along with alerts that the Leafs would be drained of all entertainment quotients. The coach countered that fans would probably take dull hockey over losing hockey any night, because winning is never boring. The Leafs just didn't have the horses for firewagon hockey anyway. Meanwhile, back in Montreal, Burns's successor Jacques Demers had been promising "creative" hockey, a clear shot across his predecessor's bow. That rebuke ticked off Burns, and the chip on his shoulder about Demers would never quite disappear—even when, years in the future, Canadian Senator Demers fought ceaselessly to get Burns into the Hockey Hall of Fame while he was still alive to savour the honour.

Game one of the 1992–93 season was no defensive gem, however, and assuredly not dull. Leafs showed pluck against the Washington Capitals, a team thirty-one points better than Toronto in the standings the previous year, twice tying the score but ultimately falling 6–5. Yet they'd shown determination and liveliness and, yes, entertaining hockey. The fans were delighted, but the coach was not similarly impressed. "We're not the type of club that can get into a pissing match with a skunk. We don't have the firepower to do that. If we do get five goals, we should win."

As remedial instruction, a testy Burns put the team through merciless "hamburger drills" in the days that followed in preparation for a western road swing. At the Saddledome on October 10, he deployed a twenty-one-year-old rookie netminder, Félix Potvin, instead of his veteran ace, Grant Fuhr. Potvin, jittery, immediately surrendered three goals. After the first period, Burns delivered an angry lecture in the locker room, upset that his players were allowing the Flames to run roughshod over them. "Our guys had their heads so far up their you-know-whats they were coming out their noses. I can't sit and watch that. It makes my stomach turn. I was vocal. Let's just say everybody was listening." Leafs, attentive, fought back gamely and lost 3–2. "There are going to be threats and they are going to be carried out," Burns told reporters. "I won't be embarrassed in the first period like that again. Some guys didn't compete, and I'm starting to find out who they are. I guarantee that we'll have a lineup that will compete every night." True to his word, Burns remodelled the lineup in the following game at Edmonton, with five new faces. Yet again, Toronto trailed 3–0, but this time they showed gumption in a comeback 3–3 tie.

Between-period lashings were quickly becoming a fixture. Burns unloaded again when the Leafs trailed lowly Tampa Bay, and his tirade sparked a trio of third-period goals, giving Toronto its first win of the season, 5–3. But he remained perplexed that his canon wasn't sinking in. "I just don't understand. This has nothing to do with systems. It has to come from the heart and the brain." To a journalist, he offered an exposition on the reality of coaching. "It's not as glamorous as people think. When the team wins, the players get the credit. But when the team loses, it's the coach. How many times have you seen somebody wearing a hockey sweater with the coach's name on the back?"

Toronto beat Norris Division rival Chicago, and that improved his disposition, marginally. But a 5–1 routing by Minnesota had him apoplectic. So puny was Toronto's power play that he even dispatched Gilmour to the point. "I was ready to go out there myself with my booming shot," Burns said, sarcastically.

Next morning, he tried blowing off steam by jogging to the Gardens. He was living in a spacious waterfront condo near Harbourfront with girlfriend Tina Sheldon. They'd met in Montreal when Burns had been corralled as celebrity shill for a line of pre-packaged weight-loss meals. He hated the food—it made him violently ill—but he liked the marketing lady who'd landed him for the account. Tina was a dark-haired, blue-eyed dazzler—and married. She separated from her husband and quit her job to accompany Burns to Toronto, and the couple happily set up house. "She set her cap for him," says the man who'd made the original introductions. And Burns was more than receptive.

By October 26, Toronto had surprisingly racked up five wins in their last six starts. And still most sports fans were far more preoccupied with baseball. Burns rather liked it that way, even when the Gardens crowd broke off to applaud Jays score updates on the scoreboard. "It's a tough feeling for the players, hard to concentrate with all the baseball cheers. We're tied for first place in our division and probably nobody knows about it. Hey, I'd like to take my guys over to the Blue Jays' locker room and have them rub themselves all over those guys."

Up next was a home and home series with Detroit, the first major test of the young season for the Leafs. They got ripped 7–1 as the visiting team. "I'm really wondering if we have the stuff to play with the top teams in this league," Burns seethed. "If it happens again in Toronto, then we'll know we can't do it against the good teams. This was just godawful." He advocated the K-I-S-S principle: Keep It Simple, Stupid. Toronto did, and rebounded with a 3–1 win, then sent a further message by knocking off mighty Pittsburgh 4–1 at the Gardens. "The game probably opened a lot of eyes about coming into this place. We always wanted to make this our building."

The coach was preaching the Burns 101 syllabus: No long shifts; if you lose the puck, put yourself in a position to get it back; short and crisp passes; if outnumbered, dump it out of the zone or into the other team's end; never lose the puck between the blue lines. Burns's motivational mastery was the added element. He did have the unfortunate tendency of picking on his "whipping boys," as Gilmour describes those who were most subjected to the coach's blasts, young Rob Pearson a favourite target. But Burns had no reservations about nailing even Gilmour to the pine for a period if displeased with the effort.

It was early days still, but, as unlikely as it might have been, Toronto had a piece of first place in the Norris, shared with the North Stars, and tied for fourth overall in the NHL. Potvin was a critical component in that chugging-along phase, the number-one goalie of the future bidding to make that future now.

Louise Burns was in the stands when Toronto polished off the Senators in Ottawa 3–1, and still her son wasn't happy, barking in his players' ears on the bench. "I got mad because Félix was standing on his head in the first period and we were standing there watching him." By mid-November, not only were the Leafs atop the division, but they had the league's best defensive record, though Burns got shirty whenever hung with the "D" descriptor. "Don't call it defensive hockey or call me a defensive coach. I call it hard work. The message is getting through. We're trying to make the playoffs, and there'll be no passengers on the Maple Leafs. There's no system, no ABCs. It's just making everyone understand their roles." He acknowledged being surprised himself with Toronto's fine start, but grateful because "it's going to be a dogfight to the end."

He remained relentless about instilling pride and never took his foot off the pedal. "Passion is a word that Pat used a lot throughout the year," says Foligno. "That was a team with a lot of passionate players, a lot of leaders who'd been captains on other teams. And we were following our biggest leader, which was Pat. We believed what he said; we wanted to play the way he told us to play. When he saw us get so emotionally involved in a game, he got into it too."

There weren't enough superlatives for Burns to invest on Gilmour, especially. He was Killer's number-one fan and said so at every opportunity. After a game against the Kings in which Gilmour had broken Tomas

Sandstrom's forearm with a two-handed slash, league president Gil Stein assessed a weird penance: Gilmour was suspended for eight *non-games* and fined $30,000. Burns was infuriated, quickly coming to Gilmour's defence. "The Kings are always crying about something. They ran our goalie twice. But every time someone gets hurt, there has to be a suspension. L.A. and Pittsburgh, you can't touch them without getting suspended. People have been too quick to condemn Gilmour. Who knows if Sandstrom's arm was even broken on that play? I looked at the tape and I didn't see anything. Why does everyone want to hang Doug Gilmour by a rope until he's dead? That's hockey. Guys get whacked all the time." A columnist with the *San Diego Union-Tribune* nominated Burns as "North American Bozo of the Year" for that screed.

For Gilmour, it was one of the oddest periods in his career. He wasn't allowed to practise with the team but could dress for games. "After a couple of days, Burnsie says to me, 'What you been doing?' I said, nothing." So the coach arranged to have Gilmour practise with the University of Toronto varsity squad. "These guys are in the middle of exams," recalls Gilmour. "Their season is pretty much done but they're still practising. I show up and they're, like, 'Are you kidding me? Does that mean we have to skate hard now?' After the first day, I took them out for wings and beer at the Loose Moose. The next day, we were supposed to practise at two o'clock and I was still hung over. I went in, packed up my equipment and left. I told Burnsie, I can't skate with those guys anymore."

On December 1, Toronto lost 8–5 to the Devils. "It was the worst game that I've been behind the bench for in my life," Burns raged. "We can only win one way and that's by playing a very simple kind of hockey, grinding it out with discipline. But our guys had to get fancy. Obviously, they listened to someone other than the coach." As punishment, he dragged the team into the conference room at the Drake Hotel in Chicago, the next stop on their road trip, and forced them to sit through a long video session. "Instead of going shopping and eating, we're going to watch game film. Hey, I stayed up to 1:30 in the morning watching the [expletive deleted] film. It's like a dog who craps on the carpet. You have

A late arrival: baby Patrick with his parents Alfred and
Louise and (clockwise from top left) siblings Lillian,
Sonny (Alfred Jr.), Violet, Diane and Phyllis.

The former homicide cop joins the Montreal Canadiens: At the conclusion of the 1987–88 season, the scandalously carousing team was in need of a man like Pat Burns.

Renewing the Leafs, 1992: He told the players to hang up their jerseys carefully after each match. Mike Foligno recalls: "Even something as small as that, never letting . . . the logo touch the ground, was about bringing back pride in the club."

Playing a part, 1993: While coaching in the NHL was a dream come wildly true, Burns had other fantasies—guitar picker, cowboy, Hells Angel—and often dressed the part.

Facing an uncertain future: As the 1995–96 season got under way, few observers could have predicted that Burns's shelf life in Toronto was ticking down rapidly.

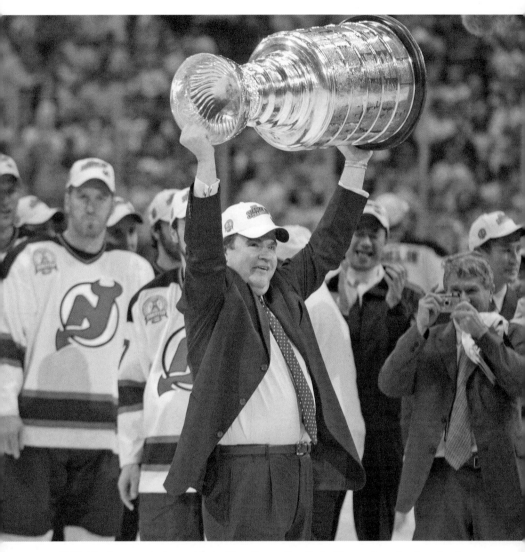

NHL Finals, 2003: At last, with the New Jersey Devils, he'd won the only silver hardware that matters. "My son Jason and my daughter Maureen came in from Montreal. . . . My wife was there, friends and family from Quebec. I pointed the Cup at them because sometimes you forget the people who are behind you, who were there when things don't go so good."

Aréna **Pat Burns** Arena

"I know my life is nearing the end, and I accept that": At the news conference in March 2010, where it was announced that an arena would be named after him in Stanstead, Quebec.

Line Burns carries her husband's ashes: The Stanley Cup urn was requested by Pat, who had also asked for a small funeral, conducted by a parish priest. What he got was a grand affair fit for a statesman.

to rub his nose in it, so he'll stop. You have to rub their noses in it sometimes."

The team was suddenly floundering, on a 2–7–2 skid, the longest slump Burns had ever experienced in the NHL. Fletcher cast about, trying to pick up useful parts, claiming winger Bill Berg off waivers from the Islanders. That's when Burns uttered his famous wisecrack: "Don't ask me about him. I wouldn't know him if I ran over him with my truck."

A big win over Detroit—five power-play goals from a unit Burns had earlier described sneeringly as the "powder play"—restored life to the squad and seemed to reverse the downward slide. Wrong. When the Leafs blew three leads, and finally the game, 5–4, to Buffalo on December 20— their ninth loss in thirteen games—Burns reached for the sledgehammer. Borrowing a page from the Mike Keenan handbook, he staged his postgame press conference smack in the middle of the visitors' locker room. "I'm having this press conference in the dressing room so all my players can hear. The tail has been wagging the dog for too long around here."

The tactic had the aroma of a staged scene, carefully orchestrated, designed to put maximum pressure on his underperforming players. The Leafs had now gone a full month without a road win. He ranted, he raved, he lambasted, saying the only thing preventing him from shipping some of them out was a league moratorium that halted all transactions for Christmas week. Players crept sheepishly in and out of the room. "I remember that," says Todd Gill. "What Pat was saying was the truth and nobody wants to hear the truth when things are going bad. But you stand up and listen. The hardest thing for an individual to do—and I think Pat taught all twenty-three of us on that team—is you can go as far as you want to go, you just have to push each other. And we started doing that. One thing I loved about Pat Burns is you'd get two or three shifts and if you didn't hold up to what he thought was good enough, you'd be sat for that period. And then the next period you'd get one more chance. He always gave you that second chance. There were no third chances, but you always got a second chance." Burns gave Gill another small but useful piece of advice. "When I didn't have it going and Pat was getting on me, I'd go in the dressing room between the first and second period, gear right down, jump in the shower, get re-dressed and say, okay, I'm starting new. He told me to try that. I did, and things seemed to go better when I could convince myself that I was starting new."

Gilmour dismissed the rant as a "scare tactic." Wendel Clark, the focus of swirling trade rumours, shrugged and said he hadn't actually caught a word that Burns spoke. In his off-ice passive way, Clark pushed back. "No player has ever quit since I've been here. And there won't be any players quitting."

Burns was bidden to a meeting with Fletcher the next day and, when reappearing for reporters, seemed somewhat subdued, even a bit chagrined by the tantrum that he rated as 8.5 on his own personal eruption scale. "Hockey players are like your children sometimes. You don't like anybody else criticizing them except yourself. I don't want people to think I yell at my players constantly because I don't. I praise my players when praise should be given and I scold them when I think I should. I don't like to lose, and I want my players to hate losing—not be satisfied with what happened in Buffalo. All I want to do is make this club respectable." More waggishly, he reached for a metaphor, referencing the horseflesh belonging to Toronto's new owner, Steve Stavro, who also owned the successful Knob Hill Stable. "It's like Mr. Stavro said. He treats this business almost like a horse stable, and he's right. These guys are thoroughbreds. You've got to beat them, you've got to whip them." Then, laughing, he added, "But if we break their legs, we promise we won't shoot anybody."

With the trade moratorium lifted, the Leafs did indeed attempt to peddle Clark to Edmonton, but the Oilers backed out at the last minute. When reporters got a whiff of that aborted deal, the captain—only five goals on the season—was put in an awkward position. Burns seemed to damn Clark with faint praise. And he was well aware of what he was implying. "I love Wendel Clark, but are we expecting too much of him? He's a great team guy and a great role player. His role is to go out and give us a lift once in a while. Maybe we're looking for the wrong guy to turn us around. Maybe Wendel is more of a support guy." Was he undermining the captain? Clark read it differently. "Ah, he was just pushing buttons because Pat was good at that. Sometimes, I think Pat was using me to get a message through to the other players. He was really talking to the guys in the room. I might grumble, but he knew I could take it. I had that *C* on my sweater and he expected more of me."

From high-decibel condemnation, Burns settled down to an almost benign absorption of a 4–4 tie in Detroit, a game in which the Leafs blew another lead. "I don't think we played all that bad, all things considered. We are in Detroit, you know."

Perhaps the club's fast start had been deceptive? The nosedive, with Toronto slipping to seventh, sent Burns back to the blackboard. He reminded the players of what had worked through the first six weeks. They were chasing goals instead of being defensively vigilant to prevent them. They didn't have the offensively skilled ponies to freewheel, and they'd all got sidetracked. "I'm taking some of the blame," he lamented. The team would revert to tight-checking hockey and damn the aesthetics.

As the calendar changed to 1993, on a night when smokers had to butt out for the first time at Maple Leaf Gardens, Toronto managed a low-wattage tie with St. Louis. But everyone was keyed up for Burns's looming return to the Forum. His old media foes from Montreal had descended on the Gardens to bang out their dispatches leading up to the game. Burns was bemused. "You guys were turning cartwheels when I got fired." The prodigal son's homecoming even bumped Céline Dion's Grammy Award nomination off the front page of *Le Journal de Montréal,* the city's largest-circulation paper. Journalists did their best to manufacture a feud between Burns and Jacques Demers, comparing and contrasting their styles. Demers had been ridiculed in some quarters for his habit of greeting players when they came off the ice after a game, shaking each one's hand. Burns, perennially brooding behind the bench, always pivoted immediately and disappeared without a word, win or lose.

Before this game, Burns walked slowly, dignified, across the Forum ice surface to the visitors' bench. It was an emotional, pressure-packed match that he wanted desperately to win. From the moment they boarded their flight, his players were aware of the occasion's significance and Burns's mood; he'd paced up and down the aisle. When he stepped out of the cab at the arena that night, Burns was greeted by a phalanx of TV cameras. To the media, he professed this was just another middle-season game, of no special significance, but he was lying and nobody bought it.

Toronto came out hellbent, building up a 4–0 lead, Gilmour tallying two. And then they very nearly caved, hanging on for the 5–4 win, Mark Osborne scoring late in the third. At the buzzer, Burns windmilled his arm triumphantly and, unusually, patted every player as they stomped to the dressing room. "That was one game where Pat never said anything to us beforehand," says Gilmour. "But you could see how nervous he was. I don't think I ever saw him that emotional again. It was so important for us to win it for Pat and we did it. It was like a piano falling off his back. It meant so much to him, and then when he pumped his fist at the end . . . wow. Some guys who'd never been traded before maybe couldn't understand what it meant, but this was like Pat coming back after being traded. It was very big, for all of us." Afterwards, Burns admitted circling the date on his calendar. "I thought about it a lot during the summer."

The team was now at .500 for the first time since December 1. Later in January, in the rematch at Maple Leaf Gardens, Potvin stoned the Canadiens 4–0, his first NHL shutout. He'd firmly bumped Fuhr, sidelined with an injury, as main man between the pipes, largely due to the faith Burns had placed in him. "He's going to keep the net as long as he keeps it going. He's got to understand that it's his to lose, even when Grant gets back."

Something special was starting to happen with this club as it began to put together little win streaks, clawing its way back upward in the standings. Burns's only complaint was that the Gardens crowd was too quiet. When beer went on sale during games for the first time at the old barn, he snarked, "Maybe a couple of them will get off their hands now."

On the road, the coaching staff noticed players hanging together more instead of breaking off into cliques. Nobody ever ate alone. They were becoming a genuine collective. While concentrating on solidifying their playoff position, the Leafs found themselves just five points behind second-place Detroit.

"Everybody had accepted their role," says Gilmour. "Pat would still chew us out after a bad game, but sometimes you knew it was just an act. He had to put that face on, so we'd just sit there with our heads down. He'd never scream at me, just give me 'the look'—squinting his eye the way a cop might look at you, and I knew. The next day, I'd come in just shaking. He was a big man, right, and he could be very intimidating in the dressing room. Actually, he could scare the shit out of us. It was strange; if we were on a winning streak, he made us practise harder. If we lost a few, he gave us more time off. I don't really know where he learned to handle people, probably from having been a cop.

"The feeling that was developing on that team, I've never experienced anything like it. We didn't have the best players in the league, but we had good players. He wanted us to go out together as a team, to have a beer, to have team functions. His family was the players in the room and their families. Again, I look at all the teams I've played with. There are so many guys who are on their own agenda. That team was different." One day, they held their team meeting at a watering hole across from the Gardens, P.M. Toronto. Everybody stayed for beers afterward, coaching staff and trainers included. "Believe me, you never see that in the NHL," says Gilmour. "You just don't." The occasional tirades—which weren't much required anymore—no longer had quite the frightening impact. "We knew he loved us," says Gilmour, "and we adored him."

If not quite loosey-goosey, their spirits were soaring, which triggered ridiculous rounds of internal pranks. Gilmour lost count of the times he arrived at his locker to find the heels of his socks cut out—by dastardly Burns. Almost every day, the coach pricked pinholes in the dressing-room paper coffee cups. On one memorable occasion, when the team was in Minnesota, a couple of players balanced cups of water atop the door ledge, expecting to douse the next teammate to walk in. Instead, it was Burns. "He's got his suit on, his hair's all perfect, and four cups of water drop on his head," Gilmour howls. "Todd Gill fell off his stool, he was laughing so hard. And Burnsie just says, 'I'll get you back for this, guys.'" When Burns was an hour late for practice in Florida, the players subjected him to a kangaroo court and issued a fine. On another road trip, Burns secreted a pair of women's panties into a suitcase belonging to assistant GM Bill Watters. His wife found them, just as the devious Burns had envisioned.

At game fifty, Burns met the players individually for one-on-one discussions. There was really no need. They were all stoked. "Even I can't think of the right things to say right now," Burns admitted. Fletcher cashed in his biggest insurance asset and sent Fuhr to Buffalo for Dave Andreychuk and backup goalie Daren Puppa. Andreychuk was a true goal scorer and precisely what Burns had been pleading for. "I kept saying to Cliff, 'I need somebody to play with Gilmour.' He kept saying, 'Be patient.' Well, now I've got a guy."

The only fly in the ointment was the status of Wendel Clark. The captain had angered Burns by going on an All-Star break vacation to the Turks and Caicos Islands while still recovering from a strained rib muscle. Burns wondered aloud why Clark was unfit to play but fit to frolic on the beach. The coach was irritated over yet another prolonged injury absence by Clark, insinuating he was being too cautious about returning to game action. "I'm not dogging it," Clark insisted. "You can call me anything you want, but don't ever say I'm dogging it. You can say I'm a brutal player. You can say I'm brutal defensively and I can't score anymore. But don't say it's from lack of effort."

There were even whispers Clark might lose his C. But Burns backed off, insisting his captain had not fallen from grace. "Wendel was the captain before and he's going to stay captain." On his first night back after sitting out thirteen games, Clark banged with abandon and scored a vintage Wendel goal against Boston. "I wasn't out there to vindicate myself. I've been injured enough to know when to come back and when not to come back." Burns was effusive with praise. "He came out of the gate like a bull and kept raging all night. It was great to see him on the bench."

Gilmour set a team season record for assists in an 8–1 thrashing of Vancouver, smashing the standard set 16 years earlier by Darryl Sittler. "I was so proud of the team in Vancouver, I could have cried," said Burns. "I could have hugged every one of them." Red-hot Toronto was now gunning for its eighth straight game without a loss, in San Jose. Burns nevertheless found stuff to agonise about. "There's enough time we could still, heaven forbid, go into a slump. Dougie Gilmour, heaven forbid, could get an injury. Something could happen to Félix. I could think of all sorts of ways we could get [expletive deleted]." They were ten games above .500 and flattened the Sharks 5–0. "And I'm supposed to be a defensive coach?" Burns teased. Todd Gill, who'd been a special rehabilitative project of Burns, said: "This guy commands respect. He hates to lose and he has made his players scared to lose."

Glenn Anderson collected his 1,000th point in the Vancouver game, and Burns double-shifted him throughout the final two periods, which was appreciated by the player's three dozen friends and family in the stands. It seemed as though benchmarks in career stats were being reached every night as the season hurtled towards a conclusion. "As we approached the playoffs, we sensed this team was special," Foligno reminisces. "We started hitting numbers, reaching little milestones on a personal level or statistics-wise as a team—little accomplishments. Pat would make a point of saying, 'This is so-and-so's whatever game to have played,' or consecutive face-offs won or a road record—things that helped us get focused so that we wouldn't bury ourselves by looking too far down the road."

There was no big secret to the Leaf surge; the team's best players were leading the charge and the foot soldiers were playing their hearts out. And they were extremely well coached, as illustrated by the club's defensive record. Just two points behind second-place Detroit, they were now chasing a forty-two-year-old club record of eleven games without a loss. In little more than two months, the Leafs had gone from one of the worst teams in hockey to one of the best. Burns tried to tamp down the giddiness in Toronto, but everybody could tell this team was for real, not an illusion. He grumped about playing at home, "where fans think you can walk on air."

Bob McGill, who'd been a member of the 1985–86 Leaf team that had established a club record for futility with only seventeen wins, could scarely believe the squad's good fortunes and gave all the credit to Burns. "In years past, we had different coaches and a different philosophy every year. There was always turmoil. Guys weren't happy and we weren't a team."

This was a team, cohesive. The unbeaten streak came to a screeching halt in Detroit on March 5, however, when the Red Wings made the Leafs look lousy, 5–1. This was worrisome because it seemed increasingly likely Toronto would face Detroit in the first round of the playoffs. But they wasted no time getting back on track, soon afterward dumping the Tampa Bay Lightning 8–2. "I think we've woken a lot of people up," said Burns. "Deep down, some of them might be saying, 'Ah, they're a bunch of phonies riding a big streak. But I think other teams are starting to notice. If you're going to build on that, you have to keep working hard. You can't get to a certain point and then relax." At practice before that Bolts game, Burns unleashed some rage, shattering his stick against the glass. "I'm just doing my job. I have to make them realize that you can't go through the motions at this time of the year. If you want to keep the fire burning, you have to outrun the wind." He'd been working on that quote for a while, as was his habit to keep reporters satisfied.

With eleven games remaining, Toronto was flirting with first place in the Norris Division—penthouse territory, though no one was allowed to even mention that in the dressing room. The Leafs locked up a playoff spot on March 28 by trouncing the equally hot Flames 4–0. Predictably, Burns saw the glass as half-empty. "We haven't done diddly yet. We haven't won anything yet. We haven't won our division, we haven't won a playoff round. There's nothing to get excited about. We can't fly our flags and say, 'We've made it, we're done.'"

Yet the players had clearly fallen in thrall to Burns's unfancy approach to success. They were 25–8–3 since January 6—no other team in the NHL had been better over that stretch—and had just garnered seven out of a possible eight points on their last road trip. In Toronto, many Leaf fans, after weathering misery for so many years, had to pinch themselves and ask, "Are we all hallucinating?" On April 4, the Leafs won their forty-second game, surpassing the franchise record, set in 1950–51 and matched in 1977–78.

But then there was a slight wobble, a few setbacks that put first place in the division all but out of reach. McGill's season was ended by a broken jaw. Andreychuk hadn't scored in five games. A 4–0 defeat by sad-sack Philadelphia, which snapped the Leafs' twelve-game undefeated record at home, took some of the glow off. That loss guaranteed Toronto a third-place finish in the Norris Division, behind Chicago and Detroit, where first place had been a possibility just a week earlier. Burns waved off suggestions the season of enchantment had spent itself. "Everyone seems to be looking at us thinking we're going to choke and fold. Good. Let them think that."

The final three games were mostly meaningless, though two goals from Foligno in a 4–2 victory over Hartford set a Toronto franchise record for most points in a season. Beating the Blues 2–1 in OT, earning their twenty-fifth home ice victory, established another club record. Their last game was a 3–2 loss to Chicago. The Leafs finished the season with 99 points; the year before, they'd had 67. Everybody was just anxious and eager to start the postseason. "It's going to be fun," promised Gilmour. "We've got to be happy with the season we've had, but not satisfied. We've got a little bit of work ahead of us still."

In an interview with the *Toronto Star*'s Damien Cox, Burns acknowledged that he was dreaming of a Stanley Cup. "There's no better feeling than looking up on that out-of-town scoreboard and realizing you are one of only two teams still playing. I think about it every day. There could be a chance this year."

While Fletcher was originally cool to the idea, Burns convinced the GM the team should go north to Collingwood for several days of rest, practice and seclusion before the playoffs. When Gilmour's grandfather died, he wanted to return home for the funeral. "I asked Pat, 'Can I go?' He said no. He said, 'Your grandfather would want you here.'"

On the day before they flew to Detroit to open the playoffs, Gilmour was strolling to the Collingwood rink with Wendel Clark. "There was this guy in an old Camaro. He's honking and waving at us." Gilmour smacks his hands together. "Bang! He drives right into a pole. The guy had a kid in the car with him, so Wendel and I run over to make sure they're not hurt. And this guy, he's saying, 'It's okay, we're okay, don't worry.' Oh man, it was the wildest thing. We couldn't believe it."

And it was just the beginning. Over the next forty-two nights—during which the Maple Leafs would play twenty-one games—all disbelief was suspended.

Chapter Twelve

Twenty-one Games in 42 Nights

"Pressure? What pressure?"

THE LEAFS used an old bucket of a chartered Air Ontario plane that felt like it was held together by spit and chicken wire. "You'd be sitting there on takeoff, clutching the armrests, never knowing if the damn thing would get up enough speed to lift off the runway," says Doug Gilmour, shuddering at the memory. Only later on, at the start of the conference final against Los Angeles, did owner Steve Stavro upgrade the team's transportation arrangements, renting a sleek and spacious 727 with polished attendants serving catered gourmet box lunches. One reporter from each major news outlet was permitted to hitch a lift with the club.

The spring '93 playoffs were a heart-stopping thrill ride: twenty-one games in forty-two nights for Toronto—three consecutive seven-game series. No other NHL team had done that before, and Pat Burns burnished his reputation as coaching virtuoso. It would be a dreadful metaphor to say the postseason flight eventually crashed and burned for the Leafs, and all those along for the breathtaking spring whirl. But everyone who was there, up close, will never forget the experience—the hockey, the whole splendiferous and exhilarating adventure.

———

"If I told you, I'd have to kill you." That was Gilmour toying with a reporter who'd inquired about the Leafs' strategy against Detroit, Toronto's first-round opponent. Pat Burns had been equally cagey about what he had in mind as the series opened. Toronto had allowed only 241 goals in 84 games for a 2.87 GAA, the best since 1971–72. Cliff Fletcher had constructed a compelling club out of the wreckage left behind from the '80s. But this was also the oldest team in the NHL, with an average age of twenty-eight. And now Toronto was going up against the offensively flashy Red Wings and their formidable power play. Hustle and desire had been contagious among the Leafs, but would that be enough to cramp the superior talent and prowess of Steve Yzerman, Chris Chelios and their Motor City crew? "The crack in the door is there for every team," reminded Burns, noting Toronto and Detroit had split their head-to-head series through the regular season. "I know I believe that, but I don't know if all the players believe it." Then, mimicking the traditional Olympics declaration: "Let the games begin!"

Stavro had Maple Leaf Gardens director Terry Kelly hand-deliver a lucky tie to Burns on the eve of the series. He chose not to wear it for game one at the Joe Louis Arena. It might have helped, as things turned out. If the coach did have a game plan, it must have gone unheeded. Leafs turned the puck over in their own end, took bad penalties, failed to contain the Red Wings' speed, missed passes, blew checking assignments, couldn't even execute a viable dump-and-chase and got pushed around absurdly. The Leafs looked not only nervous but afraid. At one point, trash-talking thorn-in-the-side Dino Ciccarelli—he'd staked out territory directly in front of Félix Potvin, practically planted a flag, and was left unmolested—screeched insults right in the young goalie's face, and nobody made a move to dislodge him. "If a guy's going to put his rear end in our goaltender's face, we've got to do something about it," Burns complained.

Before the game, Todd Gill paced anxiously in his underwear outside the Leaf dressing room. The teamwide tension could be cut with a knife. The Leafs took the boisterous crowd at the Joe out of the equation by scoring first after killing off a two-man disadvantage, but they were frantic, undisciplined and overwhelmed thereafter, thrashed 6–3. Octopi plopped on the ice in whoop-whoop celebration. Burns had to salvage something from the atrocity to alleviate his players' despondency. "It was one of those nights. What you don't want to do is bury your head. You've got to stick it up proud and get right back at it." An invitation to the dance is how Burns had characterized Toronto's first playoff inclusion after more than a thousand days and nights in the wilderness. But the Leafs had been stomped, staggering in their incompetence. The coach was among those who marvelled at Detroit's awesomeness. "You should have seen it from ice level. Whoosh—and they were gone. That team can kill your dreams in ten minutes."

Ten minutes, five shots, four goals: goodbye dreams.

Bad-ass Bob Probert, the NHL's heavyweight champ, mocked Wendel Clark, practically slapped a white glove across the captain's face. "You really couldn't find him out there on the ice," he sneered. Probert had almost ripped off Potvin's arm in one drive-by collision and then mugged passive defenceman Dmitri Mironov with nary a shove-back. "Probert was pretty much allowed to do what he wanted," Burns groused. "But I don't have a forklift to move him out of there."

There was more bad news: Toronto right winger Nikolai Borschevsky collided with Vladimir Konstantinov in the third period, striking his head on the lip of the boards. He fractured the orbital bone below his right eye. When Borschevsky tried to blow his nose, his eye puffed up grotesquely because air was forced through the crack in the bone. The injury was expected to keep the not-so-husky Siberian out of the lineup for at least seven days, doctors saying he wouldn't be able to play with a face shield once the swelling went down because air could leak into the eye and explode the orb. Meanwhile, Todd Gill suffered back spasms after lunging for a puck. The eviscerated lineup had Burns wringing his hands over what might ensue in game two. "Often, you get the smell of blood when you lose players. The other team gets going like wolves." As personnel adjustment, Burns dressed Mike Foligno, who'd been a game one scratch. "Maybe Foligno might have a couple bounce in off his bum."

Next morning, propped on a stool and balancing on the tip of his skates as he faced reporters, Burns tried to sound philosophical. "When I got up this morning, the sun was still shining," he said, evoking Pierre Elliott Trudeau after the Night of the Long Thousand Knives. That evening, a bunch of Leafs went to Tiger Stadium to take in the ballgame against Seattle. Handing out ducats, PR director Bob Stellick added, "You also get a coupon for a free hot dog and drink."

Toronto put in a better effort in game two, showed more zip, but the result was the same: a 6–2 loss. As the score mounted, things got ugly with lots of slashing, spearing and stick swinging. Potvin grew so exasperated with Ciccarelli's abuse that he laid a two-hander across his irritant's shins with his goal stick. The Joe crowd, meanwhile, taunted the oddly docile Clark: "WENDY! WENDY!" In the regular season, Clark had outpunched Probert in a memorable title fight, but now he turned the other cheek. Probert was a menacing presence every time he stepped on the ice, while Toronto's lauded team grit had turned to team silt. Clark had sought calmer waters at the edge of repeated frays, noticeable only for his absence—the absence of malice. He was excoriated by reporters for his meekness. "Pat had told me not to fight Probert," Clark says now. "But I wasn't allowed to say that I'd been told not to fight him."

Perhaps there had been a breakdown in communication between coach and captain. "I told Wendel and the others that they had to create some havoc to get this thing turned around," said Burns. "Nobody's asking him to fight Bob Probert—that's not it at all. Probert's not the problem. We've got to hit their good people and not waste our time and energy on guys who can't really hurt us." Burns was livid over Probert questioning Clark's manhood and stories written about Toronto's captain. "You can question Wendel's ability to score. You can question his ability to shoot. But nobody will ever question Wendel's toughness or his heart. That's bullshit, pardon the expression. Wendel Clark is not a guy that's going to skate away from anything. Nobody here will ever question Wendel Clark's courage." Steaming, the coach stalked off. Yet later, privately, Burns took aside a columnist who'd been especially merciless in print about "Pretty Boy" Clark. "You're not entirely wrong," he confided.

Detroit coach Bryan Murray claimed to be appalled by all the lumberwork. "It was certainly one of the most vicious games I've been involved in. There are lots of people who don't want fighting but, if that's the result of no fighting in hockey . . . boy." For Burns, the only saving grace was leaving Motown behind for a while, with few chroniclers of the Leafs misfortunes— outscored 12–5—expecting the team to return there that spring. "We're a good club," Burns said defiantly. "At least we're going back home. Let's wait and see. I hope our fans are as vocal as theirs." He repeated the Leaf gospel preached all season: "Everything this team has accomplished has come from hard work and second effort. It seems to me, we coaches showed them all these films and diagrams and explained matchups at length, and at some point, they said to themselves, 'Hey, this is going to be easy, as long as we follow those plans.' Well, it's never easy. Never has been. Never will be."

In Toronto, Burns convened a meeting to address leadership, dismissing the idea that Clark was guilty of leaving a void in that area, pointing fingers instead at veterans who'd won the whole enchilada elsewhere. "The guys with Stanley Cup rings have done (bleep). But I've talked to them about it and I made them talk a bit too. If we believe we're beat, then we're beat." Team psychologist Max Offenberger was tapped to make a dressing-room house call. Of more direct influence was Burns's decision to neutralize the distraction of Ciccarelli. Simply put: Ignore him. Let the guy chirp and harass Potvin. Render him invisible. Potvin signed on to the strategy. "I'm not going to touch him. I won't let him bother me. I'm going to try to see through him." Potvin says Burns made a point of bucking him up. "He came to me in the room saying, 'I don't want you on the ice today for practice. Make sure you rest and are ready for game three.' Right away, that cleared any doubts I may have had in my head."

Following a brisk practice, assistant coach Mike Kitchen booted a garbage can in anger when he saw the media swarming around Clark's stall. The captain was his usual stoic and straightforward self when queried about whether he still had a leadership role on the club that extended beyond the ice. "I don't know. I'm not that deep. I'm a farmer, for God's sake. I show up and play, and that's the only part that's in my control."

The team's psyche was fragile, and its big guns had gone silent. Gilmour had two goals in two games, one on the power play. Dave Andreychuk, saddled with a reputation as a playoff vanishing act from his years in Buffalo—"Andy-choke"—had yet to score. Gilmour suggested the squad had been too uptight in Detroit. "We've been nervous. We've been scared out there because we didn't want to lose." Crucially, as Burns emphasized, they needed to wise up, avoid being drawn into taking penalties that were killing them. "We have to be smart and keep our energy for when the clock is ticking, not for the scrums and the fights. We can't worry about out-toughing them."

In the third game, Toronto came out flying and banging bodies. With a little more room to operate and the advantage of the last line change, Gilmour and Andreychuk cranked up production. Although the Leafs wasted three consecutive first-period power plays, the extra-man situations gave them the momentum needed to jump into a 2–0 lead. But it was Clark who silenced his critics with a commanding, muscular performance. Several Wings were nearly quartered by his bone-crunching Clarkian body slams. He scored the goal that gave Toronto a 3–1 lead—parked at the edge of the crease, taking a pass from Gilmour behind the net and stuffing a backhand between the legs of Tim Cheveldae—and shoved the Leafs back into the series, Toronto winning 4–2. In the locker room afterwards, the unassuming warrior made a press pack wait for twenty minutes while he had a long chat with a young fan in a wheelchair. Then Clark stood in the media circle, braces still latched around both gimpy knees, and offered only a gentle retort. "You know the media is going to throw things at you. I just put my skates on, play the game."

Burns spread around the praise. "The fans were just great. The guys on the bench were just jumping. It was the first time I've seen everybody on the bench just jumping." A series of tactical coaching moves had contributed significantly. Using last line change to his advantage, Burns deployed ten different line combinations in the first period alone. "And be sure to leave Dino Ciccarelli alone in front of the net. Why get into a wrestling match with him?" The pest was not a factor. "It took us two games to get used to playoff-style hockey, but we're in control of our emotions now and we still don't feel like we've played our best hockey."

The yapping between opposing coaches, each trying to secure a psychological edge, was bordering on silly. Murray even whined that Burns had a leg-up because of the eight-inch riser behind the Leaf bench. He complained that it gave Burns a better view and made him more imposing to game officials. Burns sniped right back, noting that the visiting coach's office in Detroit was in the men's washroom. "That's not bad, except when a security guard came in to use it. The place smelled for half an hour." By the start of game four, Murray had his own riser.

It was another chippy affair. While Gilmour and Andreychuk performed superbly, it was the supporting players who stepped up, Burns issuing kudos in particular to his ferocious checking line of Peter Zezel, Mark Osborne and Bill Berg for containing Detroit's top troika. Zezel won three crucial faceoffs in the Leaf zone with a minute left in regulation, goalie pulled, Toronto up 3–2. Raised in Toronto's Beaches neighbourhood, Zezel spoke reverently about donning the blue and white. "Every time the sweater is put on, there's a price. As soon as that sweater goes on, guys go for their guns."

With the series tied at two games apiece, Burns was jubilant. "It could have been the hardest I've seen them work. There is a lot of pride on this team." Andreychuk had potted the winner and was asked if he'd finally shed the "Andy-choke" handle. "Not by any means. I've still got a long ways to go." Little did he know.

Everybody was banged up and bruised, none more than Gilmour, with several stitches threaded to close an inch-long cut below one eye and a crescent-shaped cut above the other eyebrow. That owwie occurred when Steve Chiasson drove Gilmour's head into the boards in the second period. Later in the game, Mark Howe tomahawked his left wrist, at the base of the thumb, sending Gilmour straight to the Gardens medical clinic cupping the hinge, Dr. Leith Douglas in pursuit. He returned to action a minute later, taped up. "Your heart stops," said Burns. "But he's tough. He came back." No worries, said Gilmour, the wrist wasn't broken. "I've got X-ray eyes, so I can tell you it's only a bruise."

"It's a new series now," Burns crowed. "That's what happens in the playoffs. Things go from hot to cold and from cold to hot. That's the fun of the playoffs, what makes it exciting. This could be a long series. We're an ugly team to play against." There were smiles of delight, too, when, contrary to predictions, Borschevsky suddenly returned to practice. Gilmour assured inquisitors his wrist wasn't busted, even joked about doing pushups and lifting weights. Stepping off the ice after practice, he feigned a severe limp. There were serious concerns, however, about what the hard-smashing series was costing Gilmour. Burns was constantly double-shifting his go-to guy and Gilmour's weight was dropping dramatically, despite all the pasta carbs he was ingesting. "After games, they just laid me down on a table and threw IVs at me," Gilmour recalls. "With all those electrolytes, I'd walk out of there feeling like I hadn't even played a game. Then I'd walk home. At the time, I was living right next to the Gardens on Wood Street, so it was a short walk."

Returning to the mosh pit of the Joe, Toronto purloined a game they probably had no right winning, overcoming a 4–1 deficit. They exploited Detroit's weak link in goal, beating Cheveldae twice on long shots by Dave Ellett. A fluke goal by Clark midway through the third sent it into overtime. Hero of the night was Mike Foligno, who'd begun his NHL career as a Wing. Clark dug the puck out from a scramble at the left boards and passed to Foligno, who fired a shot through a maze of bodies from between the circles, winning the game 5–4. Then he executed his joyful victory hop, jumping so high in the air his knees almost touched his chin.

"It was jubilation on a number of counts," says Foligno. "One, obviously, was that I hadn't even known at the start of the season if I was going to be able to come back and play again. Two, I used to play for Detroit and felt like I had some unfinished business there. And then, to have scored that overtime goal, oh man. I remember Wendel's work on the wall and Mike Krushelnyski's screen in front of the net. When I scored, I threw off my gloves. It's funny; I don't even know why I did that. Then a whole bunch of other guys threw their gloves in the air, Todd Gill and Peter Zezel. Oh my God, it was like a Stanley Cup championship game. There was so much emotion. Everybody was happy we'd won the game, but I think the guys were happy for me as well. It had been such a tough grind I'd gone through. That win in overtime was so much *fun*. And you know what? The feeling we had that night, we wanted to get it again. That's when we really got a taste of winning, for the feel of winning, and wanted to taste it again." Burns was thrilled for Foligno. "The old guy bopped one in for us." In overtime—and there would be many more OTs to come that spring—Burns had unshakeable confidence in his players, harking back to the harsh workouts he'd put them through in practices throughout the year. After one such gruelling session, he'd barked: "There'll be a night next April, in overtime, when the work we do now will pay off for us."

The Red Wings were aghast. Toronto had put itself in a position to clinch at home in game six. The city, gaga with hockey fever, welcomed the Leafs back with full-throated gusto at the usually mausoleum-hushed Gardens. But they left the arena in distress. "We got our asses kicked," says Gilmour. Surrendering five unanswered goals in the second period—two of them shorthanded—Toronto was drubbed 7–3. At the start of the third frame, Burns replaced Potvin with Daren Puppa. "He told me on the bench, 'Just take a break, because you're going back in for game seven,'" says Potvin. "That showed he still had confidence in me." Burns could find little that was positive to seize on in the rout. "We can't be any worse than we were tonight. That's the only good thing." A concussed Zezel left the building leaning on his father, Ivan, with instructions that he be awakened every two hours. Reporters took to their computers, chiselling a headstone in advance for the Maple Leafs. Burns shielded his players. "A lot of experts around here said we'd be out in six and we're still here." He did reclaim the underdog stance that was always a favourite posture, telling the players: "Nobody believes in us. It's poor little us against the world. However, you men can show them all how wrong they are. It all comes down to determination and desire."

Who would have bet on the Leafs at that point? They'd stolen one in Detroit, but to do it again, in a game seven? Dream on.

"We were still learning how to win in the playoffs as a team," Foligno says. "Detroit had come back with barrels a-blazing in our building. I remember us getting scared but saying, 'You know what? We've still got a chance here.' Pat warned us we might not have the lead to start in game seven, but 'Let's learn from our last game, don't quit no matter what the score is.' And we did learn. We let them get the lead [in the second period] and we battled back and we were able to take the game into overtime again, and the rest is history."

Burns had pulled out all the clichés: backs against the wall, do-or-die, no tomorrow, when the going gets tough . . . Yet it was the Wings who looked more tightly wound, nursing a one-goal lead through half the game. Before the third frame, Burns addressed his troops, keeping the pep talk short and focused. "It's there for you, guys." In the third, Detroit was up 3–2 after an exchange of goals. With just two minutes and forty-three seconds left in regulation time, Clark pounced on a loose puck in the corner and passed to Gilmour in the slot, who beat Cheveldae to even the score, sending the game into overtime. "All of a sudden, *boom-boom-boom,* we were back in it," says Gilmour. "When I tied it, I felt in that moment, the pressure hit Detroit."

During the OT intermission, in the corridor outside the dressing room, Burns smacked his palms together. "I love this. This is the kind of hockey I get off on. This is great!" What he told the players was, "Just throw everything at the net." In fact, Toronto mustered only two shots in OT, but Borschevsky—"Nik the Stick" to his teammates—made one of them count. Gilmour, who'd been centring Andreychuk and Glenn Anderson, had just got back to the bench with his wingers. Burns turned him right around, sending him out again with Clark and Borschevsky. At 2:35, the little Russian with the broken orbital bone who'd not been expected to heal quickly enough to rejoin the series, wearing a plastic shield, redirected Bob Rouse's goalmouth pass, stabbing home the winner. Yowza.

As the Leafs swarmed over Borschevsky, jumping and dancing in an orgy of celebration, Burns and assistant Mike Murphy shared a bear hug. Up in the press box, Cliff Fletcher buried his face in his hands. Then Burns turned and pointed to Fletcher with an outstretched arm. "Except for that first game back in Montreal, that was the most emotional I've ever seen Burnsie," says Gilmour.

In the dressing room afterwards, Borschevsky was besieged by reporters. "The doctors told me ten days. But I say I play today." Then he raised his arms in surrender. "I'm sorry. I no speak good English. Maybe tomorrow I talk better." In another corner, Todd Gill wept tears of joy. Burns, making his way to the interview podium, got in one zing: "So much for the experts." He said the win was "almost like an apology to our fans" for game six. "For the past few days, I've been telling everyone who would listen that this series would go seven games and that we'd win it in overtime. Of course, I also said that Glenn Anderson would score the goal."

Changed into street clothes, the Leafs straggled towards the bus that would take them to Windsor, across the Detroit River, and the flight home. Wendel Clark carried a case of beer under each arm.

Bring on the St. Louis Blues . . . and all that jazz.

With Detroit relegated to postseason footnote, the Norris Division final loomed as the Tale of the Cat and the Dog: Félix and Cujo. For his part, Burns was annoyed to be denied the underdog role, even as he pointed to such big-game St. Louis horses as Brett Hull and Brendan Shanahan. Toronto held a 4–0–3 edge in regular-season play, but Curtis Joseph, from Keswick, Ontario, held the hotter hand, standing on his head when the Blues swept Chicago. Solving the Cujo riddle was now Toronto's challenge. Burns allowed the Leafs one optional practice before the series opened at Maple Leaf Gardens, but otherwise granted them no rest to savour the Detroit triumph. "He didn't give us a chance to breathe and enjoy the win because he said we hadn't achieved anything yet," says Gill.

"To be fair to Pat, he was hard on everybody. Usually, your best players get away with a little bit. One thing I loved about Pat is that he was as hard on Dougie as he was on the rest of us." (At the time of this conversation, nineteen years later, Gill was coaching the Kingston Frontenacs, the junior team managed by Gilmour.)

Joseph was allegedly vulnerable high to the glove side, but he held the Leafs off the scoreboard in game one until there was under a minute left in the first period, John Cullen tucking in his own rebound. Philippe Bozon got that one back midway through the third. And there the score remained for what seemed an eternity. Back and forth the teams swung in what the advance billing had conjectured would be a dull, defensive goaltending duel. There was nothing boring about the battle between net men. Not until 3:16 of the second overtime, as the clock approached midnight, threatening to turn the TV broadcast into *Hockey Morning in Canada*, after Joseph had faced sixty-two shots and been clunked on the head by Foligno's skate, did Gilmour, the former Blue—hero one more time, with gusts to legend-in-the-making—prick the cocoon of apparent invulnerability. Every other Leaf was tied up by frantic checkers when Gilmour darted out from behind the net with a swirling, spinning, dizzying wraparound goal that confounded Joseph. "It was the longest game I've ever played," says Gilmour, who'd skated miles, logging Herculean ice time.

With the pounds still falling off, he looked emaciated, sometimes seeming no more than a black-and-blue smudge inside a jersey. "I should take that little runt home and force-feed him," joked Burns.

The perspiration had barely dried off when the puck dropped on game two, the Gardens a sweat-soaked sauna. With no air conditioning, muggy air clashed with cold ice surface, creating a misty fug at ice level. Potvin knew he had to match Joseph save for save; there was clearly no margin for error in this showdown. "It was tough because I knew I couldn't let anything get by me. But at the same time it was fun. Because Curtis was so good at the other end, I knew I had to be equally good. And honestly, I grew up a lot from the first series against Detroit. Now it was about taking care of business."

Hull scored on the Blues' third shot of the game, stunning the crowd. But Gilmour, quickly ascending to the ranks of the immortals, made it 1–1, scooting in from the corner to stuff the puck behind Joseph. Garth Butcher, St. Louis defenceman, immediately and sharply—almost quicker than the eye could see—scooped the disc out of the net. The episode went to video review, scrutinized from several angles, before referee Paul Stewart, after an interminable wait, signalled it was a good goal. In the next frame, Gilmour was clipped in the face with a high stick. He fell to the ice, writhing, and the partisan crowd held its breath. Finally, he stood up again, gave Stewart an earful for not calling a penalty, and the game proceeded.

Again there was no further scoring in regulation. Again, it went to overtime. Again, it went to a second overtime. Again, Joseph withstood a Leaf barrage. Again it would be a 2–1 verdict, but this time for the Blues. At 3:03 of the fifth period, St. Louis defenceman Jeff Brown pounced on a rebound and hit the open side of the net, Potvin down. Through six playoff games, including the opening round against the Blackhawks, Joseph had now stopped 252 of 261 shots. His jackknife splits and Venus-flytrap glove snaps were jaw-dropping. "He's playing right now as if he was four hundred pounds and four feet wide," said Burns. As the series switched to St. Louis, the coach had little advice to impart. "Put the puck in the net more, that's all I can say." Despite hammering Joseph with 121 shots, the Leafs left Toronto with no better than a split in the series.

Looking to change the dynamics, Burns decided to dress the sparsely used Mike Krushelnyski for only his third outing of the postseason. The veteran had enjoyed a splendid first half of the season, but then went frigidly cold. Still, he was the only Leaf to play in all eighty-four regular-season games that year, albeit with reduced ice time. "Fifty-two players had come and gone through the door that season," Krushelnyski recalls. "That's tremendously hard on a coach, juggling players and trying to fit in all the pieces." What sticks out in his memory is one especially punishing practice. "We'd lost the night before, and Pat bag-skated us for forty minutes. If he'd have gone even one more minute, there would probably have been a huge revolt. But Pat wasn't there to be our best friend. At times you loved him, and at times you hated him."

Wendel Clark scoffs at the notion of either/or. "The whole thing with a coach isn't whether you love him or hate him. It's whether you respect him. Pat had a lot of respect."

Game three was mercifully shorter, but no sweeter for Toronto, a 2–0 lead vanishing into a 4–3 loss. Gilmour had a new track of stitches across the bridge of his nose, but a St. Louis columnist had more fun mocking Burns's signature pompadour. "What's the deal with coach Pat Burns? Why has this beefy, tough-guy former cop made himself over to look like oily lounge singer Wayne Newton?"

Alarm began to creep up the Leafs' spines. "Fear is knocking on our door, and the way we have to answer it is with faith," said Foligno. "We've got to believe in each other. I know we do." Then he lightened up the mood. "As a team, our goal, our whole reason for being here, our very existence, is to try to put a smile on the face of Pat Burns. And we've actually done that a few times this season. But we want to do it some more." Burns, grimacing, was simply sick of listening to encomiums for Curtis Joseph. "It's been Joseph, Joseph and more Joseph. We finally got three goals against him, but the trouble was we gave up four."

In the game four matinee, Toronto exposed Joseph as merely human. Leafs crashed his crease, threw him off balance, Foligno and Krushelnyski creating most of the traffic. "They've given us good hockey all year," said Burns of his two inelegant but useful marauders. "They played the style we wanted: move your legs, take a punch in the face." Joseph yowled to the referee about the liberties Toronto was taking with his turf. The ref had a word with Burns. "We're just bringing the puck to the net," he responded, angelically. "That's our job." Roused by a Burns pre-game speech, the players threw their bodies around with purpose in the 4–1 victory. A sizzling Potvin, who'd sweated off nine pounds of water in the game, outplayed his St. Louis counterpart.

As the series reverted to Toronto, the two teams had developed a serious hate-on for each other. Except for tree-hugging Glenn Anderson. "Hatred isn't in my vocabulary," he sniffed.

In the fifth game, Toronto continued its domination, outchecking, outscoring and outsmarting the Blues, clobbering them 5–1. A win in the sixth game, at decrepit St. Louis Arena, would give the Leafs their first Norris Division title since moving from the Adams in 1981 and send them to the Campbell Conference final. Back in the Gateway City, the temperature was scorching. Foligno, warning that the Blues would not roll over, inverted a cliché with a spoonerism. "We've got to make sure we hold our heads, uh, our feet, on the ground." Burns found time to tweak his opposite number, St. Louis coach Bob Berry, who'd been going through agonizing withdrawal as he tried to kick the smoking habit. The Toronto coach sent over the obligatory lineup sheet to the Blues dressing room with a cigarette taped to it.

Inside the muggy barn, Burns's pompadour was wilting as he pounded his beat behind the bench. With Toronto leading 1–0, watching his players dilly-dally as if victory were assured, his hair practically stood on end. "I could feel it when we left Toronto. There was all this talk about Stanley Cup, Joe-Sieve [the moniker hung on Joseph by Leaf fans], stuff like that. You can't talk like that in the playoffs."

The Blues prevailed 2–1, and now the situation was reminiscent of Toronto's previous series against Detroit, when the Leafs had failed to put the Wings away in six, inviting the excruciating tension of a deciding game seven. Afforded the chance between the smooth and bumpy road, the Leafs again opted for the latter. "We played with fire and we got burned," the coach sighed. "We've really put gas on the fire now."

Foligno admits the Leafs felt a sense of foreboding going into St. Louis. "They had so much pride, the Blues. They didn't want to lose in front of their home fans. So that's what we told ourselves after. But when we got back home, there was absolutely no way they were going to beat us in our own building. We were convinced we would raise our level in the next game to the point that all our passes were going to be on the tape, everything would be executed properly, and that's exactly how it turned out. It was unbelievable; we played the game that mentally we'd seen ourselves playing."

Still, staring down another game seven, Burns was fretful. "There's no doubt about it, the visiting team has the advantage. The pressure's on us. I've told them to go find themselves a way to put on the jersey at 7:20 and say, 'This might be the last time I put it on.' Seventh games don't come down to tactics. They come down to what you have within you. They've got to reach deep into their hearts and understand what this means." Gilmour deadpanned: "Pressure? What pressure?"

Who could have foreseen what would befall the Blues that night at Maple Leaf Gardens? Curtis Joseph, like Icarus, must have flown too close to the sun. He melted. Wendel Clark scored two goals and ripped Joseph's mask off on another bazooka slapshot that struck the goalie flush on the mug. Four goals in the first period took all the starch out of St. Louis in a 6–0 defeat. All Gilmour did was pick up a goal and two assists, to give him 22 points in the postseason, surpassing Darryl Sittler's club record of 21. Game, set, match. "Pat had us so prepared for that game," he says. "He didn't do it with a lot of loud speeches, either. He just spoke to us quietly."

Outside, the city went crazy, a good crazy. Foligno, who lived downtown near the Sutton Place Hotel, waded through the crowd as he walked home, weaving through the impromptu parade on Yonge Street. "I always tell people that I've been to a few victory parades in my life. There was one in Colorado, when we won the Stanley Cup. There was the one when the Blue Jays won the World Series. And there was the one after our series against St. Louis. I had a bunch of family in town and they joined the parade. I remember walking down the alleyways to get to my house because I could not walk down the street without being mobbed. It was amazing."

Chapter Thirteen

Gilmour vs. Gretzky; Burns vs. Melrose

"If he thinks calling me a doughnut is going to distract me . . ."

FROM HIS SEAT towards the back of the plane, Pat Burns was glaring. Of course, this was his face in repose, brow perennially furrowed, grave stare, expressionless yet speaking volumes. And on this morning, Leafs bound for Los Angeles, he was deeply annoyed. Cliff Fletcher was really the target of his ire, but there wasn't much he could do about that. "The Boss," as Burns called his GM, had opened up the team's travelling entourage to spouses. A convivial sort, Fletcher invited wives of the coaching staff and management staff to accompany the club on their sojourn to California. That's what really got up Burns's nose. "I'm not for it," he huffed. "This isn't a vacation, for Chrissake."

So opposed was Burns to domestic intimates tagging along for games three and four of the Campbell Conference final that he had deliberately withheld knowledge of the invitation from his own girlfriend, Tina Sheldon. She found out about it only after receiving a call from Fletcher's wife, Boots. So then he was in double doo-doo. "Don't you want me there?" Tina had asked, hurt. He was forced to admit, "No, not really." Being Burns's significant other could be a trial. While affectionate and usually considerate—a "big teddy-bear," as Tina described him—the love

ROSIE DiMANNO

of his life was really hockey, and everything, everyone, came second, at least during the season, and most definitely during the playoffs. But once Boots Fletcher let the cat out of the bag, Burns was caught lying by omission. He surrendered to the inevitable, not graciously, issuing a disclaimer: "Don't expect me to go for no hand-holding walks on the beach." In fact, Burns would take that promenade stroll, though in unexpected fashion.

Fletcher threw matters of cost to the wind. The Leafs, he figured, deserved all the coddling his franchise could afford as the gruelling postseason ground on. Players were liveried from the L.A. airport to their posh oceanfront hotel in Santa Monica. While agreeing that sequestering the team outside Los Angeles was a good idea, Burns was testy about the location: too much sand and surf, entirely too laid-back and la-la. There may be fewer temptations farther from the bright lights of Tinseltown, but the hotel was also a considerable distance from both the practice rink and the Great Western Forum in Inglewood. Burns spent plenty of hours sitting in the marble lobby, Buddha-like, casting an arched eyebrow around the joint, making note of players' comings and goings. Few were tempted to loll poolside with frothy drinks, though brisk constitutionals along the boardwalk or out to the Santa Monica Pier were advocated as therapeutic. Burns did fret about sunburn, reminding players about the time Jacques Lemaire got so scalded on his balding pate that he was unable to pull helmet over head come game time. "Remember sunscreen!" he bellowed.

After sixteen games in thirty-two nights, transcontinental travel was the last thing the Leafs needed. But in Wayne Gretzky's fifth year as a King, Los Angeles had knocked off Calgary and Vancouver. The speed-laden Kings were all glitz; the Leafs a lunch-bucket crew, with a blue-collar integrity they carried with pride, and very much an extension of the man behind the bench. The character of the squad was but one reason—apart from winning—that hockey had returned to its rightful place in Toronto's bosom. "Not just Toronto, the whole country," says Dave Ellett, who'd emerged from a prickly first few months of the season under Burns's custodianship of the team to become one of the coach's most trusted rearguards. "We had a bit of a rocky start, kind of butted heads. Pat was a defence-first type of coach, and I liked to jump in on the play. He hated when defencemen passed the puck up the middle of the ice. I always felt I had the ability to do that and I was going to continue to do that. But if it didn't work out well or the puck got turned over, I'd get 'the look.'"

Ellett and Burns both hailed from the Ottawa area. Early in the season, the Leafs were playing Ottawa on the road and Ellett was on the ice for the pre-game skate. "Burnsie came right out on the ice, made a beeline for me. I could see him coming and I'm thinking, 'Okay, what did I do? What's he mad about now?'" Instead, Burns inquired if Ellett was the grandson of Abe Cavan. Ellett confirmed he was. Cavan had been the police chief in Ottawa. Burns beamed: "He gave me my first job on the police force! Yup, I'll never forget him for that."

Now, decades later, Burns was coach of the Toronto Maple Leafs and they were one series away from the Stanley Cup final. What a strange and winding road. Yet there was an intriguing patchwork of relationships among Burns, the Leafs and the Kings. It was Gretzky who'd hired Burns to coach his junior Olympiques in Hull all those years ago. Los Angeles was a club that had been interested in Burns's service the previous summer, when he signed with Toronto. Burns got plenty of mileage recounting that story during the series, inflating the narrative— because Burns was never shy about exaggerating—to the point that he had L.A. dangling the GM title too. Majority franchise owner Bruce McNall, future felon, sharply corrected that version of history.

In any event, the Kings hired Barry Melrose, who was almost as colourful a character as Burns. Melrose, a former Leaf, was second cousin to Wendel Clark. They were also teammates on the local fastball nine in hometown Kelvington, Saskatchewan, during the summers of the early and mid-1980s, Melrose catching and Clark at shortstop. Burns's assistant, Mike Murphy, had been head coach in L.A. for one season after serving as captain of the club for six. Several players had been Kings teammates on other teams. Although operating a continent apart, in different divisions, the teams had commonalities that dovetailed.

There was no dove-cooing in the series. It got off to a rollicking start at Maple Leaf Gardens when Marty McSorley—Gretzky's personal Praetorian Guard in both Edmonton and now L.A.—flattened Doug Gilmour with a cheap-shot ambush with less than five minutes left in a game Toronto won 4–1. Gilmour completely outshone Gretzky in the affair, The Greater One on this evening, totting a pair of goals and assists, his fingerprints all over every scoring sequence. In the third frame, Toronto outshot the Kings 22–1; that's how lopsided the match had become. McSorley's blindside elbow kayoed Gilmour just after Number 93 set up Bill Berg for Toronto's fourth goal. With Gilmour prone on the ice, Clark—defender of the Leaf realm—hustled over to teach the thuggish defenceman a lesson, laying a whupping on him. McSorley would carry a shiner as memento. "Well, our best player was lying on the ice in a 4–1 hockey game," said Clark. "That's something we didn't want to happen."

During the melee that followed, fans littered the ice with debris, a crutch included among the items hurled. "Somebody's got a long crawl home," Melrose chortled. Gilmour picked himself up, skated directly to the L.A. bench, hung on to Darryl Sydor's stick and flayed the players with verbal abuse. That stand-up gutsiness awed even the Kings. "Just by coming over to our bench, he was trying to say that he wasn't going to take anything from us," Sydor marvelled.

From where he was standing, Burns went ballistic. He raced beyond the end of his bench, stood near the seats that separated the teams, screaming and gesturing at Melrose. Linesman Ray Scapinello had to charge between the men to prevent Burns from crossing over the DMZ. Mullet-haired Melrose—hair would become a trash-talking topic in this series—claimed not to have understood Burns's screed. "I thought he was ordering a hot dog." Repelling the tirade with an insolent grin, Melrose then puffed out his cheeks, mimicking Burns's jowls and nyah-nyahing, "You're fat!" That further incensed Burns. According to players from both sides, Burns called Melrose "bush" and spewed profane insults regarding the L.A. coach's dated Rod Stewart shag. "Why don't you go get a fucking haircut!"

Not exactly Oscar Wilde wit. This was infantile sassing, but it could have been worse, Melrose told reporters later. "I could have said, 'Have another doughnut.'" (It was not an original line. In the 1988 playoffs, angry New Jersey coach Jim Schoenfeld confronted Don Koharski in the corridor and the referee was either bumped or stumbled, whereupon he threatened that Schoenfeld would never coach another game. Schoenfeld: "You fell, you fat pig! Have another doughnut.")

Gilmour has more than once watched that first Leafs-Kings game, and the others from the '93 playoff run, on video. "To this day, I want to go over there and grab a piece of Barry. If they'd really got into it, my money would be on Pat for sure. That showed how much passion he had for his hockey club, so it was great to see. The same thing for when he jumped on referees. If he had no emotion, how would the players have emotion?"

After the game, Burns was still fit to be tied about the bushwhacking of Gilmour, asserting he'd never send one of his enforcers on the ice to assault a star opponent. "All I know is that if Ken Baumgartner did that to Wayne Gretzky, we'd be hung from the top of Parliament Hill. I lost a lot of respect for the Los Angeles Kings because of that. I know that wouldn't happen on our team. I certainly would not allow that to happen." In the Kings dressing room, McSorley tossed off a glib explanation. "Just call me a cheap-shot artist." Burns also took a not-so-subtle swipe at Gretzky, comparing the icon unfavourably to Gilmour. "Wayne Gretzky plays less than two hundred feet of the ice. Dougie goes back, picks up his checks and finishes them at the other end."

So there was that. The war of words, to the delight of reporters, would continue throughout the series.

The next day, with his right eye blackened and nearly swollen from Clark's pummelling, McSorley sarcastically invited photographers to take all the close-up pix they wanted. "Everybody get a good picture. A couple of stitches—big deal." Otherwise, he was the picture of innocence. Unable to resist, McNall got in on the lip-flapping, saying he had no clue what words had been exchanged between coaches. "What was he yapping about at Melrose? I thought maybe he was mad Melrose got the job Burns was begging for all [last] year." When two large bouquets of balloons were delivered to the visitors' dressing room, Luc Robitaille piped up: "One's from Doug and one's from Wendel."

Burns arrived at practice with an hours-old haircut—clearly, he was the one who'd visited the barber—patiently giving journalists a chance to comb through the feud fallout, then stated he wanted to put the kerfuffle behind him. "Irish tempers flew. I'm in a good mood and I want to stay that way. Barry can talk about it all he wants. I love the Kings today." Barry did continue to yammer, now indignant over the remark Burns made about Gretzky. "Anyone in hockey that criticizes Wayne Gretzky is not very smart. Pat Burns is making a lot of money in hockey now because Wayne Gretzky hired him to coach his junior team." He suggested Burns had had a "brain aneurysm." He revisited the November incident where Gilmour broke Tomas Sandstrom's arm, with Burns accusing the Kings of "always crying about something" when they groused about the non-game suspension. "Who's whining now?" Melrose taunted, noting the hypocrisy over McSorley's mauling of Gilmour.

Mischievous Melrose knew how to stick in the needle, though professing to have sworn off physical confrontations since the time when, as a first-year coach with Medicine Hat, he'd gone after a fan who slugged him during a game, which led to sixteen-year-old players swinging their sticks like hatchets. "I vowed not to lose control again. I was embarrassed." So he swallowed his temper, even staying cool during a 10–2 demolition by Philadelphia earlier in the year. "I had a leather strap between my teeth."

As for his much-mocked mullet, which Burns had targeted for ridicule, Melrose explained: "The only thing my dad and I ever fought about was my hair. He always made me keep it short. When I left home at fifteen, I said I would never have it short again. Everybody likes it. Well, you know who doesn't? Bald people." Ba-da-*bing*. Burns rolled with the jokes about his thinning pompadour—"I don't have much hair on top anymore"—but he was genuinely aggrieved by the punch at his paunch. "Maybe when

Barry hits forty-one or forty-two, he'll find the stomach will grow out a bit, too."

Reporters quickly noticed Gilmour wasn't on the ice for practice. Cracked Burns: "Doug has gone back to his planet for a rest." It was the only rest the double-shifted Gilmour would get.

In game two, it was the Leafs who utterly lost their composure. The raggedy match could have gone either way; neither team distinguished itself. Near the end of the first period, after McSorley swatted him again, Gilmour skated up to his tormentor with fire in his eyes and head-butted McSorley bang on the schnozz. The Kings were outraged that Gilmour was not assessed a major penalty or game misconduct, both players receiving minors for roughing.

Toronto wasted a 2–1 lead and lost 3–2 on Sandstrom's tie-breaker in the third, set up by Gretzky, who disputed accusations the Kings were a one-dimensional run-and-gun team. Indeed, L.A. had matched Toronto's grit and slow-down style in the snooze cruise, while Gilmour, as one columnist put it, "went from super-duper to super-stupor" in the space of two days. At the time, Gilmour denied head-butting McSorley, saying: "We were just head-to-head." Today, he says: "Oh, I head-butted him."

Off the ice, Melrose was wrangling with Don Cherry, who was hardly a neutral observer of the series—he planted a smooch on Gilmour's kisser on national TV after game one. "I just don't feel that *Hockey Night in Canada* should be cheering for one team over another," said Melrose, miffed. "We have as many Canadians on the Los Angeles Kings as the Leafs do." In retaliation, Melrose forbade his players from appearing on *HNIC*. Cherry fulminated on the air that Melrose "was a candy-ass as a player and he's a candy-ass as a coach." Prudently, Melrose passed on the opportunity to tell the bombastic commentator to kiss a relevant part of his anatomy.

Cherry further slammed Melrose for looking like "Billy Ray Cyprus" on account of the hair—which actually cut closer to the bone for Burns, who'd proclaimed Billy Ray *Cyrus* his favourite country crooner. Meanwhile, Melrose's wife, Cindy—notable for stripper-style fashion, all lace and bustiers—grabbed a piece of the inter-coach baiting by going on KISS radio and calling the Toronto bench boss "Fat Burns."

Toronto had not won a game two throughout the playoffs. Burns was ticked that his team had failed to show much, squandering the opportunity to take a two-game series lead. "We all seemed to sit back and wait for the Doug Gilmour Show to start. Maybe some of our guys still don't realize what this is about." Now they were winging to the coast, distaff partners in tow—but not for the players. Burns had no inkling what was about to hit him.

A Los Angeles radio station, making light of Burns's girth, urged its listeners to send a doughnut to the coach, identifying the team's Santa Monica hotel. When the Kings caught wind of the prank, officials called the station, firmly urging it to cease and desist. Not a chance. Eighteen dozen doughnuts arrived. In a quite brilliant counter-thrust, Burns and Tina distributed the pastry to vagrants in Santa Monica and Venice. "I was a king this morning. I may be the most unpopular person in L.A., but the homeless guys who sleep on the beach think I'm the greatest. I thought they were going to carry me around on their shoulders. They told me it was the best breakfast they'd had in years." Knock it off though, Burns requested. "I advise people not to waste their money, because Tim Hortons doughnuts are the only ones I eat." Good-natured about the gag, Burns put a different spin on the fans' gesture, suggesting they weren't ribbing his portliness. "I think it has to do with my previous years as a police officer. We do hang out in doughnut shops a lot, to have coffee and stay awake so we can protect all those guys who have big mouths."

He was growing weary of the shtick and the spotlight. "While all this stuff has been a lot of fun, it's time to get down to brass tacks again. Barry and I aren't the point of this thing at all. We're just a sidelight. We're here to win some hockey games, not bicker like a couple of schoolchildren." To that end, Burns put the Leafs through a lung-burning practice, rejecting any suggestion the club was physically worn down. "They shouldn't be tired. The piece of meat between their ears is tired, maybe."

Hundreds of fans came to the Forum armed with doughnuts as

projectiles to hurl towards Burns. Gilmour-badgering from spectators began halfway through the Canadian anthem. "They had these signs," recalls Gilmour. "On one side it said 'Gilmour Head Butt.' Turn it around and it said 'Gilmour Butt Head.' That was actually pretty funny. I should have kept one."

Gilmour was blowtorch-tailoring his sticks (made of wood in those dinosaur days) in the corridor of the Forum before the game. "This guy walks by and says, 'Hey you, take it easy on us.' As soon as I heard the voice, even without looking up, I knew who it was—Sylvester Stallone. I'm thinking, 'Wow, that's cool.' There were all these Hollywood stars coming to the games and we were in awe. Pat said, 'We don't give a fuck about who these people are, okay? Who cares if Kurt Russell and Goldie Hawn are in the stands? Don't even look at them. They're not cheering for you.'"

The Kings tipped Toronto 4–2, twice beating Félix Potvin on short-handed goals. While Gretzky continued to play pedestrian hockey—for him—Burns was uneasy about an imminent explosion from Number 99. He implored his players to take a long look in the mirror and ask themselves, "How much do we want this?" They must have heeded his directive, because an efficient, forceful effort resulted in game four, which Toronto took 4–2, winning all the one-on-one battles within the encounter. "We are at our best when we think we're done," observed their appreciative coach. "We have to play scared." "It's going to be a long series," Gretzky predicted. "We know that now."

There was anxious remonstration about 99. His last remaining objective in hockey was to lead the Los Angeles Kings to a Stanley Cup. But where was the tour de force performance that had been anticipated? "Wayne's Wane" went the refrain. At the start of the series, the thirty-two-year-old Gretzky declared that he hadn't felt this good in ages, but there was little evidence of that on the ice. Alas, as everyone now knows, he was saving it for the final act, the curtain-dropper.

Rattled, the Kings called in their positive-thinking guru, Anthony Robbins, the celebrated late-night TV pitchman for books and tapes on personal power and author of *Awakening the Giant Within*. Melrose was a devotee. Burns, back in Toronto, scoffed at the New Age approach to hockey; how very California. Besides, Burns said, the Leafs had their own motivational expert in team psychologist Max Offenberger. "I've got Maxie. We smoke a cigar, have a cognac and everything looks better. Anyways, Max has home-couch advantage." On home turf, Toronto's fans would show the L.A. mob a thing or two, Burns promised. "The Madhouse on Manchester will become the Crazy House on Carlton."

The coaches fired another round of verbal salvoes, each accusing the other of shattering the ceasefire. Burns believed there was an implied slur when Melrose made a comment about the Leafs having an older lineup, which forced them to play a middle ice–clogging style because they couldn't otherwise keep up stride for stride with the Kings. It was a soft lob, but Burns went nuclear. "Barry Melrose doesn't show any respect to anybody. He has been the same since the playoffs started. He thought he could distract me with that doughnut thing. I was a cop for sixteen years. I've been called a pig, a dog. I've had beer bottles broken over my head. I've been kicked in the groin. I had a woman I was arresting try to scratch my eyes out. If he thinks calling me a doughnut is going to distract me . . . I don't think Barry understands that coaching is a fraternity. We should respect each other. We're alone out there. Someday he might be alone."

There was cunning to his jawing. It was deliberately shifting media attention away from his players in the Toronto pressure cooker. "I don't know if that's something Pat learned from Scotty Bowman or if it came naturally," says Gilmour. "Scotty always had something to say about nothing. He'd complain that the benches were short or the ice wasn't satisfactory. The focus was obviously on us, and Pat was trying to deflect it. And he didn't want us reading the clippings, especially if they were negative."

Game five at the Gardens reached the sixty-minute buzzer deadlocked 2–2, Toronto clawing back from a two-goal deficit. In sudden death, Leafs carried the play by a wide margin. With thirty-nine seconds remaining in the first extra period, Glenn Anderson cut in from the left circle, skated by a crowd that included Gretzky and belted a shot that seeped through the legs of Kelly Hrudey "like a croquet ball through a hoop," as a *Los Angeles Times* story described it. "I was thinking, 'Just get a shot on net,'" said Anderson, who'd been the most inspirational Leaf from among a decidedly flat pack. "We pulled a rabbit out of the hat," admitted Burns. "But rabbits are getting pretty scarce. After the first period, we reached down and pulled out a chicken."

Toronto was one victory away from their first Stanley Cup final since their last Stanley Cup championship in 1967. Burns placed a dressing-room ban on any mention of the Montreal Canadiens—home and idling, waiting for an opponent to be determined—but the city was going bonkers. Players barely had time to register their win before boarding the plane back for L.A. "We played every other day but it felt like every day," says Gilmour. "We knew what was going on in the city, but the players were all in our own little world together. I look back sometimes and say to myself, 'Did that really happen?'" Gilmour is referring not to his heroics but his own occasional savagery, the frantic reaction provoked by Burns urging them all: "Just bleed, boys."

"People, kids, ask me all the time, but it's so hard to explain. I thought for sure we were going to win that series. I put that helmet on and, honestly, sometimes I was a complete fucking asshole. I'd take the helmet off after and ask myself, 'Did I really just do that?' It really felt like we were a team of destiny. Man oh man, it was an unbelievable feeling."

Unbelievable is how game six felt, too, even more so when looked at in the rear-view mirror, nearly two decades later. L.A. built up a two-goal lead and then Wendel Clark took over, delivering arguably the finest, most gallant game of his life. He scored once, he scored twice, he scored thrice. Two of those goals came in the third period as Clark almost unilaterally drew the Leafs into a 4–4 tie. "It was a career game," says Mike Foligno. "Wendel took it upon himself to cover all the mistakes of the team and singlehandedly get us back into it, to give us a chance to win. He showed us what kind of a man he was with that kind of a performance. That game proved to everybody why he was the captain of the team. I remember the jubilation in the dressing room, that he was able to take it into overtime for us."

Clark is modest about that glorious night. His troublesome back had been aching all day. "I took only a two-minute warm-up and wasn't even sure that I was going to play. Then I went and had therapy with team physiotherapist Chris Broadhurst. You never know when you're going to have that kind of game. I certainly hadn't sensed it. The puck just followed me all night." He pauses. "The next night, the puck just followed Wayne Gretzky."

For the rest of his life, Burns would argue there should never have been a next night, that Gretzky should not have been on the ice to score the 5–4 winner at 1:41 of overtime, a power-play goal with Anderson in the box for foolishly boarding Rob Blake, squaring the series at three apiece and setting up a third game seven for Toronto. Kerry Fraser called the penalty with 12.1 seconds left in regulation. In his press conference that evening, Burns didn't quibble much about an infraction whistled at so crucial a juncture. "What are you going to do? It was a good call."

The players, if unhappy about that penalty, were hardly panicked. "We'd come back and we thought we were going to win the game," says Ellett. "We were going to kill that penalty, no big deal. No one was mad at the ref, saying, 'We're getting screwed.' We [planned to] put it behind us, just kill the penalty and go on."

To reporters, Burns had added a postscript. "They could have called one on Gretzky, too." That was the real killer, on Killer.

What happened in overtime has assumed mythic proportions in the constant retelling. Just before he stuck a knife in the Leafs, Gretzky had clipped Gilmour under the chin with a high stick. Every on-ice official allegedly missed it, though Gilmour was visibly bleeding. In his memoir, *The Final Call*, Fraser writes: "As a referee, the biggest fear I've always had is that when I blink, something could occur in that fraction of a second that I will miss. It's also uncomfortable when a player simply passes in front of your line of vision—you worry something fateful might occur. Was this such a moment?" First off, he approached Gilmour. There was blood on his chin, "although it wasn't oozing. My initial thought was that some old scar tissue had been scraped off." He claimed Gilmour told him that "Wayne took a shot and the follow-through struck me on the chin." If that was the case, Fraser says he responded, then no penalty was warranted because inadvertent contact from follow-through on a shot exempts the culprit from a high-sticking citation. That was the rule then.

Gilmour disputes that recollection of their conversation. "I said it was *not* a follow-through. Gretz went to lift my stick and he missed. That didn't make it a shot follow-through. So, okay, Fraser didn't see it. But the linesman wanted to call it. In those days, according to the rules, Gretzky would have been gone from the game. There would have been a riot. That's why it wasn't called. It would have been four on four, and who knows . . ."

Gilmour was in the dressing room, getting eight stitches to close the cut on his chin, when Gretzky scored in OT, the puck deflecting right onto the blade of his stick off a wayward pass. The roar and rumble overhead told Gilmour what had happened, though he didn't know which King was the hero. Discovering it had been Gretzky, Gilmour's heart sank. "I was afraid we'd woken up a sleeping giant. I was like, 'Oh crap, that's the last thing you want to do.'"

The Leafs were dismayed—what a waste of Clark's splendid outing— but not wracked. They remained in L.A. overnight, had a late team meal and a few beers at their hotel. "The flight home was pretty quiet," says Ellett. "Pat hadn't really said much to us after the game. But no one was down. It was going to be our third time in a game seven, and we'd won two of them, so everyone was feeling pretty confident."

Nevertheless, some in the media did speculate that maybe the Leafs had tempted fate once too often. Meanwhile, the Kings were buoyant. "More than that game six loss knocked us down, it gave the Kings momentum," says Foligno. "It gave L.A. the confidence that, Jesus, now it's down to one game. It's in their building but we've won there before." Melrose blurted: "It's not a seventh game. It's a best of one now." He then advised his players and the L.A. media: "Pack extra underwear. We're going to Montreal."

To the media, Gretzky conceded no felonious assault on Gilmour. But he did take palpable glee from scoring his 105th career playoff goal and forcing a game seven. He teased: "I'm not superhuman. I'm not gonna get four points a night. It's impossible. But I have to make sure that when I do something, it's big." It was indeed BIG and gave Gretzky twenty-nine points in the playoffs, three fewer than scoring leader Gilmour.

With game seven set to fall on the exact one-year anniversary of his hiring in Toronto, Burns was on the same wavelength as Gilmour, fearing that Gretzky had been aroused and now threatened to do something spectacular. He was also concerned about the stamina of his tireless heart-and-soul team leader, leery that the fuel in his tank would suddenly dip fatally low. "He's held together with thread right now. We'll call that planet he's from and get some more."

You know how it ended.

"Gretzky was just Gretzky," says Clark.

"Wayne just came in and took over," says Potvin. "He did what he'd done all his career: carried the team on his back," says Gill. "That's why he's the best player that ever lived."

Ellett: "Gretzky magic. He lit it up."

The Great One pronounced it the "greatest game" he ever played. "We'd watched Wayne's career, all the broken records, the Stanley Cups in Edmonton," says Mark Osborne, the checking hound whose line, with Zezel and Berg, had shadowed Number 99 in the series—though Osborne missed game five to be with his wife as she gave birth to their daughter. "So he says that was his best game. Well, isn't that just nice for us. His greatest game and we don't get a chance at a once-in-a-lifetime opportunity to play the Habs for the Stanley Cup. Thanks, Gretz."

Let the post-mortem be mercifully brief. Gretzky rose magnificently to the occasion. His eighth postseason hat trick lifted the Kings into their first Cup final on a 5–4 victory. The Kings were up 4–3 when Dave Ellett's skate inadvertently directed Gretzky's shot—his third goal—past Potvin. "Of course, I've seen it a million times," Ellett sighs. "Everyone has to bring it up. It was just one of those things. I felt something hit my foot.

I knew right away when the crowd went silent that it wasn't good. I turned around and saw the puck in the net."

It wasn't quite over yet. Ellett, the unwarranted goat, got one right back for the Leafs. "People forget because they show that Gretzky goal highlight all the time. But I did score one a minute later. There were two minutes left to play, we still had a chance." With Potvin pulled, Toronto just couldn't get that equalizer. L.A. won 5–4. The magic had run out. In the dressing room several players wept openly. "Absolutely devastated," says Gill. "To this day, I'm devastated. When people bring it up, I still get a lump in my throat. It was *so* close. It was right there."

Then it was gone.

Burns went around the room, giving every disconsolate player a hug, saying thank you, thank you, thank you. "He was very emotional, you could tell," says Gilmour. "But he was also very proud."

At the end of the game, when shaking hands, Gretzky said to Burns: "I couldn't let it happen. I couldn't let you win."

"This team went far beyond my expectations," a raspy-voiced Burns said at the solemn press conference afterwards. "I just kept on telling them, 'You've got to kick at the darkness until the daylight shows.'" The poignant quote sounded like a line he'd worked on, tucked it in his pocket, in case. Or maybe he stole it from Bruce Cockburn's "Lovers in a Dangerous Time."

"This was a great learning process for this organization, a great stepping stone. From now on, you know if you're going to put this sweater on and wear these colours, you've got to be ready to play. I've never been more proud of a team, and I said that to them. I would have said it before but I didn't want them to think it was over."

It was over.

Chapter Fourteen

Out of Gas

"My job is to make them forget about how tired they're feeling."

WITH HEAVY BAGS under their eyes, dressed variously in jeans and summer shorts, arriving in ones and twos, the Leafs of '92–93 convened for a last time at a midtown Toronto restaurant. In their heads, they were still playing hockey, still vying for the Cup, still ice warriors. In reality, as surreal as it felt, and raw, they were just one among fourteen playoff teams that had lost their last game of the year and been sidelined.

The wake had been organized by Wendel Clark. Bob Rouse cruised in on his brand-spanking-new Harley. Mark Osborne came bearing cigars—some chocolate, some Cuban—to belatedly celebrate the birth of his daughter. All had shaved off their playoff beards. Most swore they wouldn't watch the final between Montreal and Los Angeles—couldn't bear it.

The season had been an unqualified, monster success, a grand achievement. But it was too soon for reflection and too late for fantasizing. Exhausted now that adrenaline had ceased pumping, feeling all their physical hurts, few were in the mood to look ahead—and training camp was less than a hundred days away. "I want to get on my bike and feel the wind in my hair, find some sand and sun," said Pat Burns. He'd been courted to participate as TV colour commentator for the Cup final, but declined. "I'm tired of talking about hockey."

Yet they were reluctant to let go of one another for the summer. From the restaurant, players piled into a fleet of cabs and headed for a strip club, the House of Lancaster. "Then Pat and I went to another bar, the Left Bank," says Doug Gilmour. "Dan Aykroyd was there with his entourage, so we joined them for a while. After that, we just went home. I wouldn't say that Pat was heartbroken, just drained, like me."

The coach packed his suitcase for a short vacation in Antigua, but was back by June 1, when the team was feted by the city at Nathan Phillips Square. The fact they hadn't actually won anything didn't dampen the enthusiasm as ten thousand well-wishers descended on the civic plaza. Fans crowded around the temporary stage and ringed the ramps. It was the largest gathering at City Hall since the Pope's visit in 1984. Burns was as flabbergasted on that afternoon as he'd been during the postseason, when hundreds of boosters welcomed the squad at the airport after they'd *lost* a game on the road. In Montreal, he joked, they would have sent up fighter jets to shoot down the team plane. "I've been fortunate to be part of two great traditions, the Montreal Canadiens and the Toronto Maple Leafs, but I've never seen fans like this in my life. You guys are the greatest."

On the stage, players shuffled their feet, hands thrust in their pockets, suddenly bashful in front of all this adulation in the wake of what was, ultimately, a losing cause. "We've waited a long time," said Wendel Clark, at the microphone. "I know you guys have waited a lot longer." Clark had been a year old in 1967 when Toronto last sipped from the silver chalice. "We're going a lot farther in the next few years," he promised. The loudest ovation was saved for Doug Gilmour. He'd been almost hiding behind his teammates, running his hands through his hair, staring at his feet. "I know the guys back here are very proud of what happened this year. And we'll get better as time goes on. I thank you. And these guys behind me, I thank them." Inching through the throng, signing autographs, Gilmour caught the attention of a reporter. He folded his hands together, laid them against his cheek, briefly closing his eyes. "Long nights," he whispered.

At a levee held later by the city, Burns said he was overwhelmed by the heartfelt reception. "We didn't win anything and they turn out like this. It's great, but I feel almost embarrassed about it. The fans are excited today, but they may get impatient tomorrow. The expectations are much higher, so it's going to be tougher."

A few weeks on, after Montreal had disposed of the Kings in a five-game final, Burns won his second Jack Adams Award as coach of the year. In advance of awards night, he professed to be blasé about the nomination, which was actually his third. "It doesn't really excite me anymore. It's not a question of winning. It's a question of getting up there on national television and thinking of something intelligent to say." When his name was called, however, Burns was appropriately appreciative, dedicating the award to his players. "It's a bigger honour this time. We accomplished a lot, and the club has built a foundation. I came in with my ideas and I stuck with them. I knew we didn't have a lot of explosive scoring power, but I felt we could find a way for this team to win and gain respect." Gilmour was nominated for the Hart Trophy—most valuable player—and the Frank Selke Trophy, as best defensive forward. The former he lost to superstar Mario Lemieux, who'd missed a month of the season receiving radiation treatment following the devastating news he had Hodgkin's disease, a form of cancer—and still managed to cop the scoring title with an amazing 160 points in 60 games. The Selke was all Gilmour's. He giggled when reporters pointed out the irony of winning top defensive honours when he was such an offensive force. There were guffaws as well for Gilmour's Glitter Boy 'do, backcombed out to here and shellacked/hairsprayed. Burns, tanned and mellow from his holiday in the tropics, posed with Gilmour for endless photographs. The last Leaf to win an individual NHL award had been Brit Selby, top rookie in 1965. Burns injected a note of caution into the celebrations. "I think coaches can only last three or four years in one city unless they win the Stanley Cup every year. If, four years down the road, we haven't won the Cup, there will be people looking for my head." Addressing reporters, he added: "I'd love for Toronto to be my last coaching job. But you guys will decide that."

———

Burns rented a cottage on Lake Simcoe that summer—the only off-season he would ever spend in the Toronto region, because he couldn't avoid the constant back-slapping and attention of autograph hounds in southern Ontario. They'd find him out on the lake, in his boat. The Leafs remained wildly popular through those summer months. A recap video, *The Passion Returns*, flew off the shelves, as did the "Pat's Garage" poster, with players and coach draped fetchingly across motorcycles and vintage pickup truck, studly and gritty.

As time allowed, Burns made guest appearances with the Good Brothers, a bluegrass band founded by twins Bruce and Brian Good. Their relationship with Burns stretched back to the 1991 Canada Cup, when the final games had been played in Hamilton against Team USA. It happened to be Canadian Country Music Week in the Steel City. Burns, Brian Sutter and Mike Keenan were presenters at the musical awards night. Burns ran into Bruce Good later in the evening and they went "suite-hopping" in the hotel. Coach was thrilled to meet Canadian music artists, and in return invited Bruce and his son, Travis, to the final Cup game, which Canada won. Around midnight, the Goods joined up with Burns at Team Canada's Toronto hotel base. "We partied until daylight in one of the rooms. I think it may have been Keenan's," Bruce recalls. Early the next morning, without sleep, everyone gathered for breakfast downstairs. The Canada Cup trophy was used as table centrepiece. When Keenan finally left for some shut-eye, Burns and Bruce took the trophy for a spin, popping into a local country music radio station for an interview.

In Bruce's version of events, this is what happened next: "We went back to the hotel and put the trophy on the pillow next to Keenan while he was sleeping." As he remembers it, Keenan never even noticed the Cup when he woke up and checked out. "A maid found it and put the thing in the lost and found."

Burns comped the Goods for a game in Montreal the next season, and gave them a personal tour of the "cathedral" that was the Canadiens' dressing room. The acquaintanceship warmed further after Burns moved to the Leafs. He was always keen to play with the band when asked. The Good Brothers had a long relationship with the team. In the late '70s, they'd played frequently at club parties, usually organized by Ron Ellis. The group's first album—for which they won a Juno Award—had been financially backed by a Leaf defenceman, Dave Dunn.

"That first summer in Toronto, Pat joined us for benefit shows and some regular gigs," says Bruce. "He had an excellent singing voice, but I was surprised at how good he was as a guitar player, not playing lead but rhythm. He knew more chords than any of us. It was incredible, really, when you realize that he was self-taught. He loved music. His favourite song was "Margaritaville," so we played that a lot. He had such stage presence—a natural, loved getting up and performing. Some people thought it was just tokenism because we enjoyed having the Leaf coach up there, but that wasn't true. Pat was a terrific musician, had a real knack for it. I think he could have made a career out of it if his life had gone in a different direction."

Burns had a particular fondness for Irish music as well, so he and the Goods formed a separate band called the Butcher Boys, strictly for the purpose. One night, they got together at Travis's apartment and taped an entire album of Irish music. Burns played and sang on every song. Bruce has since had an engineer transfer that old tape onto a CD. At the very end, a distinct rapping—thump-thump—can be heard. That was Travis's neighbour knocking on the wall, telling them to knock off the racket already.

In LeafWorld, Wendel Clark became the third player in team history to join the million-dollar club, and Burns politely bid for a contract renegotiation. He got it: a $100,000-per-season raise on the two years remaining. By late August, Burns was back at his office, surly over expectations for the '93–94 season and calling around to make sure his players had been observing their summer fitness regimens. "It seemed like only a few weeks had passed, and there was Pat on the phone," recalls Gilmour.

The conversation went something like this. Burns: "Whatcha doin'?" Gilmour: "Nothing." Burns: "Started working out yet?" Gilmour: "Uh, just getting at it." Burns: "Okay, just checking." At medicals on day one of camp, Burns scrutinized the fitness test results, clucking and tut-tutting.

Apart from actually winning a Cup, though, what could the Leafs possibly do for an encore? Win ten in a row, for starters.

First, there was the small matter of exporting NHL hockey to Jolly Old England, the Leafs and New York Rangers making the trek to London for a pair of exhibition matches. Naturally, Burns detested the chore. "I really don't like anything about it, but there's nothing I can do." After the seven-hour flight, he was even more disenchanted. "If I have a tourist hat on, I think it's fantastic. But as a coach I have to say, 'Geez.'" Cliff Fletcher laughs recalling that excursion. "Pat was bitching every day. He'd say, 'This isn't a goddamn vacation! We've got wives, we've got girlfriends. What the hell?'"

Players, wives and girlfriends took a cruise along the Thames, were guests of honour at Planet Hollywood, and on an off-night had their choice of either going to the theatre or attending the England–Poland World Cup soccer qualifier at Wembley Stadium.

Mike Keenan's Rangers won both hockey games.

Quasi-vacation over, Leafs returned to their Gardens HQ. "Pat will be running his usual Hitler-style camp," moaned Mike Foligno. In truth, the players were restless to get back at it, for real. "There was a feeling when we came back to training camp that we'd fallen short the year before, and we wanted to prove that we were a good team," says Félix Potvin. "The chemistry we had in the first season all translated to our team the next year." To Todd Gill, the summer respite had come and gone in the blink of an eye, but he was eager to pick up where the team had left off. "The playoffs had been such a confidence builder for us. Every player was so much better because of what he'd gone through the year before."

The season opened October 7 with sports fans focused on balls and strikes, the Blue Jays in pursuit of back-to-back World Series titles.

Roberto Alomar dropped the puck for the ceremonial faceoff. Burns always maintained that he dreaded home openers, but there was nothing nerve-wracking about game one on the schedule as Toronto dumped Dallas 6–3. And they're off.

Game two against Chicago, with hundreds of fans holding radios to their ears as the Jays simultaneously did battle with the White Sox: Leafs won 2–1.

Game three versus Philadelphia: 5–4. A nice little streak to launch the season. "I'm happy the guys played well in these three games, but I've still got my two feet planted on the ground," said Burns. "Now there's only eighty-one games to go."

Game four: Leafs barely broke a sweat dumping Washington 7–1. Burns even rested Gilmour for the last seven minutes. "That'll teach him for making so much money," the coach fake-growled. Four victories in a row, Burns exhorted the team to reap points while ye may. "We've got to be like squirrels and fill our little tummies now, get as much food as we can to put away for winter. It will be a long, cold winter."

Games five and six: A twin killing over the home-and-home Thanksgiving weekend with Detroit, 6–3 and 2–1.

Half a dozen games into the campaign and Toronto stood atop the league. Perfection. Gilmour was the NHL scoring leader. Forty-nine years earlier, the Leafs had also broken out with a six-pack of Ws. That season, they won the Stanley Cup. And yet these Leafs were still the secondary sports story locally. "I think there's enough room in the paper for us and the Blue Jays," shrugged Gill. "We don't mind page 2 for a while." Certainly the hockey scribblers had taken note as more and more copy was devoted to The Streak, the Leafs now three wins away from setting a league mark for best start ever by an NHL team. Burns pretended it was much ado about nothing much. "I don't even look at records. If it's there, it's there. We just look at points."

Game seven: The Leafs crushed Hartford 7–2. Stringbean Potvin boasted a sparkling 2.14 GAA—best in show. Burns, thawing, marvelled at the offensive output from a team that most observers had expected would encounter scoring issues. "I really don't know where they're all coming from, but it's kind of fun."

The franchise—and league—record for wins was nine, set sixty-eight years earlier and equalled by the '75–76 Buffalo Sabres. In this unfolding spectacle, Potvin had been between the posts for every victory.

Game eight: So what did Burns do in Miami, where Toronto was hosted by the Panthers? He started backup Damian Rhodes. "Dusty" Rhodes maintained the string, Toronto edging Florida 4–3 in overtime. And for the umpteenth time, "I don't care about the record!" As if.

The team swung over to the west side of the Florida panhandle, to face the Tampa Bay Lightning. Gill, in his tenth season as a Leaf, reminisced not so fondly about the bad old days. "Some of the kids on the team now don't realize how bad it once was in Toronto. My first five years, the Maple Leafs were everybody's favourite joke. You'd laugh but some days you couldn't, it hurt too much. No wonder no one wanted to play for the Toronto Maple Leafs and put up with that stuff. Now the jokes have dwindled to nothing. Now people have to take us seriously." In 2012, Gill looks back in awe. "Mentally, other teams were thinking, 'Oh God, we've got Toronto coming in.' And how long had it been since anybody had said that?"

Game nine: Mark Osborne notched both goals as Potvin shut out the Lightning 2–0 at the ThunderDome, on the same Saturday night the Jays clinched their second World Series, beating the Phillies. Whoop-de-do all around—baseball championship and streak's alive, record tied. Oh, except for Burns, who groused: "This is professional sports. You're supposed to win." Then he admitted, "We didn't talk about it much, but it was always in the back of our heads." He wouldn't let his players get fat heads about the achievement, though. "Sooner or later, every team goes into slumps. We'll have our slump, the coach won't be any good, players won't be any good and Félix won't be able to stop a table."

Could they extend the streak to ten? Going into Chicago Stadium, it didn't seem likely. Toronto hadn't prevailed there since December 22, 1989, shut out five times in thirteen losses. The 'Hawks were sharpening their talons. "If they beat us," said Burns, "they've beaten the hottest team in the NHL." In a vulnerable moment, Burns did predict Toronto would survive their venture into the sixty-four-year-old Chicago building, with its 17,000 rabid fans and the booming pipes of the Barton organ. "The jinx will be broken." Nik Borschevsky piped up: "Small rink, crazy peoples."

There was another bitsy problem: Gilmour had been ejected from the game in Tampa with less than four minutes to play in the third for repeatedly punching defenceman Roman Hamrlik. In the preseason, he'd also received a one-game suspension for head-butting Washington's Enrico Ciccone. Brian Burke, league vice-president and disciplinarian-in-chief, had reviewed the Tampa video and was considering supplementary punishment. Gilmour was indignant. "It's a joke. I'm going to get suspended for fighting? If I'm suspended, I'll be really, really disappointed."

Burke travelled to the Windy City for the hearing. Burns accompanied Gilmour to the grand inquisition. Judiciously, Burke deferred his decision, ensuring Gilmour would be in the lineup that night against the Blackhawks.

Game ten: Jinx broken, Leafs fearsome in a 4–2 victory. Potvin stopped forty-two shots according to the game sheet. Burns was skeptical. "If a fan gets hit in the head with a puck here, they count it as a shot." Ten wins and counting, and the beat goes on. Up next: Montreal. The match was weighted with melodrama. Not only was this yet another return of Burns to the city of his debut fame, but Leafs-versus-Habs loomed as the Stanley Cup final Toronto had been denied in the spring, the storybook final that never was. "I helped build that team, though I don't take credit for them winning the Stanley Cup," said Burns, sounding as if he was doing exactly that. Jacques Demers could barely contain his excitement, wound up over the showdown between Potvin and Patrick Roy. "It's like Sandy Koufax versus . . . versus . . . versus . . ." Stumped, his voice trailed off. He switched analogies. "It's Joe Montana versus Dan Marino. That's it. Montana versus Marino. It's the cream of the crop. The best against the best. You can't ask for better. On national TV! Wow. What a confrontation."

Demers, who seemed always to be seeking Burns's approval, no matter how many times smacked down, tried to pay his predecessor a compliment.

"Pat Burns has that team well programmed. There's no luck involved. They are very, very well coached. He has taught them how to win. He's one of the elite coaches in the league." Burns, rudely, rejected the bouquet. "You don't teach a team how to win. You teach them how to play better. They learn how to win on their own."

Game eleven: They didn't. Win, that is. Ex-Leaf Vincent Damphousse scored a hat trick as the Habs whipped the Leafs 5–3. Streak over. Fletcher mischievously reminded his coach about the displeasure he'd expressed over the London sojourn. "Ten-and-oh, Pat. Yup, a terrible training camp. Those wives and girlfriends must have been a real distraction." Yet Burns was almost relieved when the streak ended. Now he could rightly revert to curmudgeon mode with something to groan about.

The coach was correct to have warned that what goes up inevitably comes down. The Leafs did get slumpish following their extraordinary start. Indeed, they finished the season fourteen games above .500, meaning they'd played only four games above .500 between The Streak and season's end. Gilmour's point production dropped drastically. At the trade deadline, Fletcher obtained speedy sharpshooter Mike Gartner from the Rangers for Glenn Anderson, but Toronto still stumbled through the final month. Burns occasionally employed a weird new tactic: perching at the locker stool of an underperforming Leaf. It wasn't one of his more brilliant ideas. Clark, at least, needed no motivation; he had a career year with 46 goals in only 64 games. He and Dave Andreychuk combined for 99 goals, by far the highest total for any two wingers on one team that year.

Last match of the regular season, Toronto dominated the Blackhawks 6–4 in Chicago, and the Leafs finished second in the Central Division. The game was a playoff preview, as the 'Hawks would be their first-round opponent. In Chicago's favour was goalie Eddie Belfour, who pretty much owned the Leafs, with a 16–6–4 lifetime record. But Belfour collapsed in the opener, allowing three soft goals as Toronto, as instructed by Burns, fired a barrage of long-range artillery. Leafs easily pocketed a 5–1 victory. "Because we won 5–1, we should be overconfident?" the coach asked rhetorically, adhering to his underdog theory. It had been a bruising encounter nevertheless. The combined rapsheet read: hooking, hooking, cross-checking, elbowing, tripping, hooking, interference, tripping, roughing, roughing, slashing and roughing, spearing and game misconduct, hooking, fighting, fighting and game misconduct, fighting, fighting and game misconduct, roughing, slashing, cross-checking, interference, roughing.

Prior to game two, Burns enlightened the media with some stats he'd collected. According to the coach, teams that captured the second game in a septet series triumphed 75 per cent of the time. "The first win doesn't allow us the luxury of anything. What are we supposed to think, that the series is over?"

Hardly. The 'Hawks and Belfour buckled down as the scoreless match moved into OT territory, where Todd Gill's blast through Clark's partial screen nearly three minutes in earned the thrilling victory. Potvin was merely spectacular, straining credulity on one airborne save, catching glove outstretched as he sailed horizontally.

But now they were facing the scary spectre of raucous Chicago Stadium for two. The Blackhawks eked out a 5–4 win in game three—Tony Amonte, guns blazing, scored four—and won the fourth 4–3 in overtime. "I'm not surprised," Burns said. "And I'm not down." Tripling his negatives, he added: "I'm not negative about nothin'. We're going home. They gotta win in our rink now." Burns accused his crew of having patted themselves on the back after taking the first two games. "Then the pat on the back turns into a kick in the ass."

For game five, Gilmour reprised his role as playoff catalyst, inspiring the Leafs to a 1–0 triumph, though he wasn't actually on the ice for the final result. He was brusquely upended by Gary Suter in the third period, right ankle taking his weight awkwardly. Immediately sensing something was seriously wrong, he threw stick and glove in disgust. Assisted to the dressing room—Mike Eastwood beat Belfour while Gilmour was absent—he returned for a single power-play shift but otherwise remained on the bench as one-man cheering section.

Team officials assured Leaf Nation that Gilmour was fine. This was not remotely true. He was gobbling painkillers and limping noticeably on his twisted ankle when the squad boarded a charter for Chicago. There was doubt that Gilmour would dress for game six, though the 'Hawks weren't buying it. "His ankle is a long ways from his heart," said coach Darryl Sutter. X-rays allegedly showed no broken bones. "If he can walk, I know he'll play," said Burns. That Gilmour could skate was attributable to the two pre-game freezing injections he received. Mindful of their leader's agony and courage, Toronto shut down the 'Hawks, playing patient, Katy-bar-the-door hockey, winning 1–0—on Gartner's power-play poke—for the third time in the series. "I just wanted to get this thing over with," said Gilmour. "That's probably why I played. It made sense to take a day off, but it made more sense to win and take three or four days off instead."

Wresting the series in six games, Toronto ensured there would never be another NHL game at Chicago Stadium. The team moved into the new United Center the next season, their beloved old arena slated for demolition. The music had been silenced.

The Leafs turned their attention to San Jose, stunning slayers of Western Conference champion Detroit. The Sharks, a third-year expansion franchise coached by Kevin Constantine, personified dull, lacklustre, soporific hockey—Toronto's forte, actually, if one was being honest. In game one at the Gardens—chomp-chomp—the Sharks plodded their way to a 3–2 decision on Johan Garpenlov's winner with 2:16 remaining.

"We had trouble with them all year," Burns reminded. "We're in it up to our knees." Leafs were shocked to hear some of their fans booing them off the ice and pleaded for a bit of patience.

Toronto evened the series by pounding San Jose into 5–1 submission on three power-play goals and Mark Osborne's shorthander, nicely neutralizing the "OV" Line of Igor Larionov, Sergei Markov and

Garpenlov. Taking pity on the clearly ailing Gilmour, Burns sat down his go-to knight for the second half of the third period. "We didn't need him anymore," he kidded. "We tossed him aside." Now, under the playoff format adopted that year, they faced three in a row in the often-turbulent Shark Tank. The coach finger-wagged, unleashing shock-therapy Burnsian rhetoric, as if his charges were unaware of the dangers that lurked. "'You might never come this close again.' That's what I've been drilling into them. I told them I can absolutely guarantee that some of them will never get a better chance at the Stanley Cup than the one they have right now. There'll be changes on this team next year, maybe a lot of them. Who knows if any of us will get this shot again?"

And what happened in northern California? The Sharks undressed Toronto 5–2, Ulf Dahlen the spark plug with three goals. It was San Jose's first playoff hat trick in their, um, ten-game playoff history. Potvin, revolted by his performance, went back to his hotel room and watched the movie *Tombstone*, which could have been a SpectraVision metaphor for Toronto. Burns tore a strip off his troops. Duly admonished, they responded with majestic ferocity, trashing the Sharks 8–3. Clark set the tone early with a thundering hit on Jeff Norton, bending him over backwards on the boards, the defenceman lying alarmingly still on the ice for several minutes. Then Clark flattened Dahlen for good measure. Leafs used their size advantage on tiny netminder Arturs Irbe, who absorbed a pounding in his crease. Dave Andreychuk came out of playoff narcolepsy with a pair of goals, and Gilmour tied a franchise playoff record, with five points—a goal and four assists.

But, damn it all, upstart San Jose kept coming. Who *were* these guys? The Shark Tank was so loud for game five that, as Toronto columnist Bob McKenzie wrote of the stentorian Leaf play-by-play broadcaster, "Joe Bowen was asked to speak up." The Sharks' 5–2 victory restored their one-game edge in the series, and Toronto was on the ropes, one loss away from elimination as they flew back cross-country. Burns was running out of tricks. He'd tried cajoling. He'd tried cussing. He'd tried extra-hard practice. He'd tried no practice. "It's very frustrating for me, for the whole coaching staff. I'll tell you this: we're not going to be a popular team if we blow it."

One Leaf was certainly popular, in the fatal attraction sense. It emerged that Gilmour had been targeted by a stalker, a woman who zigzagged crazily from love to hate. She'd made threats over the phone to Gilmour's brother, David, at the bar he owned in Kingston, hissing that she wanted to kill Doug. That had been a few months earlier. Then she attempted repeatedly to get past security at the Gardens, succeeding on at least one occasion to convince staff she was a friend of the player's. Gilmour hadn't taken the threats seriously to begin with, but now he informed his coach, who brought in the police. For weeks, undercover cops followed Gilmour and girlfriend Amy Cable back and forth from games and practices. Additional officers were stationed behind the Leaf bench. No charges were ever laid. Gilmour said he never worried about his own safety, only that of family and friends. Sports celebrities had been seriously attacked before—Monica Seles stabbed courtside by a stranger and Nancy Kerrigan whacked across the knee with a pipe in a plot hatched by the husband of skating rival Tonya Harding.

On the ice, crunch time in game six arrived with overtime. The teams were knotted at 2–2, Clark scoring both regulation-time goals for Toronto. A minute into the extra frame, Garpenlov teed up a slapshot from eighteen feet out in the slot, a rocket that had Potvin clearly beaten, but bounced off the crossbar, the clang heard around the Gardens. "I don't actually remember the clang," says Potvin, possibly the only person on hand who doesn't. The tension was excruciating until Gilmour set up Gartner for the winner.

"Whew," said Burns as he stepped up to the microphone for his postgame presser. "You guys have no idea what it's like to coach a National Hockey League team in overtime. Want to feel my armpits? My shirt is soaked with sweat from my armpits to my belt. Yes, it was a draining experience."

On the off-day before game seven, Burns was even brooding about brooding. "Chuckling, dancing, laughing—that's not my character. I wish I was a jovial person, but I'm not." Superstitious, he was stricken to learn that Kevin Gray, star of the hit musical *Miss Saigon*, would be onstage at the

Princess of Wales Theatre and thus unable to sing the national anthem. Burns had come to think of Gray as a talisman in the postseason. "*Aaaaaccchhh!*" he said when hearing the news. "No, don't tell me that. Ah, give me a break."

The Leafs, if not quite nonchalant about game sevens by now, sucked up the stress. Luck, good or bad, had nothing to do with the outcome—a 4–2 win constructed from Clark's two goals and Potvin's outstanding goaltending. "Who was worried?" said Burns, tongue firmly in cheek. "It was never in doubt." No way, Jose.

Burns thought the 2–3–2 playoff format was an abomination. Most observers felt the same way, arguing the configuration favoured the team without home-ice advantage. If visitors split the first two on the road, a series could end in a hurry. Against Vancouver in the Conference final, it would be scratch-and-claw, Burns figured.

"I wish we didn't have home-ice advantage playing both San Jose and Vancouver," says Dave Ellett, looking back. "We were put in a difficult position. Losing one at home and now we've got to go into their building for three in a row—boy, you want to talk about pressure? It was a tough, tough gig. The style we played, hard hockey, every game a battle, had put a lot of mileage on us. For that Vancouver series, we were playing on fumes."

Valiant Gilmour was still getting double syringe stabs on his foot before games and the San Jose seven-pack had taken a bite out of everybody. Burns knew his guys were fatigued. He exhorted them to keep digging down. The final would be a Tale of the Two Pats: Burns and Quinn skippering the biggest, most physical teams in the NHL. Both coaches also had big hair. The Canucks had knocked off Calgary in seven and Dallas in five, so were better rested when Quinn led them into Toronto. Quinn, the former Leaf defenceman who'd famously almost separated Bobby Orr's head from his torso on a thundering, clean check in the 1969 playoffs against Boston, was raised in Hamilton, his father a firefighter. "I'm an ex-Maple Leaf," Quinn said. "I still have a tattoo on my butt there someplace. That we're playing in Toronto, the jewel of hockey in Canada, is very satisfying. I'm really happy to be here."

Game one was a homely dump-and-chase encounter, the only dazzle supplied by Tom Cruise and then-wife Nicole Kidman in the stands. Peter Zezel, with two goals, won it for Toronto in OT, pouncing on goalie Kirk McLean's blunder—the Canuck goalie had elected to skate into the corner in pursuit of a loose puck, was checked by Bill Berg, and the puck squirted to Zezel, who had a totally unguarded net to shoot at.

In game two, Gilmour assisted on all three Leaf goals, two by Ellett, but Toronto lost 4–3, and the worst-case scenario was unfolding as Burns had feared. "I kept telling the players, the [game one] effort wouldn't mean a thing if they didn't win game two as well. The Vancouver Canucks came in here looking to split, and they did. They understood what was at stake. We didn't, apparently." Mark Osborne recalls: "We were flat. And now we're going to Vancouver for three and it was, like, *aaaggghh.*"

Quinn—coach, GM and president of the Canucks—complained his team was suffering from a media-generated eastern bias. Insults were flung between coaches, even drawing in Fletcher, as old grievances from regular-season games were dredged up. "They're resurrecting stories that Captain Cook read in the newspapers when he came through here," Quinn quipped.

Countering with their own celluloid star power, the Canucks had Mel Gibson in the stands at the Pacific Coliseum for game three. Leafs were never in it. The match, won 4–zip by Vancouver, was punctuated by a third-period brawl that started when Gilmour was checked behind the net by Tim Hunter. It was completely legitimate, if bone-rattling, contact, but Rob Pearson took umbrage and rained punches on Hunter, who refused to fight back. Within seconds, fights broke out all over the ice. As Pearson departed for the dressing room, Burns could be seen mouthing, "Good job." Five players, including Gilmour, were ejected.

Up in the press box, Vancouver's director of player personnel, George McPhee, apparently enraged watching Bob Rouse whaling on Jeff Brown, angrily pounded his fist against the glass pane, shattering it into smithereens. Shards of broken glass went flying, so startling off-ice official

Gary McAdam that he toppled backwards in his chair, knocking himself out cold against an iron bar.

Burns had a sick feeling in the pit of his stomach. He sought to breathe a second wind into his players. "It's now or never for this club. If we're going to win a Stanley Cup, it's got to be this season, immediately. We had a chance a year ago. We've got a shot now. I don't think we could expect to have the same opportunity next season with this group of players." But, as he confided to a friend, he knew; after game three, he knew. "We've run out of gas."

At practice the following day, Burns delivered an eloquent monologue on the harsh beauty of hockey to a rapt audience of reporters, speaking about ethics and honour and childhood Cup dreams. "It's still my dream." On the subject of rejuvenating his players, he said: "My job is to make them forget about how tired they're feeling, to make them forget their injuries. If we lose because we're not good enough, we'll have to accept it. But I think we're good enough. That's why we're not going to quit. We're never going to quit." He railed against the "cheap shots" the Canucks inflicted on his Leafs. "There used to be a code of honour in hockey. That's the way I still coach. I would never tell my players to go out and make cheap hits. Is that what we've come to? Is that where we're going?"

Where the Leafs were going was to a second consecutive shutout as Vancouver took the fourth game 2–0. McLean was lights-out. Toronto was on the precipice, teetering, and Burns was all out of stirring speeches. At the team hotel, he shared a quiet poolside lunch with Gilmour, Wendel Clark and Todd Gill. The coach admitted he had no more rabbits to pull out of the hat. "Maybe a bunny, but not a rabbit." Later, the team enjoyed a relaxing cruise in Vancouver harbour, Burns standing at the rail, looking pensive. "Guys, we're going to have to all hold hands together and pull in the same direction. Who knows what can happen?"

The inevitable happened, albeit in dramatic fashion. Gill, who'd injured his ankle, took a freezing injection, just like Gilmour, and begged to play, but Burns wouldn't permit it. "It was the right call; I realized that after," says Gill. "But at the time, I wanted to play so bad and Pat was worried I'd hurt myself worse. I said, 'But I got the damn thing shot up, let me play!' The thing is, Pat really did care about his players. I respect him for that, but at the time I was ready to kill him."

At the start of game five, before the opening faceoff, Burns moved slowly along the bench, patting every Leaf on the back, leaning over to speak words into their ears. Enlivened, Toronto built up a three-goal lead in the first period and then watched it evaporate. Locked 3–3, they played on into double overtime, Greg Adams scoring fourteen seconds into the fifth period, giving Vancouver the 4–3 win and the series. The Leafs, again, were done, Vancouver moving on to face the New York Rangers in the final, losing in seven. "That week in Vancouver, never winning a game, was the longest week I'd ever spent," says Fletcher.

Burns offered decidedly cool congratulations in his requiem. "The Vancouver Canucks will represent Canada very well in the Stanley Cup finals. But I won't admit they were the better club. I won't admit that."

Chapter Fifteen

Locked Out and Loaded

"Who am I going to play with Sundin?"

"IF THEY WANT TO STAY with the team they've got, then maybe it's time for me to move on."

There was no subtlety to Pat Burns. He wasn't going anywhere, although the Nordiques were making overtures, clandestine lest they be accused of tampering. GM Cliff Fletcher would soon put a stop to that, with a two-year contract extension and honking-huge raise. Burns's tacit ultimatum, delivered through the media, was the coach wailing for a roster shakeup, fidgety because the squad as constituted had regressed, was living on borrowed time. So, in the weeks after Toronto was eliminated from the playoffs—final four once more, but no further—Burns lobbed his mini-grenade.

It was widely agreed that personnel adjustments were required. Nobody, however, sensed the shock wave coming. On June 28, 1994, the first day of the NHL entry draft in Hartford, Fletcher made the knock-me-over-with-a-feather announcement that Toronto had traded Wendel Clark to Quebec for Mats Sundin. Oh my. Among Leaf fans, the disbelief was staggering, the outrage instantaneous. Trade Wendel? How could they? Reached at home by the *Toronto Star*, Don Cherry sputtered: "This isn't

April 1, is it? This must be a joke. I hope somebody's kidding me that you would trade Clark for Mats Sundin."

It was no joke. The audacious Silver Fox had done the inconceivable, the unimaginable. The blockbuster trade involved six players, but Clark was the price for obtaining twenty-three-year-old Sundin, the number-one draft pick overall in 1991, who'd been in the 100-point district two out of three seasons. Despairing Leaf Nation went into paroxysms of grief, feeling genuinely betrayed. Fletcher knew he'd be vilified. He'd tossed and turned the night before, vacillating over the deal. Nordiques GM Pierre Lacroix had approached him with the idea. At that point, moving Clark hadn't been on Fletcher's radar. It was later suggested Burns had been a fifth columnist, scheming to put a whole lot of gone between himself and Clark. Theirs had been a distant and sometimes strained relationship, lacking the symbiotic intensity that existed between Burns and Doug Gilmour. "They hated each other," says one Leaf who was there at the time. "It made Pat crazy that Wendel wouldn't play hurt and basically did nothing in practice." Certainly, the coach had, on several occasions, publicly challenged his captain. "We got along well enough," counters Clark. "He was a good coach, not like some who wish they were players instead." And Burns acknowledged that, in the clutch, Clark had usually answered the bell. Now, the captain was about to get his bell rung emotionally. "It broke my heart," Clark says.

Burns did not promote the trade, says Fletcher. "I cannot recollect Pat ever coming to me saying, 'We have to trade Wendel.' What happened was Quebec had lost to Montreal in the playoffs. In their minds, they had been physically intimidated in that series. Lacroix started talking to me about Wendel. I said, 'Well, we've never even thought about trading Wendel. But I might look at it if Mats Sundin would be coming our way.' When they agreed to that, it was something we had to do. Mats was young, he was big, he was a horse. You had to do it."

Jettisoning the captain was agonizing, though. "Wendel Clark had been the hope of the Maple Leaf franchise for years, the only thing they had," says Fletcher. "Wendel represented eternal hope in Toronto, and I appreciated that." A Leaf icon, undoubtedly, but Fletcher was being paid to make the burdensome decisions to better the team, and this was a club verging on old and spent.

Clark had spent that day filming a breakfast cereal commercial in Toronto. Bowled over by the news when Fletcher called, he went home, where reporters quickly gathered on his doorstep. A white stretch limo idled in the driveway. In the back seat was close friend Tie Domi, then a Winnipeg Jet, sipping a beer. Sundin, meanwhile, was at Borje Salming's hockey school in Sweden when informed he was now a Leaf. The legendary defenceman assured Sundin all would be well, that he'd love playing hockey in Toronto. Sundin never spoke with Burns until the big Swede arrived in town for training camp. Said Fletcher, "I don't think we'll be as good a team October 1, but I'm hoping by March we'll be a better team."

When the draft was over, Burns was booked on a puddle-jumper back to Montreal. At the Hartford airport, he ran into Pat Hickey, longtime hockey reporter for the Montreal *Gazette*. Their flight was delayed and the two Pats repaired to the bar, where they were joined by Jacques Lemaire, who was coaching the Devils at the time. Burns and Lemaire spent the next three hours sipping martinis and talking hockey—"What a horseshit job it was to coach the Canadiens," Hickey recalls. The flight was eventually cancelled, but the trio—two of them well refreshed by now—were put on a plane to Boston, with a connection to Montreal, arriving shortly before midnight.

Hickey didn't have a car, so Burns offered him a ride. "Burns found some coffee at the airport, we found his truck and we sat there for about thirty minutes while he made some phone calls. While we were waiting, an RCMP cruiser came past, and it stopped when the driver recognized Pat. Jacques Demers was in the cruiser because he was looking for his truck, which had been stolen. Demers yelled out at me, 'I see you're getting a ride with the ex-coach!' At which point, Pat replied: 'I still have a job, you fat fuck!'

"I live about ninety kilometres from the city, and Pat was another thirty kilometres further," Hickey says. "He was driving about 140 kilometres an hour in the rain, and at one point, I reminded him that there was a speed trap near the Bromont exit. He said he wasn't worried about a ticket because he was part of the brotherhood. As we approached my exit, Pat wanted assurances that I didn't live too far off the autoroute because he was getting tired. I told him it was only a kilometre and offered him our guest room, but he said he wanted to get home. About thirty minutes after he dropped me off, I called his cell to make sure he got home okay. There was no answer. I called again five minutes later, and Pat answered. He said he was in his driveway and he thanks me for calling because he had stopped the car but had fallen asleep with the engine running."

Gilmour, as expected, inherited the *C*. Fletcher and Burns had sat down, looked at each other, and immediately agreed. "There wasn't even a discussion," the GM told a media gathering. "We both knew it was Gilmour. I expect Doug to play with the Leafs until he retires. And he'll be captain as long as he plays." Really, general managers should watch those declaratory statements.

Burns flew to Toronto for the formal announcement of Gilmour's captaincy at the Hockey Hall of Fame, then went directly back to the Eastern Townships—didn't even stay overnight. On Lake Memphremagog, he had a new neighbour in Félix Potvin that summer. "If you want to get away from it all, I'll tell you a place," the coach had advised. Potvin purchased the property where he still resides. "My mom and dad came to visit and we decided to take a boat ride," Potvin remembers. "Mom asked me to show her where Pat lived. I said, 'No, I don't want to go there on the boat. What if he's outside and sees us spying on him?' But I steered the boat by Pat's place and, sure enough, I see him coming down the dock. He recognizes me, waves us over. We talk for a while, have some beers. He was great with my mom. Away from the rink, Pat was a really fun guy, a different person. But he never mixed his job and his fun time."

Burns's "local" was a little pub called The Owl's Nest. Another habitué was revered author Mordecai Richler. "He smokes like a chimney but never buys cigarettes," Burns snorted. One night, the two sitting together, Richler complained that he couldn't find anyone to do maintenance work around his house. "You do know," said Burns, "that you have to pay them?" Richler cast a beady eye around the regular cast of tipplers and picked one at random. "Hey, do you know how to paint?" The fellow said, sure, he could do that. "Okay, you're hired. Start tomorrow. Come over when you've sobered up."

Ominous clouds hovered over hockey in the weeks before camps opened. League and players' association were stalemated in talks over a new collective bargaining agreement. It was rumoured Commissioner Gary Bettman intended to abort any day, with clubs shuttering their rinks before medicals. Tentatively, with nobody taking bets on whether any season would unfold, the camps opened and exhibition games proceeded. Sundin was booed at the Gardens. "I remember coming to Toronto not knowing what to expect. My first meeting with Pat, he called me into his office. Any time a coach brings you into the office, you get worried, and Pat was an especially intimidating guy. He was sitting at his desk, doodling, and he says, 'What do you think I want to talk about?' I was nervous, so I laughed a little. 'Uh, I don't know, Coach.' All he said was, 'You just keep working as hard as you did in Quebec and everything will be fine. Don't feel like you have to replace Wendel. Be your own guy.' I tried to be that for him because Pat was the best coach I've ever had in my career. He put all his passion into his teams."

Seven Leafs from the previous season were gone, including stalwart defencemen Bob Rouse and Sylvain Lefebvre. Departed also was a frequent target of the coach's wrath, Rob Pearson, who practically did somersaults fleeing Toronto as a restricted free agent. Some could cope with Burns's incessant demands; others, like Pearson, couldn't, and never escaped the doghouse.

Shaving off his beard was Burns's signal that he was now in full coaching mode. The potential of this '94–95 squad tantalized him. "It's going to be like a whole new team. We're going to be younger and I think we'll be more aggressive. But it's going to take a while before we get everybody pulling in the same direction. There are definitely question marks. Who am I going to play with Sundin? It's going to be interesting." There had been a vast turnover, "but we've still got our TCB guys." TCB stood for "Taking Care of Business," the Bachman-Turner Overdrive anthem that was played at every Leaf home game, along with Thin Lizzy's "The Boys Are Back in Town," the team's other musical standard.

Prospects for an NHL season were bleak, however. Burns could only look on in silent incredulity as his players shook hands in solidarity with opponents after exhibition games. Before a game with Detroit, Gilmour and NHLPA president Mike Gartner went to the visitors' dressing room for a confab. Red Wings coach Scotty Bowman found the door closed to him when he tried to enter, so he went across the rink for a pre-game commiserating chat with Burns. Coaches, sighed Burns, were "neither fish nor fowl" in this labour impasse. He took the team to their usual Collingwood resort for a three-day bonding interlude. "I'd be devastated if we didn't keep playing. I hear all kinds of things and I have all kinds of hope. Not that I know anything, because I don't." Whistling in the wind, he prepared the club for their season-opener against Washington. It would not come to pass. Owners pulled the plug, and rinks went dark October 1.

Months dragged by. Would both sides be so foolish, so averse to compromise, that they'd sacrifice the entire season? Behind the scenes, Fletcher spearheaded conciliatory discussions. "I got involved because the ownership of Maple Leaf Gardens was not happy with the lockout at all." As a contingency plan, Fletcher presented Toronto's board of directors with cost-cutting schemes that included layoffs and pay cuts for himself and the coaching staff, but Steve Stavro rejected it. This was all foreign territory for everybody. Burns was still being paid, but there was nothing for him to do. Fletcher dispatched him to scout junior and minor-league games in Quebec. "It was more or less to give him something to stay busy. But we were all just waiting."

Restless, Burns retreated to the cabin he'd bought in Austin, also on Lake Memphremagog, that summer. It was decidedly rustic and held no charms for Burns's girlfriend, Tina Sheldon, who visited only once during the 105-day lockout. Burns rode his bike while the weather held and was endlessly on the phone to Fletcher—"What's the word? Any news?" He accepted an invitation to open a community rink on Broughton Island in Nunavut, flying up to the Arctic territory on an RCMP plane. Informally, he coached youngsters in the Magog area.

At the Gardens, ice was rented out to punters at $500 for seventy-five minutes, resurfacing included. The Leafs and their union brothers had dispersed to play in leagues overseas or in charity games in the U.S. and Canada. Rules prevented coaches from even speaking to their players. Burns paced and prowled, fretful about the players' conditioning and having to start from Square One if this labour standoff was ever resolved. Not that he necessarily observed the no-communication order. By mid-December, he was covertly calling players, whispering that an agreement would be reached by the end of the year. Burns imparted workout proposals to the guys he most trusted, to pass along. When Toronto reporters discovered a large group of Leafs conducting lively drills at a suburban rink—wearing their Leaf jerseys inside-out—it was assumed Burns was present in spirit. Dave Ellett, sharply managing the drills and scrimmages as pseudo coach, denies receiving any coded instructions from Burns. "No, no, we weren't allowed to talk to coaches." But Burns had admitted as much to a reporter: "I've told them what I'd do, and what should be done."

The squabbling NHL sides mustered for three days of meetings in Chicago with a news blackout imposed. Fletcher repeated warnings that a deal had to be reached by the end of the first week in January to salvage a half-season. "I've never felt so useless in a situation in my whole life," Burns moaned. "It's getting scary. I'm almost starting to think like a fan, where I don't care anymore. Just tell us if we're playing or not."

At the eleventh hour, plus about two thousand, they settled it. Camps reopened January 13, 1995, for five days of manic preparation before a truncated forty-eight-game season, within the conference only, and regular playoffs that could stretch into July to follow. Leaf players anticipated a reign of terror from their boss. "We're just going to have to hack and whack our way through it until we get in shape," said Burns. "My focus is going to be on a playoff spot, nothing more. There'll be no chance to think of where we finish—just get in there and pray we're healthy and ready. Patience is out the window. I can't afford to wait. Somebody not producing—sorry pal, you're gone. We coaches have had a mess dumped on our laps, to be fixed in a hurry. There's only one way I can do it here—to be more demanding than ever."

Contract stipulations restrained Burns from whipping his charges into shape with Simon Legree fury; workouts for Training Camp II were limited to three hours a day. At the first afternoon session—Leafs on the ice minutes before Bettman formally declared "Game On"—the coach winced and shook his head. When players were slow on line changes during scrimmages, he barked: "C'mon! This is for the playoffs, the third period of the playoffs!" Skaters gasped, but didn't gag. "Actually, it wasn't that bad," summed up defenceman Jamie Macoun. "He didn't kill us."

Twenty-six teams were entering unknown terrain. For the Leafs, with so many new faces, there was the added issue of trying to revive the chemistry that had served them so well over the past two years. They put their faith in Burns, though concerned about his threat that laggards would be heaved over the side. "I don't have a magic formula. The only good thing is that everybody is in the same boat. I hope nobody takes it easy. You can't go pacing yourself in a forty-eight-game schedule." In Vegas, bookies pegged Toronto at 4–1 odds to win the Cup.

The players looked awkward and sloppy in the first game against L.A., a 3–3 draw on the coast. Then they lost 3–2 in San Jose. Burns juggled his lines maniacally, searching for instant alchemy. At one practice, when sticks went up between Todd Gill and Dave Andreychuk and they exchanged gloved jabs, Burns smiled. "That's good. Maybe the brotherly love will go away a little bit and we'll be a little meaner." In the Gardens opener, Toronto spanked Vancouver 6–2, Mats Sundin superb, selected as first star, if not yet forgiven by fans for the crime of not being Wendel.

There was no sense of continuity or cohesiveness, however, as the season sprinted by. Toronto's expected offensive prowess wasn't evident. The sked was front-heavy with road games for Toronto, and Burns claimed he was aiming for merely a .500 record by the All-Star break and somewhere in the region of .700 after that as the team bore down. But this team was clearly having difficulty gelling. Players were also afraid of making mistakes that would get them benched. "Maybe we're not as good as everybody thought we were," Burns whined. He was perplexed that the distinctive Leaf passion, the one-for-all ethos, had gone AWOL. "They hesitate to crack jokes or say the things that develop chemistry among a group of men. The togetherness isn't there yet. Camaraderie is just building."

Burns no longer had a reliable checker-wrecker line. Gilmour was having trouble getting untracked: The defence had maddening lapses. It quickly became apparent this Leaf squad would go as far as Sundin could take them. After a dispiriting loss to Los Angeles, the dressing room door stayed closed for longer than usual as the players held a team meeting to air out feelings, leaving the Chancellor of Austria—waiting to pose for meet 'n' greet photos—to cool his heels in the corridor. Burns's postgame pressers got shorter and brusquer. "It's got to come from them," he argued. "For the last couple of years, this team has been finding ways to win; now we're finding ways to lose." Twenty-six games into the abbreviated season, Toronto was a middling team. "We have to win our share the rest of the way because the bottom's coming up," said Burns. "We don't want to risk devastation. I hope the players understand that. This is getting to be a life-and-death situation." As the trade deadline approached, a rather bitchy Burns put his players on alert: "I wouldn't buy any groceries this week."

It was a line stolen from Tie Domi, who'd made the observation in Winnipeg, where his status was a subject of debate. Leafs had just played the Jets in Winnipeg. Domi, a right winger, was lining up for a faceoff, back to the Leaf bench, when he heard somebody yapping at him. He turned around, glaring. "Nobody's mouth was moving. Then I looked at Pat. He said, 'Yeah, you heard me. I'd like to have you on my right side.'" Why Burns coveted Domi was unclear. He already had a proven enforcer in Ken Baumgartner, who famously shouted "Daddy's Home!" when wading into a scrum in support of teammates. But Baumgartner got little ice time. "We had toughness, but in a lot of games Pat wouldn't use those guys," says Fletcher. "He wasn't comfortable putting them on the ice because the games were too important. Pat's feeling about Tie was this is a player who can skate, who can play in all situations." Fletcher made the deal, sending Winnipeg Mike Eastwood, and pulling off four other trades that revamped the lineup. Burns had presented his GM with a shopping list, and Fletcher got to it.

Domi received the call from Burns at 3 p.m. "Told ya." Huh? Who is this? "It's Pat Burns and you're a Leaf. Get on a plane. I want you in the lineup tonight." Domi caught the first flight available, gleeful at being returned to the franchise that had selected him twenty-seventh overall in the 1988 entry draft, though appearing in just two NHL games before being dispatched to the Rangers. He made it to the Gardens minutes before game time. "I never even saw Burnsie before I got on the bench. I was in the dressing room, changing, and he was on TV doing an interview." It wasn't until the next day that they spoke one on one in the coach's office. "He's sitting there in sandals and boxers, wearing glasses. I started laughing. 'What's so funny?' I said, 'That's quite the sight, Pat.' And from that moment on, he loved me."

There was only one month left to get the reconfigured Leafs sorted out, right side up. Burns had his replenished assets, more skill and speed on his roster. Yet he didn't ease up on the reins or adjust a defensive system designed for the players who were there before. "We had a different team, and we needed to play a little bit of a different style," suggests Ellett. "I think Pat had trouble coming to grips with that. I mean, that's why we'd traded for Sundin, right, to open up? But Pat wouldn't let us."

In a blur of fits and starts, the Leafs lurched to the finish line, no more disoriented than other clubs. While Montreal was being eliminated from postseason contention, Toronto finished fourth in the Central Division, which meant another first-round tango with the Blackhawks, who had home-ice advantage. Burns didn't give a rat's patootie about that, but first rounds always scared him, as they did all coaches. "It's the toughest round of the playoffs. If you can get by the first round, you're all right."

When the playoffs opened, they certainly seemed all right, taking the first two games of the Western Conference quarter-final, Potvin stealing the second with a shutout on forty-two saves, a tall glass of water. "Not much makes me nervous. My dad used to tell me, 'You'll never die of a heart attack.'" The team stayed overnight in Chicago after game two. And that's where the trouble may have begun. "Some guys went out after," says Sundin, who wasn't one of them. "They got back late. Pat heard about it and was not very happy." There was more to it than that. A group of players who hadn't dressed came back to the hotel and got raucous—to the point that there were complaints to management. Burns was roused from his sleep in the wee hours by the night manager. "Please tell them to stop." The coach was outraged, and not just about having his beauty sleep interrupted. Did these fools not understand what was at stake? He seethed during the charter flight home and ordered the squad directly to the Gardens. "He bag-skated us," says Sundin. Domi: "That was the first time I'd seen him really pissed off. Old-school bag skate, no pucks, and here we were two games up. He made his point."

Toronto was halfway there, halfway out of the chaotic first round. The S-word—sweep—was verboten. "The only advantage we have right now is that we have to win two games and they have to win four," said Burns. "The 'Hawks are a proud team. Nobody's dead until they've been buried and the funeral rites have been given." Chicago didn't lie down for the Leafs to kick dirt on them. Led by Eddie Belfour, they went tit-for-tat on Toronto and swiped a pair right back. The series was tied, all Leaf cockiness having vanished. When the 'Hawks won their third game in a row, at the United Center, it felt like the Leafs had fallen down a manhole. Now the underdog status Burns embraced was no longer an act. "We play better when we're desperate. There's no one here who's laid down their guns and said, 'We surrender.' The big question is, how much pride are we going to have?" Typically, Burns had stripped the situation down to bumper-sticker platitudes, as if self-regard could compensate for execution and discipline, which had gone down the flusher. And the team did respond, though they were fortunate to escape elimination with a 5–4 overtime win in game six after blowing a 4–1 third-period lead, the crowd bellowing boos. Journeyman spare part Randy Wood—a Yale boy, actually—popped the winning shot ten minutes into OT, after Sundin swung the puck out front on a wraparound attempt. "It's nothing to be proud of," admitted Burns, wiping perspiration from his brow, shaken by the third-period collapse. "We found a way to win even when it seemed we were dead as doornails." The Leafs had merely earned the right to play their fifth game seven in three years. "The pressure is on them, not us," Burns insisted. There was just enough time between games for him to get clocked speeding by photo radar on Highway 427, his third violation since moving to Toronto.

The deciding encounter was a nightmare for Todd Gill, a reprise of what had been his worst moment as a Maple Leaf—the final game of the '88–89 season, when his giveaway at Chicago Stadium resulted in a goal that put the Blackhawks into the playoffs ahead of Toronto. This time, fate cruelly revisited at 11:53 of the third, Leafs trailing 2–1 but pushing hard for the equalizer. Gill attempted a backhand pass to defence partner Dmitri Mironov that an onrushing Joe Murphy knocked down and turned into a breakaway, flipping the puck over Potvin. Twenty-six seconds later, Chicago scored again to remove any chance of a miracle comeback, an empty-net goal added to wipe out the Leafs 5–2. Toronto, a club conceived to win it all in the wrangled wreckage of a mutant season, had not survived the first round.

"Everything unravelled," says Potvin. "To be honest, I don't have many memory souvenirs from that season. It felt like we were just running to make the playoffs and then we were out." Ellett: "Of all the losses, that was the probably the most disappointing, for Burnsie and for everyone involved." Nobody could figure out what had gone so catastrophically wrong, how the Leafs could have relinquished a series that had been under firm control. "Up 2–0, you should be able to prevail," says Fletcher, as flummoxed as anyone else, even years later. "We got beaten."

Chapter Sixteen

Hitting Bottom in Leafland

"I believe Pat basically fired himself."

CLIFF FLETCHER WAS URBANE, suave and cultured. Pat Burns was unrefined, blunt and coarse. One was cut from cashmere, the other from broadcloth. Two more diametrically opposed natures could scarcely be imagined. Yet, in hockey terms, they complemented each other. With apologies to Tom Cruise in *Jerry Maguire:* "You complete me." It wasn't a buddy-buddy relationship, hanging out together on the road, because Burns always remained somewhat diffident about suits with GM honorifics in front of their names. He was the employee and Fletcher "The Boss." Away from the game, they had nothing in common. Inside the game, they were intuitively bonded, while allowing each other space to operate in their divergent jobs. "Pat was very independent," says Fletcher. "He wanted to run things his way, which was my management style. I was never a frustrated coach."

Their rapport was thus easy, never fraught. Over the occasional drink, in airport terminals, Burns continued to regale Fletcher with stories from his cop days. They make him crack up still in the retelling. Like the time Burns was on a drug stakeout in a gay bar, semi-dressed in drag. He was dancing with a male partner and hissing into his lapel microphone, urgently calling in the raid by police waiting for the signal outside. Except his colleagues took their sweet time entering because they were laughing so hard at the image of Burns swaying in a man's arms. "The scariest time was when they put him in undercover as a convict at Kingston Penitentiary for a month," Fletcher remembers. "The only person in the world who knew he was there was the warden. Pat said he kept having nightmares that the warden was going to have a heart attack and die. He was never so frightened in his life. You hear these stories, and it's easy to see how Pat developed the personality he had—think fast on your feet. That served him well in coaching."

Were all the stories true or were some inventions? Does it matter? Burns may have buffed his cop resumé, but the coaching biography was for real, self-evident, and that's what counted. The rest was amusing backdrop. Fletcher certainly valued the "instant credibility" Burns had brought to the Leaf franchise. "He got the whole town buzzing. From that point forward, things just got better and better—for a few years. He was everything the Maple Leafs could have asked for in a coach." But Fletcher had been around hockey for three decades and recognized the underlying traits, strengths that could become weaknesses, in so peppery and zealous a bench boss. The pattern of diminishing returns became more starkly evident later in Burns's career. "Pat was the type of coach who would never have a long tenure in one place because he was so demanding and got so much out of everyone," says Fletcher. "After a number of years, if he had that same group of players, they just collapsed. They had no more to give."

As the 1995–96 season got under way, few observers could have predicted that Burns's shelf life in Toronto was ticking down rapidly, his coaching bona fides headed for the remaindered bin. The playoffs had been a profound disappointment but were generally viewed as an anomaly, an unfortunate twist of fate, the kind of unforeseen consequence that frequently occurs in sports, even to good teams, which is precisely what keeps fans riveted. Only a handful of commentators with a personal axe to grind against Burns, because he'd mistreated them repeatedly, raised any alarm bells or detected fundamental problems on a squad that had been significantly retooled. Some mild speculation about Burns's future provoked a self-pitying response. "For two years I was king of the city and now I'm a pauper. But I went through the same thing in Montreal, and you'd expect to feel the heat in any high-profile hockey city." There was rationalizing for a first-round bounce: injuries, including Gilmour's two herniated discs, the derangement of a lockout-shortened schedule, not enough time to transition following Fletcher's flurry of trade-deadline deals. But surely there was no rot at the Leaf core, eroding what GM and coach had built. The house was sound.

Burns, in the final year of his contract, hadn't asked for extension or raise—wanted the former, didn't think he deserved the latter. It would get done, no rush, both sides assured, Fletcher now dealing with Robin Burns, the coach's first cousin, as agent. It did appear suspicious, however, and possibly antagonizing to the franchise, that the coach was making unilateral endorsement deals, taking care of number one through side arrangements that could have been interpreted as slightly insubordinate. When the Leafs signed with one radio station, Burns promptly sold his services to a rival broadcaster. When the Gardens struck an exclusive signage contract with one car maker, Burns walked across the street to a competitor.

A report in *The Globe and Mail* in early August claimed Fletcher had tried unsuccessfully to dump Burns and been rebuffed by owner Steve Stavro, who didn't relish paying out the $750,000 remaining on his coach's salary. Fletcher was quick to shoot down the story, saying, "There is not one-millionth of one per cent of authenticity" in the assertions that had been ascribed to two anonymous sources. GM immediately phoned coach to quell any anxieties. Burns had just returned from a fishing trip to New Hampshire and found dozens of messages on his answering machine: queries from journalists about the *Globe* story and further scuttlebutt that had him headed for Pittsburgh or Chicago, a report on French-language radio claiming he'd been terminated in Toronto, condolences from friends. "I hear I've been fired," Burns said to Fletcher. "Don't be stupid," Fletcher responded. They both had a laugh about it. It was all the usual off-season prattle, given a bit more credence because this was the first time Burns had encountered any controversy in Toronto. More chuckles greeted the confirmed news that Burns, along with Jacques Lemaire, had been appointed by Gary Bettman to a committee examining ways to reduce the neutral-zone interference that had slowed down the game by epidemic proportions. Burns and Lemaire were the two coaches guiltiest of employing that hockey style. Burns saw the irony.

Fletcher landed some key summer acquisitions via trades and free-agent signings. Strapping Sergio Momesso arrived from Vancouver. Classy playmaking defenceman Larry Murphy put his John Hancock on a three-year, $7 million contract that made him the highest-paid Leaf—a distinction that would fuel the caterwauling of fans when he failed to perform as advertised, the boos and jeers so relentless that the tortured player would be traded within two years as an act of mercy. By then, of course, the team had imploded and even Fletcher would be torpedoed.

Those convulsions were still far in the future when Toronto opened the '95–96 campaign in Pittsburgh, routed 8–3 by Mario Lemieux—back from a seventeen-month health hiatus—and the Penguins. Just a freakish thing, Leafs maintained. It happens. The team braced for the return of prodigal son Wendel Clark, who'd been traded a week earlier from Quebec to the New York Islanders. Due to intra-conference play in the lockout season, Clark had not crossed the Gardens' threshold since leaving Toronto. He had to remind himself to veer towards the unfamiliar visitors' dressing room. Mats Sundin, ceaselessly self-effacing, tried to downplay the event. Leaf fans gave their ex-captain a standing ovation. But Clark wasn't a factor in the game and Sundin dazzled with a four-point performance that propelled Toronto to a 7–3 win.

The other memorable episode in October occurred with *KA-POW* shock when Toronto hosted Tie Domi's one-time team, the Rangers. Seemingly unprovoked, Domi cold-cocked Ulf Samuelsson with a gloved left hook with sixty-four seconds left in a game Toronto would lose 2–0. *POW* in the mug and Samuelsson went down, immobile, lights out. Even according to the code of enforcers, and with scant sympathy for Samuelsson, among the dirtiest players in the league, this was an extraordinary assault. Burns was not impressed, describing Domi's loss of temper as "disappointing."

"Samuelsson called me a dummy," says Domi, revisiting the incident. "'Come on, Tie Dummy. Come on, Tie Dummy.'" Domi took that as both a personal slag and a slur against his late father, mocking the family's surname. "So I fucking dropped him." When Burns demanded an explanation afterwards, Domi recounted Samuelsson's baiting. "Pat goes, 'Oh, okay then. He deserved it, good job.'" The mugging earned Domi an eight-game suspension. He did not, however, fall out of favour with his coach.

While Burns remained devoted to Gilmour, Domi was his pet poodle, the one player he took for walkies outside the rink, adopting him as quasi-date for promotional appearances or just tootling around town. "He took me to luncheons, things like that, and I was happy to do it. Pat would say, 'Come on, you're coming with me.' I got to know him as a person, away from the rink." Burns was also intent on cultivating Domi as a player with more dimensions than just toughie and guardian of Leaf talent. "He was the first to tell me I could be a playoff-type player. He made me established and accountable. He *liked* me. And when Pat liked you, you were like his son."

Burns was also a lonely man in those days. He revealed little of what was going on in his private life, but he and Tina were clearly headed for a breakup. Quite a few years younger than Burns, Tina had adjusted well to her new life in Toronto. At first, she did marketing for a cookie company, then landed an upwardly mobile position in the promotional field with Nesbitt Burns, the investment firm. Burns was pleased that his girlfriend's career was blossoming. He didn't want her to be merely an appendage to his existence, yet a chasm had opened between them. Tina hadn't gone to the Eastern Townships at all that summer. She'd developed friendships in the world outside hockey. There was no longer any talk of marriage. Burns told a friend that Tina wanted children, and he could understand that, but he wasn't about to reverse his vasectomy and had zero appetite for child-rearing again. When Burns came back to Toronto for training camp, he noticed that several photographs of him and Tina as a couple had disappeared from their waterfront condo, tucked away into drawers. What he inferred was that, in his absence, Tina had taken steps to erase him from their shared dwelling. Burns assumed Tina had been seeing someone else—as indeed he had been over the summer. By Christmas, they agreed to go their separate ways. It was a gentle parting, and they remained friends. Burns even let Tina stay in the condo for however long she liked, while he moved into the Sutton Place Hotel.

But Burns was distracted and occasionally mopey over another failed relationship. One night, he was drinking alone at a waterside bar, the Purple Pepper, on Queen's Quay. A group of young people were also on hand, paying absolutely no attention to the Leaf coach sitting by himself in the corner. "All of a sudden, the bartender brings us a tray of shots," recalls Mandy McCormick, who was in the youthful tippling party. "He says, 'These are from Pat Burns and he would really like you all to leave him alone.'" The group was puzzled. "First of all, none of us even knew who he was or had even noticed him. We took the shots, though, and 'left him alone.' I thought he was being a tad egotistical, but free booze is free booze."

Around the team, which was having a so-so season, the jelling that Burns anxiously sought was apparently coming to pass. Silly dressing-room pranks were once again common, coach included in the shenanigans. There was the afternoon when somebody poured oil on the rocks in the Gardens sauna as Burns was stripping down to use it. He stepped in and the sauna filled with smoke. "He's running through the dressing room naked, screaming: 'There's a fire in the sauna!'" howls Domi, doubling over in hysterics at the memory.

Hijinks among players should have augured well. There were no divisions within the dressing room evident to outsiders. When his charges deserved it, Burns still unloaded with a tirade, but these were fewer and farther between. One evening that he did go ballistic was in New Jersey between periods, after Todd Warriner—who absorbed more than his share of scolding from Burns—had made a touch pass to a teammate. If there was one thing guaranteed to send Burns ballistic, it was a Leaf gambling on the touch pass—a quick pass from one player to another, in one movement after receiving it, that is vulnerable to turnovers. In the room, he hit heights of fury not witnessed in a long time. "There's a guy in this room, I'm pretty sure he doesn't wear 66 or 99, but he makes a one-touch pass! There's only two guys in the world who can make a one-touch pass, Lemieux and Gretzky, and I don't see either of them in here!" He glared around, looking for the culprit. Wisely, Warriner had taken refuge in a bathroom stall. "Over here, Coach," came a small voice. Just as wisely, Burns didn't invade the player's privacy. From then on, Warriner was known to his teammates as "One-Touch."

Beneath the surface, there were a few clues that Burns's psychological methods might be losing their effectiveness. After Toronto was subjected to a 6–1 drubbing by the Florida Panthers, the coach again pushed the self-respect button. At practice at Forest Hill Memorial Arena the next day, he spotted a youngster playing on an adjoining rink. He summoned his players—who'd been booed off the ice the night before—and directed their attention to the lad. "That's the pride. That's what it's all about. There's a kid going around in a Maple Leafs sweater, adoring you guys." Some of the players smirked and rolled their eyes. That would never have happened a year, two years, earlier. Burns took note of the disrespect and put the players through a punishing ninety-minute workout. If sentimental words didn't get their attention, maybe hard-ass labour would.

The team couldn't put together a string of wins, gather any momentum. They were playing .500 hockey, no better, and there wasn't any excuse for it. A western road swing, three games in four nights in three different time zones, sapped everybody's energy, with modest results 1–0–2. Through early November, the Leafs did rouse themselves somewhat, losing just one out of six with a couple of ties. The fact was, Toronto had not managed three consecutive victories in almost twenty months. They professed no undue worry. Theirs was a veteran team, inured to mental fragility and withering of confidence, the typical precursors to stagnation and a standings crash. They'd come around.

From November 1 through 21, Toronto went 7–1–2, then 6–1–1 through the first half of December. The tidy record saw them jump seven games above .500 for the first time since their ten-game winning streak at the start of the '93–94 season. Just before Christmas, Gilmour hit the 1,000-point plateau, the third player in franchise annals to do so in a Toronto uniform, collecting 350 of them in 285 matches as a Leaf. On the same night, Burns marked his 300th game as an NHL coach, 126 of them behind the Leaf bench. "It's a great feeling, and I hope I'm around for 300 more, although that might be asking too much. Some coaches don't even last 300 games." A reporter wondered about the Grinch (of Dr. Seuss fame) tie that Burns was wearing. "I always thought the Grinch was misunderstood," he smiled. "He's really a lonely guy. I've always been a Grinch fan."

Burns was about to hear a "Who" in the new year: Who will take the blame for this suddenly, catastrophically, freefalling Leafs team?

On January 5, 1996, the Leafs were in Buffalo, clearly tired as they played their sixth game in nine nights. The 3–1 loss upset Burns disproportionately. At his press scrum, he went abruptly haywire, delivering a jeremiad that went far beyond message via media. For inexplicable reasons, he cryptically suggested there was a disconnect in the dressing room, a serious no-no for any coach to reveal. "Some players feel a coach's message isn't important anymore. Don't get me wrong, we've got a good bunch of guys on this club. I'm not saying everybody, but I think there's a couple of individuals that are trying to hold other individuals back."

What in the world was Burns babbling about? "I don't know what goes on in the dressing room," he said, "but maybe some guys say, 'This is the way we should play, not the coach's way.'" Naturally, reporters trotted off to the players for their reaction. They were taken aback, and at least some were angry. "If Burns has got a problem with some players, then that's something that he should say to them," snipped Macoun. "If he's got a problem, I don't know who it's with. He didn't say it to me." Todd Gill, very much a liege to Burns, was baffled. "You'll have to ask Pat who he's talking about. Every game I've ever played for Pat Burns, we've had a game plan and we've tried to follow it."

The coach had opened a can of worms, though a lax Toronto media contingent didn't stick their fingers in deep to poke around. Burns generally avoided singling out players for criticism, preferring the generic reprimand. On the bench, if annoyed by a Leaf's misplay, he'd bend over and speak directly in the player's ear. "Why'd you let your guy go? Just sit there for a while and think about it." Out of character, though, after an earlier loss in Montreal, he'd chastised the "leadership" of the club, which upset several players, notably Gilmour. Veterans should have been less sensitive about light slaps on the ego. Yet they were genuinely miffed that Burns had taken the matter—what matter?—outside the dressing room. Alerted to a possible power struggle on the team, some reporters started to pay closer attention. In fact, there was an ember of dissension within the inner sanctum that would in quick time flame up. "It was a team dominated by older guys," says Domi, choosing his words carefully. "Some guys are fragile and can't take constructive criticism. We were in the middle of a changeover between guys who had a long history with Pat, who'd been there for those final-four playoffs, and younger players. Pat was trying to make that transition with us, but there weren't enough young guys around to do it. Maybe some players didn't like that changeover; I'm not sure. I wasn't part of that older group. I was Burnsie's guy and everybody knew it."

It didn't help matters when *Le Journal de Montréal* quoted Burns as saying he might bolt the Leafs in the coming summer if a rival club made an attractive offer. It was now known that Burns had an escape clause in his contract that gave him three weeks to weigh other job offers once the season ended; otherwise, he would remain Leaf property. "If I were to receive a three-year offer from another team, I would have to seriously consider it," Burns told *Le Journal*. "These are things that happen only once in a lifetime. I'm no dumber than anyone else. I like security."

Along with Terry Crisp, Burns was at that point the longest-serving bench steward in a league of coaching musical chairs. Instead of agreeing to a formal contract extension or negotiating a new deal, Burns and the Leafs had signed a "letter of intent" that included the opt-out clause, essentially making Burns a limited-opportunity free agent. If Burns chose to defect, the Leafs would be off the hook financially. If he decided to come back and the Leafs wanted to keep him, a one-year guarantee was in place. But if Toronto didn't want him, they'd have to pay that year's salary, $850,000, for Burns *not* to coach. This would become a critical detail.

Trade rumours in January engulfed the team, adding to feelings of uncertainty. "It's starting to weigh on certain individuals," said Burns, while straining to undo the damage his Buffalo eruption had caused. "There is no dissension here. The door is never closed. There's nothing going on." As for his own status, no longer unimpeachable: "Who knows? Maybe Cliff might say he's had enough of me. But I'm not looking to move. I fit in fine here. It's the media that keep talking about the contract. I'm not restless. I don't want to leave. I love Toronto. Why does everybody say I want to go?"

To *Toronto Sun* columnist Steve Simmons, Burns justified his remarks about being receptive to a better deal elsewhere. "If you were in my shoes and you were offered a one-year contract and a three-year deal, which one would you take? You'd take the three-year deal, right? So is it wrong to say that?"

Burns was practising gamesmanship with Fletcher and, frankly, he was out of his league. It would have been smarter to button his lip. But he thought he had ammunition and expected to have more of it when Toronto got to the playoffs. They would make it there, that spring, but without him.

Fletcher augmented the roster in a complicated three-way trade that brought Kirk Muller to Toronto. He made no immediate impact. A winless streak had crept in the window, seven and counting. When they were stoned 4–0 by St. Louis at the Gardens, fans booed and bayed lustily. Players were embarrassed. "They want to face the music," Burns insisted. "We all want to do that together. Nobody's going to hide. Nobody's going to be in shame around this city. We know we're on our own right now. We can see by the reaction of the fans. We can imagine—by the reaction of certain members of the media—that we're going to have to stick together."

Yet the Leafs were coming unhinged. Maddeningly, Burns rejigged and re-rejigged his lines, sometimes shift to shift, seeking a spark. He explained his endless experimenting, pleading for time as the club adjusted to trades and injuries: "I've slept on it, showered on it, put names in a cup and thrown them on a table. It's going to take some time—be patient, and wait to see what the right chemistry is going to be."

Zero wins in eight games and just fourteen goals in those matches—scoring droughts being a chronic problem on teams coached by Burns. "A dark cloud follows us all over the place," he grumbled when the team landed in a San Jose rainstorm. This was Toronto's longest skid since Burns had taken over the club. "You start to ask yourself, 'Are we ever going to win another game?' We'll take a win against anybody. We've got to win a game now." It wouldn't be against the Sharks, Leafs pathetic in a 6–4 defeat.

One week into February and the change in Toronto's fortunes was stunning. On New Year's Day they had sat comfortably, eight games above .500 and contemplating a shot at first place in the Western Conference. Now they were winless in nine, one off the record of ten set during the '66–67 season. Fletcher was so distressed that he left a general managers' meeting in Arizona and joined the club in Anaheim. Squelching speculation the coach would be canned, he declared Burns was staying behind the bench for the rest of the season and "he's our coach for next year, too, if he should decide to return. His future is no different now than it was when he got us to the final four two years in a row." Fletcher did hold a closed-door meeting with the players. "I wouldn't say I read the riot act. That's dinosaur stuff. But we do have some players playing at less than their potential. I had some things to say to them. That's it. Period."

Burns was grateful for the vote of confidence but admitted worry nonetheless. "I'm sure a couple of players are questioning themselves right now, saying, 'Pat could be gone.' Some might even be happy with that. But others might say, 'Hey, it's not his fault.' I haven't been unfair to anyone on this team." He bristled at suggestions his charges had perhaps tuned him out. "I don't feel the players have quit on me, and I'm not going to quit on them." Gilmour, when asked if the team's ineptitude could be attributed to their coach, snapped: "That's a bunch of crock. Not one guy on this hockey club has a problem with Pat Burns. Pat has been very, very calm and very, very positive. We should be thanking him for staying so positive. We just have to go out there and work harder for him and work harder for us."

Toronto edged the Ducks 2–1, Burns ditching the spectacles he'd worn most of the season. "Maybe I was just afraid to watch," he joked. But in Los Angeles, the winless streak was reset at one, the Leafs repelled 4–3. "This puts us right back where we started," Burns moaned. On that night, as it happened, Dan Aykroyd had arranged a birthday party at the House of Blues for fellow Kingston native Muller. The Leafs weren't flying home until the next morning and were expected at the restaurant following their game against the Kings. Instead, Burns ordered all players on the team bus by 11 p.m. Defiant, the players simply moved the party to one of their hotel suites. House of Blues had baked a towering birthday cake that they delivered to the hotel. Some of the players heaved it on a cart, pushed it to the coach's room, knocked on his door and then ran. It was not true, as later rumoured, that someone had written on it: 'We hate you.' Still, Burns was not amused. In the midst of the team's horrifying downward spiral through the standings, there should have been no revelry, he fumed. The players should have gone directly to bed to ponder their sins.

Eight of their eleven previous games had been against teams below .500, and yet the Leafs had gone a deplorable 1–6–1 in those matches. The team was in utter disarray. Returning to Toronto, an exasperated Burns committed what was arguably his worst mistake—publicly throwing up his hands in what certainly sounded like surrender. "I don't know what more we can possibly do. I've tried yelling at them. I've run the crap out of them. I've tried reasoning with them. What else can I do?" A coach never, ever, waves the white flag. By admitting he'd run out of answers to fix what was wrong, he stabbed himself in the front, giving the franchise an excuse to dump him.

Close friends who spoke with him in those harrowing days suspected Burns was deliberately tempting his own execution. "I believe Pat basically fired himself," says Chris Wood, a Toronto businessman who had a summer residence in Magog and had become tight with Burns. "Even strong people sometimes doubt themselves. Near to the end, Pat would call and say, 'I'm going to get fired, I know it.' It was a self-defeating thing, a self-fulfilling prophecy. It's almost like he made it happen himself."

The sense of gloom around the club was oppressive. Toronto had one win in one month. Frantic, Burns banned newspapers from the dressing room. Up 2–0 on the Sabres, the Leafs had to settle for another tie. The coach's discomfort in media scrums after practice and games was palpable. He looked like a man headed for the gallows. There was a slim bright side: Toronto was in fourth place in the West before the team began its jaw-dropping slide and they were still in fourth place. Also, the Leafs had a brief resurgent period, 3–1–1 in five outings. Burns promised he would halt the discombobulating line tinkering, try to afford his players a bit of consistency. And then the second slump struck.

Leads blown, undisciplined penalties and four losses plummeted Toronto below .500. Repeatedly, Fletcher stated, "I've never fired a coach in midseason and I don't intend to start now." At their Have a Heart charity dinner, Burns excoriated his troops to reporters who came sniffing. "I don't know how the players can walk around Toronto. I have a lot of trouble walking around this city. I'm embarrassed." He was coming undone. An eighteen-game tailspin isn't a slump; it's almost one quarter of a season. But Fletcher gave him a stay of execution. "It's his job, period. That isn't even an issue." Quietly, however, he met individually with the players. Five weeks of virtually uninterrupted funk prompted the club to bring in an outside sports psychologist. Even Burns submitted. Beleaguered, the coach was saying one thing publicly and another privately to confidants. "More than ever, everything that has been written and said has made me want to come back next season even more," he told circling journalists. "If Cliff will have me back, I'll be back. Toronto is the greatest place to coach if you're winning, and I'll win again. I didn't get dumb in three months." Offstage, he was telling friends he couldn't take it anymore.

In Winnipeg, the team choked and squandered a 3–1 lead, falling 4–3. "I've never in my life felt as much strain and stress," Burns admitted. "I can't sleep at night. I lie awake for hours, trying to figure out what we have to do to break out of this slump. I've never experienced anything as bad as this before." His outspoken dismay further discomfited the players. One, quoted anonymously, suggested the breakup with Tina had thrown the coach for a loop from which he hadn't recovered. Nonsense, Burns told the *Globe*'s Marty York. "First of all, I'm glad we're not together right now because, even though I had a fine relationship with this woman and we remain good friends, I'd rather be on my own during tough times like this." He snidely pointed out that Fletcher had also separated from his wife, Boots, on Boxing Day. "I'm sure the players who think I'm distracted by my personal situation also think Cliff is distracted by his. Well, I don't think any of this has to do with our problems."

Something had to give. Slipping out of a playoff spot, the team embarked on a three-game road trip to Winnipeg, Dallas and Denver, Fletcher feeling the heat. He went on the road with the team. "We can't go back to Toronto with nothing to show for this three-game trip." But Toronto lost all three, pounded by the Avalanche 4–0 in what would be Burns's last game behind the Leaf bench.

In the midst of that trip, despondent and deeply paranoid, Burns called a friend in Toronto, complaining bitterly about a rump group in the dressing room that was playing to lose, playing to get him fired. Burns identified Jamie Macoun as leader of the alleged cabal. Fletcher, looking back at that dismal period, rejects this out of hand. "Jamie Macoun is an off-the-wall type of guy. He says what he thinks. But no professional athlete would purposely not play well to try to undermine a coach, because what they could end up doing is put themselves right out of a job. No, I don't buy that. Jamie Macoun, like most professional athletes, loves money and wanted another contract. When things go bad, everybody looks after number one—themselves. There was no doubt some of the players were feeling sorry for themselves and felt it was the coach's fault. But that happens in every dressing room. Nobody was going to blame themselves. They've always got to point the finger at somebody else." Dave Ellett adds: "Macoun and Pat didn't have a good relationship. But I can honestly tell you nobody on that team tanked. We were feeling the heat, too. Jesus, it was a miserable time." Mats Sundin: "Pat was so quiet that last week, not like his usual self at all."

After the Avalanche game, Burns walked away from the bench with stooped shoulders, face darkened. "For the first time in his career, he was at a complete loss," says Ellett. Toronto had lost sixteen of their last twenty-two games.

The Leafs spent that night in Denver. Early the following morning, Fletcher summoned Burns to his hotel room. Whether the GM fired Burns or Burns asked to be relieved remains sketchy. What needs to be remembered, though, is that if Burns had quit, he would not have received the $850,000 remaining on his contract.

"I wanted him to continue," insists Fletcher. "I said, 'Pat, we can get through this together.' But Pat felt that he'd lost the team. He really didn't think he could continue. I'd watched him behind the bench the night before and he looked so frustrated, so dejected." Tears swim in Fletcher's eyes as he remembers their solemn meeting. "Coaches can sense it, when they have command of a team and when they start to lose it." He likens the situation to university students having the same professor for four years, for every class. "By the end, you'd have a hard time paying attention to what was said, you're no longer hanging on every word like you were the first year. It's the same thing for a coach. It's hard to keep everyone's interest, to continually motivate a group of athletes who've already heard everything you've had to say over the course of time. In a coach's mind, he knows full well when he's not getting through anymore."

Fletcher remains stunned at how drastically everything went to hell in a handbasket over six weeks. He had immense pity for the man who sat before him in that Denver hotel room. "I'd seen coaches struggle before, but not like this. Pat was so much in charge of the situation all that time. In his mind, to have it unravel and not have any control over what was happening, knowing he had to win . . . it just got to him. I was hoping to buy time. But Pat wasn't having anything to do with buying time."

The humane act was to relieve Burns of his burden. It's what the coach wanted. "It was a mutual decision," says Fletcher, whose parting gift would be that one-year severance, never begrudged. But they told no one, not even Burns's assistant coaches, and certainly not the travelling media when the team boarded its flight home. Fletcher outright lied to reporters, including the second wave that met the team upon landing in Toronto, assuring everyone Burns would be behind the bench for the next game against New Jersey. He makes no apologies about giving his severed coach a head start out of town. "He asked me for it. And he deserved it, if that's what he wanted. Pat had done so much for this franchise, brought back the Leaf fever. He called me later that night, said, 'Cliff! I'm in Kingston.' I said, 'Okay, Pat, I'll have fun tomorrow morning at the press conference.'" It was morbid humour. Softly, he adds, "I loved Pat."

It was a firestorm Fletcher walked into at the Gardens, as news of Burns's termination had finally leaked. He was flayed for fibbing, but remained unrepentant. Nick Beverley, a cog in the Leaf front-office wheel, would take over the coaching reins on an interim basis. But the spotlight was now squarely on the GM to salvage the season. It had all been a bust. Most players said the right things—poor Pat, not his fault. Some were sincere, others not. "Let's put it this way," says Ellett. "When they fired Pat, there were a few guys who were pretty damn happy." Gilmour was not one of them. "I don't think any of the guys were playing to get him fired. But no one will ever admit to that. It's very possible that some guys did."

Burns made a few calls during that long night of driving in the sleet to Kingston, where he holed up. Phoned Gilmour to thank him for the years together, dialled Domi to impart some career advice, voice low and strained. "He said, 'Good luck, kid, I'm done.' It was really emotional."

Told his children he was headed home. Told best mate Kevin Dixon, who says, "He was relieved." Relieved at being relieved.

For the previous month or so, Burns had been back living in his waterfront condo. Tina had finally moved out, taking nearly all the furniture, with Burns's blessing. The unit was left spartan, uninviting, depleted even of cutlery and dishes so that Burns had to make an emergency shopping trip for the bits and pieces he needed to survive. When he got in his truck that evening, he left two dozen suits in the closet, and all his shoes. Before departing the condo forever, he also phoned his Toronto friend, Chris Wood. "Pat said, 'Woody, I'm leaving, I got fired. There's a pair of skates here that I got for you.' His boots, he said, 'Just give them to the doorman.' Pat was very generous." It was Wood who later sent one of his company trucks to collect the items Burns wanted transported, including the large framed blowup photograph of him astride his Harley, shot by a *Star* photographer at the zenith of the coach's celebrity in Toronto.

He'd made just a brief stop at the Gardens—glancing around one last time from the bench that was no longer his. The ex-Leaf coach got in his truck and disappeared into the night. He left behind a team in ruins, an angry press corps and, at the Toronto Zoo, a Siberian tiger that a besotted admirer had sponsored, paying five hundred bucks for the magnificent creature to be given the name "Burnsie."

Chapter Seventeen
Butting Heads in Beantown

"The Bruins in 2000 are Saigon in 1975."

IN THE BOSTON DRESSING ROOM, the two men eye each other intently. Harry Sinden is looking for a coach and Pat Burns is looking for a job. The applicant is indisputably qualified, yet Sinden feels a tug of unease. There is so much conflicting history, vivid scars from old wars. Sinden has to ask: "Pat, you were a Montreal Canadien. I'm having a tough time believing you could ever be a Bruin. Can you? Can you be a Bruin?" When Burns answers, Sinden studies his body language carefully. "If I'm on this team, Harry, I'll be the best Bruin you've got."

Says Sinden: "He convinced me."

Michael Jackson and Lisa Marie Presley. Tie Domi and Belinda Stronach. Charles and Diana. Odd couples that just didn't fit together, doomed from the moment their orbits collided. Add to that list the dominant-male-on-dominant-male pairing of Sinden and Burns. Not because they had so little in common, but probably because they were so much alike temperamentally: volatile, and thus destined to trigger each other's firing pins. Immovable object, meet irresistible force. Sinden was president and general manager of the Boston Bruins, penny-pinching feudal lord of all that he surveyed on Causeway Street, especially with a majority owner, Jeremy Jacobs, who preferred living in Buffalo. Forever mythologized as the skipper who led Team Canada to victory over the Soviets in the '72 Summit Series, Sinden never quite shed his coaching skin. Whoever prowled behind the Bruins bench would have Sinden peering over his shoulder as meddler and quibbler. The man couldn't help it.

Mike Milbury, prototypical Bruin and no trembling faint-heart, tells a story. "I'm coaching my first year in Boston and we get to the All-Star break, two games left to play. We play in Hartford, win that game, now we have one left before a four-day weekend, and we're in first place overall. It's my first year coaching and I'm feeling pretty good about myself. We get back to Boston at one o'clock in the morning. I call off the morning skate for the next day, but I go in to look at some tape. I get a call from Harry: 'Come up and see me in my office.' So I walk in, first place, won the night before, nothing really to worry about. I sit down and Harry says, 'You fucking think it's over, Mike? You think the break has fucking started, don't ya? You think you're gonna come in here tonight and win this fucking game, two points, but you're on vacation already, just like the rest of these fucking guys.' I was sweating bullets. I left, came back at five o'clock, locked the dressing room door, kicked over chairs, screamed at everybody. And wouldn't you know it—that was one of the best regular-season games we had all year. See, one of Harry's favourite expressions was, 'Hockey isn't like bridge; you can't pass. You have to show up and play.' He was an outstanding coach. But he came in talking like a guy who had coached a Stanley Cup championship team and a guy who had coached the Canadian national team over the Russians in 1972. Harry was demanding on his coaches because he felt—and with good reason—that he knew the right approach to coaching. And Pat Burns was not one to shy away from a confrontation, either. He did not have, shall we say, a politically correct nature."

That they joined forces in 1997 took hockey people aback. "It would have been unthinkable forty years earlier," says Serge Savard, recalling the playoff-driven hatred between Montreal and Boston that all but precluded coaching in one franchise and then the other, even with a Toronto stop-off in between. "I don't know why Pat went to Boston," says Cliff Fletcher, shaking his head. "It was ridiculous what happened there."

There was no mystery to it. Burns was a supplicant, driven to distraction after spending an entire season on the sidelines, with his thumbs up his arse. After getting the hook in Toronto, he'd retreated to Magog, content to sit tight for a while, thoroughly anticipating that job offers would be plentiful over the summer. It appeared likely there would be vacancies in San Jose and Vancouver, to name just a couple of possible destinations. To keep himself occupied in the interim, Burns accepted a six-week contract to provide daily hockey commentary on a Montreal French radio station, CKAC, during the playoffs. He also leapt at a short-term gig to express his thoughts in English during intermissions of first-round playoff games for The Sports Network. Encroaching a tad on Don Cherry's domain as king of the two-cent coach's corner opinion, these rhetorical sessions provided a nice temporary focus for Burns's energies and kept him in the loop. To his own bemusement— because he'd crossed over, however fleetingly, to the media dark side—the unemployed coach proved adroit at extemporizing and opinionating. The time-filler cameos expanded so that eventually Burns was making use of his vocal cords on several AM stations. "You can do radio with your hair messed up," he snickered. "You can be lying on your couch with a beer." Radio also led to his encounter with a divorced mother of two adolescent children, Line Cignac, who was working in promotions. Burns fell head over heels. "I've met someone," he told close friend Kevin Dixon.

Where real hockey was concerned, Burns thought he had the luxury of being choosy, cheques still coming in from that one-year-outstanding Toronto salary. Perhaps vainly, he considered himself a hot commodity. Surely another club would come knocking? As the months flew by, however, GMs were not beating a path to his door in the Eastern Townships. He started to squirm. "What happens if the phone never rings? What happens if no one wants you?" When the next season got under way, Burns wrung his hands over maybe being yesterday's man. He had to accept the fact that his road back to the NHL now depended on some other poor coaching fraternity mook getting canned.

There are always in-season firings. Perplexingly, overtures to Burns were more of the just-looking, not-buying variety. In February, he popped up in Toronto to promote a new line of snowmobiles and provided sound bites for the local press contingent, refraining from making any negative remarks about the chaotic Leaf franchise. "Brother, do I miss hockey, the scrap and challenge of it? I can't wait to get back at it, and I will, but only if the situation is right." In fact, Burns was regularly on the blower, urging his agent-cousin Robin Burns to shop his services around at any whiff of an opening. As a between-periods commentator for Montreal's RDS game broadcasts, he kept himself close to the franchise where his NHL career had sprouted. When the Habs were ushered out of the playoffs by New Jersey in five first-round games and sophomore coach Mario Tremblay was given the heave-ho, Burns expressed interest, with reservations. "I'd have to think about it. I want to coach again in the NHL, but do I want to coach here? I'm on television now; I'm nice and popular. You become the coach, you become a target."

Quietly, he did throw his hat in the ring, formalizing his candidacy. Simultaneously, other vacancies arose—Phoenix, Pittsburgh, San Jose and, most enticingly, Boston. The Bruins, finishing dead last in the NHL and missing the playoffs for the first time in three decades, had fired phlegmatic coach Steve Kasper. Another Original Six team, however currently sad-sack, had Burns licking his lips. But he was not Sinden's first choice. The GM was wooing Boston University's Jack Parker, the most highly regarded coach in the U.S. college ranks. Only when Parker rebuffed the offer did Sinden turn his beady eyes towards Plan B—Burns, who was on his way back from a Florida vacation when Sinden invited him in for a feeler chat.

"Pat reminded me a lot of a couple of coaches that I'd had—I'm referring to Don Cherry and Mike Milbury—in his attitude, his demeanour, his personality," says Sinden, recalling that long meeting in May 1997 that took place in the Bruins dressing room, assistant GM Mike O'Connell also present. "He wasn't a tactician or strategy guy as they were, but I thought Pat had handled his teams the same way. His background was similar to mine. He grew up in the city streets and had been a cop; I was a guy who'd worked at General Motors. It seemed to me that he would be a good fit for us. I just had this feeling that he could be a Bruin."

Burns later recounted that interview conversation to his pal Chris Wood, who was flabbergasted at the career choice. "He called me up and said, 'Woody, I'm going to BAWWSTON.' I told him, 'Listen, I was a big Montreal fan and I became a Toronto fan because of you. But the Boston Bruins? Love you buddy, but no way can I be a Bruins fan.' And Pat chuckled, 'You know, Woody, neither can I.' But, honestly, why wouldn't he have gone to Boston? It had been a long period between Toronto and the Bruins' offer. All coaches second-guess themselves, worry about never getting another job. I don't think Pat had any other serious offers. And it was a lucrative deal for him, his first (almost) million-dollar contract. But Harry turned out to be a tyrant."

Others tried to dissuade Burns as well: Get a grip, Pat. This is so not smart. He pooh-poohed the negative advice.

For the interview, he arrived in Boston with Robin Burns and Kevin Dixon. Robin, former NHL journeyman and successful entrepreneur—his hockey equipment company, Itech, became third largest in its specialty—had taken over from Don Meehan when rule changes prohibited agents from representing both coaches and players. "Harry had put us at a hotel on the other side of town. Pat signed in as Patrick Jonathan. We were really being hidden away. I guess Harry didn't want people to know that he was talking to us. But the first guy we run into in the lobby goes, 'Hey, Burnsie, you here to sign with the Bruins?' Big secret."

Burns enjoyed a degree of celebrity in New England, at least among those who followed the game. Dropping into a Lake Placid bar during his sabbatical from coaching, a ballsy waitress once beseeched Burns to autograph her bra. "So he signed, right on the hooter," Robin laughs.

Following the discussion with Sinden, the Burnses and Dixon retired to their hotel suite and promptly got pie-eyed. Dixon dipped into Burns's bag, removed all the underwear, soaked the skivvies in water and tossed them out the window. "Pat's yelling at us—'You fuckers! You better have kept a pair for me to wear tomorrow!'" It was Robin who hammered out the contract details. "I told Pat, 'We're going after four years because Harry will fire you after three.'" Burns pulled a face. "I'm not going to be fired." Robin warned: "Listen, Pat, I'm telling you the truth. Harry will fire you." So Robin Burns pushed for that deal and got it, with seasonal raises that brought the contract to $950,000 in the fourth year. "I knew Harry didn't want to break the million-dollar barrier, psychologically. But we had what we wanted. And that first year in Boston for Pat was . . . magical."

In Boston, Burns was no longer the son of a French-Canadian mother but the son of an Irish father, his cop cred the cherry on top. What could be more seductive for Beantown, with its romanticized Irish working-class ethos and police-shield stock characters? At his introductory press conference—held a week after Slick Rick Pitino was anointed Celtics coach and Svengali—Burns even revised that oft-told childhood anecdote about crying over the Chicago Blackhawks sweater a relative had bought him. Now it was a Boston Bruins jersey with Johnny Bucyk's name on the back. "This was when Rocket Richard, Montreal's No. 9, was the hottest thing since sliced bread," he told a local media corps instantly charmed. "I had to fight my way on the ice, off the ice, and all the way home. But it was mine." Whatever. He went so far as referring to his off-season home "in Vermont." Magog hadn't moved across the border, but Lake Memphremagog did dip partway into the U.S. state.

With his four-year pact, Burns became only the second man (Dick Irvin the other) to lead half of the NHL's six traditional teams. In a city of dynamic Big Coaches, Burns could more than hold his own. He affixed a black-and-gold Bs licence plate to his Chevy 4X4 and slapped a Bruins sticker on the side of his Harley. Red Sox pitching ace Roger Clemens had just defected for Toronto. It was only fair that Boston got charismatic Burns as compensation.

Pshaw, Burns scoffed to media queries that he might come to grief with the club president. "Everybody is afraid of the myth of Harry Sinden. Harry Sinden believes in one thing: being loyal to a team and winning.

He's an old-school guy, and I like that. I think it's important to be loyal. Don't you think it's about time we started getting back to that?" Sure, he was schmoozing the boss, but Sinden was glowingly approving in this first-trimester phase of their relationship. The notoriously skinflint Bruins organization had assured Burns they'd loosen the purse strings and sign quality talent. Sinden was agreeable when his coach quickly reached out to Dave Ellett, a favourite from Toronto days. Ellett was a free agent. "It was the first call I got, Pat phoning me directly. He said, 'I want you here—what's it going to take?' I was nervous about going to Boston. The organization had a bad reputation and my agent tried to talk me out of it. But I had discussions with Pat and he assured me that things had changed there." Ellett became a Bruin. Then Burns coaxed Ken Baumgartner—enforcer with the face of a damaged angel and part-time MBA student—into the Boston fold. "You guys are gonna love the Bomber!" he crowed to reporters.

The Bruins had just come off a ghastly season in which they'd committed the double crime of being both bad and boring. In Burns, Sinden had banked on a persona who would help fill the seats at the new FleetCenter and staunch the bleed of bailing season-ticket holders. A high-profile coach was part of the blueprint to rebuild the franchise. The other pillar of Bruin rejuvenation was a seventeen-year-old by the name of Joe Thornton, Boston's salve for finishing last in the then-twenty-six-team NHL. The six-foot-four-inch teenager was the first-overall selection in the entry draft and the most highly touted hope since Bobby Orr. With their second pick, eighth overall, the Bruins took Russian mini-bull Sergei Samsonov. "I patted him on the shoulder," marvelled Burns. "It was like patting a rock."

So, the Bruins had legendary defenceman Raymond Bourque, a couple of projected stars who could just as easily flame out, and a bunch of other guys Burns admitted he'd never heard of. Assembling his new charges at training camp, a chaw of tobacco shoved beneath his upper lip, the coach declared, "Unless you're Raymond Bourque, I don't know you." As an aside, he added: "I have ties and underwear older than some of those guys out there."

Rapped as a coach who cleaved to veterans and couldn't manage youngsters well—as if he'd never developed kids in juniors who stepped directly into the NHL—Burns pledged to be patient with his fledglings and balance sternness with praise. There was no doubt at camp that he had his players' attention. They were obedient and energetic, glad to have someone in charge who brought structure to their game plan, even though Burns could never be described as someone who excelled at Xs-and-Os instruction. As one columnist observed, "Burns is the kind of coach, who, when he senses a lull, refers to the front and back cover of his playbook; either side will suffice when used for hitting someone upside the head."

Burns was insistent, however, on bringing "Jumbo Joe" Thornton along slowly, with baby steps. "I will not make the same mistakes some teams do with their number-one draft choices." But he forgot who was really calling the shots. Here was sown the seed of his initial contretemps with Sinden. For the same reason Sinden had peeled open Boston's clammy wallet to pay Burns, he wanted full bang for his multimillion-bucks investment in Thornton. Just eighteen now, the curly-haired youth would put fannies in the seats and surely provide goal production spark. Burns wanted him to ripen in the minors. "Is it better to keep him here and not play him?" Burns asked, making his case in the media. "Or is it better that he go down, play in the World Junior tournament? We'll all have to sit down, management and the coaching staff, list all the fors and againsts. What's the best and proper decision for Joe Thornton?" Coach and GM argued heatedly about it, but this wasn't a battle Burns could possibly win. "We had this big stud, number-one pick," says Sinden. "He was the next Eric Lindros in everybody's mind. Pat looked at him and said, 'He's not ready.' But I felt that we couldn't send this kid down." The kid broke his arm in an exhibition game, slashed by Pittsburgh's Stu Barnes, so that deferred the issue for a bit. But he was in the lineup by game four of the regular season. Sinden—and his assistant, O'Connell, who concurred—could foist the youngster on Burns, but the coach controlled Thornton's ice time. Turning a deaf ear to Sinden, he eased the youth in gently, usually deployed on the fourth line, occasionally scratched entirely, such that, by his twenty-first NHL game, Thornton didn't have a single point. This was not going to earn the putative Boston saviour rookie-of-the-year laurels. "We kept him here but he didn't play much," says Sinden, reflecting on poor choices. "He was ready in some ways, but Joe was still a kid. Some of them come in at eighteen and they're fairly mature. Joe wasn't." With the wisdom of hindsight, Sinden concedes that Burns was on the button. "Pat was right on that one." It was Samsonov, with a year in the International Hockey League under his belt, who provided the buzz that year—and copped the rookie award at its conclusion.

The '97–98 Bruins came charging out of the gate, Burns, as was his forte, squeezing the most out of marginal players. "Pat's strength was that he got everyone in their right roles," says O'Connell. "It's really what he does best—gets people to become a team. He motivates each player to perform his role for the betterment of the team." It was big-yawn hockey, rigid and risk averse, but, in the coach's defence, he didn't have much to work with, and defence could be taught. A newspaper cartoon depicted Burns hypnotizing fans by dangling a puck like a watch fob. Queried about the merits of "The Trap," dead-zone hockey, he got his back up. "We had to give it a name, that's the worst thing we ever did. The positional play you're talking about? We don't play the trap. We play a positional game, and that has been going on for twenty-five years."

O'Connell fails to see the difference, as practised by Burns, while acknowledging management had known exactly what they were getting. "It was a trap mentality. Pat liked big, bruising guys but his was not a style that forced the issue. It was more of a classic 'let's wait, get in our position, and wait, and wait, and then we counter.' He'd done that everywhere he'd been. The trap was developed in the Montreal system, and that was Pat's belief. Everybody knew he was going to do it, but still, he was very good at getting them to do it, better than anyone else. And we won playing that style. Some of his ideas you might not agree with, but it's a very successful way of playing which many teams have adopted. It does enable teams without talent to win. It gives them a chance because of how it's structured. The NHL today, the way I look at it, there's five not-so-good teams and the other twenty-five are about the same."

On New Year's Eve 1997, Boston tied the Leafs 2–2 in Toronto, the first time Burns had graced the Gardens since packing hastily in the night. The Bruins were 17–17–7, vastly improved from the squad that had finished in the cellar eight months earlier. Their hockey may have been wincingly dull, but it was adequately effective because players had bought into the coach's vision. At the All-Star break, they ranked a solid sixth in the Eastern Conference, light years removed from the pitiful lot that brought Burns in as Original Six fix-it man. The postseason beckoned again. "You want to get to that 'Spring Dance,'" Burns enthused, "you'd better bring your Kodiak work boots and not your patent-leather shoes." A 4–1 win over the Islanders clinched the playoff berth on April 9, and Burns's name was touted once more for a Jack Adams award.

"The best coaches are the ones that keep people on their toes, keep players honest in terms of knowing what's expected of them," says Ray Bourque. "Pat made what was expected of us very clear from the beginning. He was a coach I learned a lot from. I'd never realized how detailed he was as a coach. This was a guy who believed you had to play defence—not just defencemen but centres and wingers too. He kept harping on it, and that's how his drills were set up. These are the drills I've brought along with me, coaching my sons' teams, and if I were ever to coach in the NHL—not that I would—the drills I would use. We practised them two or three times a week. Every single forward knew exactly what he had to do in the defensive zone. We were very, very well coached."

The turnaround was remarkable: the Bruins were thirty points better than the previous year. "It was a combination of things," says Bourque. "We had those two first-round picks. Sergei probably had a bigger impact than Joe off the bat. But we'd also signed some free agents and got a lot better in terms of talent and character, special guys like Rob DiMaio and Timmy Taylor, role players but major leaguers who were really important in the room. Probably we were a team that overachieved because a lot of people were not looking at us to have that kind of jump. And Pat was the one who jelled everything together."

Against Washington in the first round, the Bruins' Brigadoon season dissolved in six games, two of which went into double OT. Before game six, Burns shaved off the goatee he'd worn most of the year, hoping to change his team's luck, to no avail. Yet elimination didn't dampen the enthusiasm of a club that had pulled itself off the scrap heap. If Sinden and O'Connell yearned for razzle-dazzle, it was incumbent on them to lasso the talent in the off-season. Bring me the horses, said Burns, "and I'll give you tic-tac-toe. I don't think our style is boring, but you have to adapt to the team you have. Firewagon hockey, that's what we called it in the old days, like in the past with the Flying Frenchmen and the French Connection. That's all nice and fine if you have that personnel. But if you don't have it, you have to adapt."

Could the coach be any clearer? Or, with a third Jack Adams bestowed in June, any taller in the saddle? "This is our Academy Awards," Burns beamed in accepting the accolade. "We've directed films all year long, and there are stars of the movies . . . and you have the directors, who are the coaches." In a serene state of mind, he took Line to the Caribbean for a holiday. At the time of his hiring in Boston, Burns had warned his girlfriend, "I'm different in hockey than out of hockey." Line would find out, he said, "if she can stand me." Evidently, she could. The couple married in Anguilla. Bourque was the best man. "My wife and I were in St. Barts. We took a nice little boat ride over to where Pat and Line were." The foursome had become warm friends, Bourque's wife, Christiane, especially cozy with Line. Bourque remembers the lovely nuptials: "The ceremony was on the beach. We had dinner with them afterwards and went back to St. Barts that night."

In Boston, however, it was no longer all hearts and flowers. The first inkling that the coach's wishes were irrelevant came with management's failure to protect Ellett and Baumgartner in the expansion draft. Surviving the exposure, Ellett was relegated to bit player in his second Boston year.

He fingers assistant GM O'Connell as the villain. "He's the one who ended up pulling out the rug from under Burnsie because Burnsie didn't like him and wouldn't listen to him. That's why I got shit on there, because I was one of Pat's guys. First year, I never missed a game; then all of a sudden, in the second year, I'm in the press box. Pat told me, 'I can't help it. But once the playoffs start, it's my team and I can play who I want, and you're in.' The next year, they got rid of me."

Year two for Burns in Boston began with four key training-camp holdouts and a failed comeback attempt by Cam Neely. It soon became apparent the team seemed less cohesive than the year before. Tensions developed over ice time, especially for Samsonov, who experienced a midseason goal drought. A few stories appeared about things no longer so rosy in Black and Yellow Country. Ellett suspects some of these early anti-Burns barbs were planted by management "because they couldn't boss Pat around." Yet, to Ellett, Burns seemed happier and more relaxed. "Coaching had become more enjoyable for him. He learned that he didn't have to be as hard on people every day. It wasn't killer practices all the time, yelling and screaming. He was having fun."

The team was hard to figure out, though, consistent only in its inconsistency. O'Connell artlessly rebuked Burns's handling of Samsonov to a reporter. Stung, Burns swung back in a radio interview. "I don't question Mike's drafts. He has pressure once a year, and that's the twenty-seventh of June or whenever the draft is. Second-guessing will always be part of management and I think that's normal, but doing it publicly is another thing. I'm hurt. I would have appreciated it more if this had been talked about behind closed doors. Mike had an opportunity to coach this team before me. Maybe he thinks he should have been the coach. If Mike wants my job, he knows how to get it." O'Connell hastily apologized. "This is the last thing I wanted to happen." They kissed and made up but the war of words would escalate. "That was not a real compatible situation," says Sinden.

From January into February of that second season, the Bruins went into a 0–6–2 skid. Burns told Line to take a vacation by herself. Stress was making him more grouchy and distant than usual. "It changes your life around because you're taking it home more. Often, you'll sit there and people are talking to you and you don't hear them. My wife will be talking to me and she'll say, 'You're not listening to me.' And I'll say, 'Yup, I'm not.' It's because your mind is churning all the time."

Burns sought the opinion of everyone—from reporters to the FleetCenter's janitorial staff. "I'm not a one-man show. I listen to everybody, but I'm the one on the firing line. Sometimes I have a fraction of a second to make a decision. That's what I like about Harry. He's the best general manager I've ever had because he's been there as a coach, he knows. Serge was never there. Cliff was never there."

A late-season surge vaulted the Bruins over Buffalo into sixth place in the East. They finished with the exact same point total as '97–98 but had to work harder for it. In the opening playoff round, Boston drew Carolina as an opponent. It was a tight, closely contested affair with Bruins netminder Byron Dafoe—who racked up ten regular-season shutouts—a standout, impenetrable in two of the six games. That triumph got Boston one round further, but, for their labours, they now had to confront Buffalo and dominator goalkeeper Dominik Hasek. Bruins made the sublime Hasek look ordinary in game one of the Eastern Conference semifinals. Burns sought to extinguish some of Hasek's aura: "I think he let some goals in this year. His goals-against average was not zero, zero, zero—was it? The guy has been scored on before."

The Bruins dropped the next three. Burns rallied the troops after losing the fourth game 4–1. "It was an old-fashioned ass-booting. But it's not how you get put down on your ass. It's how you get back up." Boston staved off elimination with a 5–3 win in game five at the FleetCenter, then headed for a game six engagement at the Marine Midland Arena. "Order the chicken wings, because we're coming!" With the Sabres producing their best effort of the postseason, however, there was no rejoicing over wings and beer. Buffalo prevailed 3–2 and took the series in six. Burns shook off the disappointment. By his yardstick, the team had measured up. "We played hard right to the buzzer. You have to be proud of those guys, and I am."

Sinden wasn't, much. On the morning after playoff expulsion, the players woke up to a newspaper broadside from Sinden. With the exception of Bourque, fumed the GM, his best Bruins hadn't been up to the task. "The coaching staff did a great job. They tried traps, they tried forechecking, they tried everything. It was a player issue." He singled out Jason Allison (training camp holdout) and Dmitri Khristich (arbitration) for particular denunciation, which deeply upset everyone on the team. Standing up to Sinden, Allison shot back: "It seems like it's someone different's fault every year. How many years has it been since we got out of the first round? What has it been, 10 different coaches and 500 different players? So, it's my fault this time, I guess. I'll take the blame." Khristich snorted: "Carve everybody up. That's how it's done."

Burns was not despondent—yet. But Sinden did nothing to upgrade the roster over the summer except sign Dave Andreychuk to a one-year deal. Quality guys such as Tim Taylor were allowed to flee as free agents. Boston simply walked away from Khristich's arbitration award. Dafoe missed training camp and the first month of the 1999–2000 season, sitting at home in California while Sinden played hardball on a new contract. Consequently, the Bruins had their worst start in thirty-five years, not recording their first win until the tenth game.

The coach had a reputation for diminishing returns: year one was always marked by extraordinary enhancement; year two, a slight setback; year three, all-out regression seeps in. There it was again, the stigma: three-year coach with a four-year contract. "That was the book on Pat," says Sinden. "They can take him for a year or two and then they tune out. I wouldn't necessary say that was the case here. I wish we had been able to give him some better players." Sinden argued more strenuously for an attack philosophy—livelier, pouncing, take it to them. Meanwhile, Burns struggled to cobble together some momentum, halt the losing, and the only way he saw of doing that was to reinforce defensive discipline. GM and coach were at counter-purposes. "I felt we should be a more aggressive, attacking team and he didn't," says Sinden. "I remember saying to him once, 'Pat, I've seen teams play a 1–2–2 or a 2–3, but you play a 0–5. That pissed him off." Dogmatic, Burns reiterated: "This is the way I'm going to be, whether fans like it or not. What fans want is a winning team. That's what markets a hockey club—winning."

It was to be an *annus horribilis*, a traumatizing season for everybody, but especially for Burns and Bourque. One of them—the less likely choice—would not survive that season in Boston, would verily fling his body over the wall to escape the madness.

A dark sense of foreboding hung over the whole outfit. Burns became more vocal in emphasizing the paltry elements he'd been given to craft a team. Then he turned around and accused the players he did have of being "mopers." "We can't sit around and feel sorry for ourselves. Who are we to question how they're going to spend their money? We're not in any position to disagree. Who am I? I'm just an employee, just a number in [the] company. I've spoken to Mr. Jacobs twice in my life. So it's not up to me to decide that, and it's certainly not up to the players. You have a job to do as a professional athlete. You're paid to go out and perform. Go out and do it. We've got to quit pissing and moaning about things that have happened and get to saying, 'Hey, we have to go forward with this.' We have to get the passion back into the game. You can't win without emotion, and right now it's not there."

His emotions were close to the surface, apparent in an excessive—even for Burns—expletive-laced tirade following a loss to Ottawa. He erupted at Sinden when the GM attended a practice and made critical comments. "He was just going out on the ice, and I said something to him about the team," Sinden remembers. "And he said, 'Oh, you're so out of date on this stuff,' and kept walking. That just galled me. I hadn't been coaching the team, but I'd watched every game for about thirty-five years. I was not out of date."

By Burns's reckoning, he was staying the course. He refused to push the panic button and, significantly, the players expressed confidence in him. The ship righted itself temporarily, went on an excellent 9–1–2 roll, then heaved and lurched again, pounded 9–3 by Chicago. "Let's not get too depressed," Burns reasoned. "Let's not be talking suicide." Recklessly, he took another bite at management's shin, via his roster. "I don't care if the Lord is behind the bench and Moses is the GM. If our top line is not scoring, we can't win."

At Christmas, the doomsday chorus was *in viva voce* with rampant speculation Burns would be pink-slipped. By December 29, Boston had won just twice in thirteen games. Sinden flew to East Rutherford with the sole purpose of stifling rumours the coach was about to walk the plank. "I was as firm as I can be to make them understand that this is not going to happen," he told reporters. The Bs lost to Jersey anyway.

Boston staggered into the new year, a sourpuss Burns sparring more frequently and caustically with journalists. The pattern was repeating: It's not *my* fault. I can't score goals for them. Woe is me. Then, from Buffalo, owner Jacobs twisted the dagger. "I think our team has been managed well by Harry and Mike," he told the *Boston Globe*. "But our coaching has not been what I think it should be. I think our coaches need to do a better job. I don't feel our fans are getting what they deserve. They should be getting better than what we've done." Burns, appalled and offended, assailed on all sides, could hardly repudiate the owner. "I can understand Jeremy's position. When you own a multimillion-dollar business, you can damn well criticize who you want." It didn't help matters that, after Jacobs had invited the entire team to dinner at his second home in West Palm Beach, one player was anonymously quoted in the *Boston Herald,* dripping resentment: "The guy nickel-and-dimed us, and we all get to go see how rich he is."

Sinden gave his coach another vote of confidence. O'Connell didn't. The players had Burns's back, though, turning on one of their own, Joe Murphy, when the winger lambasted his coach from the bench during a game against the Senators, belching obscenities because he'd been nailed to the pine. Murphy was suspended for "insubordination" and no teammate came to his defence. There had been previous, vehement, squabbles between Murphy and Burns in the dressing room, but the coach had never before in his career been subjected to such blatant mutiny by a player. "It had happened on the bench a couple of times," he revealed. "I think it's a question of respect. I think the players were having enough. I was having enough, too." He added: "A great coach once told me, you're a great coach when you've been told to F-off five times. But the sixth time, you have to do something." Murphy was sent to no man's land—and then to Washington.

Following another listless loss, Burns was livid, angrily kicking a door open at the FleetCenter, slamming his office door so forcefully that the dressing room rattled. He emerged only to drag players out of the exercise room, where media isn't allowed, ordering them back to the dressing room to face the music. "Get in there right now!" he screamed.

By March, even Bourque—the most loyal, selfless of Bruins, five times a Norris Trophy winner—had reached the end of his rope with all the wackiness in the Hub. He requested a trade, preferably to Philadelphia. Sinden sent him to Colorado. His leave-taking, with a press conference at Logan Airport, the Bourque children tearfully watching Dad depart, was gut-wrenching and melancholy. The iconic captain had discussed his intentions with Burns. "Pat was always very respectful towards me," says Bourque. "He recognized how I went about my business, how I worked out, how I practised, and how I played. I was forty then—not quite Pat's age, but pretty close. I felt close to Pat as someone I could relate to. But that third year . . . it was not pretty. By then, it was a totally different team, all the character guys we'd lost. I didn't think we had much to work with, trying to make the playoffs. For the most part, we went out there and worked hard, but it just wasn't going to happen. Pat realized that, I realized that. I was always one to go to the rink with a big smile on my face, a guy that was positive. But it was tough to be positive anymore. Everybody realized, like I did at that point, there's nothing here." At the end of his last game as a Bruin, a 3–0 loss to Philly, Bourque collected the puck as a memento. *Au revoir, Ray.* (A year later, in the last game of a glorious career, Bourque and the Avalanche hoisted the Stanley Cup joyously.)

As Bourque flew westward on a private jet, Burns rued the end of an era, but advocated team reconciliation. Wrung out from all the melodrama, he urged a ceasefire with management. "I just hope the mudslinging stops. I've had enough of that. I'm so tired of it—who's at fault, what happened . . ." Writing about Bourque's departure in the *Herald*, Michael Gee humorously observed: "The surprise was that Pat Burns didn't climb onto a wheel strut before takeoff. The Bruins in 2000 are Saigon in 1975. The only sane destination is out."

Sanity, or something slightly resembling it, was restored. Sinden wasn't exactly bolstering his coach, however. "We haven't given up on Pat Burns. We'll sit down at the end of the season and we'll evaluate our situation." Media buzzards were circling, scenting carrion. In fact, Sinden was ready to drop the guillotine as the countdown began towards mathematical elimination from the postseason. And then he hesitated—a cynic might say from abhorrence of having to shell out Burns's guaranteed severance. Burns, sadomasochistic maybe, made it clear he wanted to come back the next year. Faced with widespread pushback—from reporters, from fans, from season-ticket holders—Sinden relented and stayed his hand.

"We had conversations about things changing, and I was satisfied," he says. "But things didn't change." Burns had promised to eschew his suffocating trap style, allow for more creativity, be mindful of Sinden's directives. When the season rolled around, though, the Bruins were just as static as ever, despite a couple of wins to start. Burns's respite from termination lasted for all of eight games. A dismal road trip wrote the epitaph to his tenure as a Bruin. Boarding the return flight to Boston, he was heard softly singing, "Leavin' on a jet plane, don't know when I'll be back again . . ."

Sinden pulled the plug on October 25, 2000. "We were losing and we were not entertaining. We were playing the same old way. Pat was still doing it his own way, always his own way. Mike O'Connell was the guy really pushing for it. He felt we had to make a change."

His third year in Boston, amidst the initial flurry of firing rumours, Burns had defied convention and purchased a property—a horse ranch, minus the ponies. The spread was actually situated in New Hampshire, which made him an out-of-state-coach, though he maintained a pied-à-terre in Boston. Now he was an out-of-work coach, but he and Line didn't sell the home. They loved the house, the secluded location. In the nearby town of Laconia, Burns held court with the media a few days after being axed, at Patrick's Pub, natch. By then, he had the script down pat. The firing phone call, he related with a chortle, had come at 7 a.m. "That's an early time of day to be fired."

Without acrimony, apparently devoid of anger, Burns laid out his case: he did try to adapt, he wasn't a one-dimensional coach and he had heeded Sinden. "Harry's an original." And no, of course he was not done coaching yet. "I'm just a simple guy, trying to get through life. I want to go down the road with as few problems as I can. This is just a bump in that road."

The evening before, Burns had watched the Bruins on TV beating the Washington Capitals 4–1. They were coached by his good pal Mike Keenan, a handy hire for Sinden because Iron Mike lived in Boston. Burns insisted that Keenan stepping into his shoes would not affect their friendship. Cousin Robin Burns says different. "He was hurt."

A week later, Sinden fired himself as general manager, bowing out to his protégé O'Connell, but keeping his president title. He was still, in effect, the boss. By the spring of 2012, O'Connell was long gone and Sinden still had an executive office as "senior advisor to the owner of the Boston Bruins." Reminiscing about the banishment of Burns, there's a hint of regret in his voice.

"I've got to say, there was probably some compulsion on my part. Sometimes, you make these moves compulsively, and when you look back, you think maybe you should have given it more time. You question yourself afterwards. That might have been the case with Pat. But we gave him a good shot."

Mike Keenan was released at the end of the 2000–01 season.

Chapter Eighteen
Redemption in Meadowlands

"I was out of hockey for two years and you said I would never be back . . ."

PAT BURNS PICKED UP Lou Lamoriello at the airport in his truck, brought the wily hockey sage back to his horseless ranch in New Hampshire, and introduced him to wife Line and pet boxer Roxie. That warm June afternoon, they spent three hours on the front porch, talking.

It doesn't take long in hockey to become yesterday's man. The coaching merry-go-round routinely discards passengers deemed to have taken one spin too many. Predominant styles alter, assets become liabilities, what was new gets old. As with athletes, those coming up through the ranks push out those suspected of being on a downward trajectory. The game, impatient, never stands still. Hubris is visited upon the ego-driven. Stanley Cup rings are no guarantee of future employment, and Burns didn't own such bling anyway. The nakedness of his fingers was not necessarily due to a quirk of fate. Of all his teams, in three Original Six cities, only one had persevered into a Cup final. In a thirty-club NHL, regular-season winning percentage equated to no more than a false positive—just another also-ran.

A dozen years behind the bench, more or less, and what did Burns have to show for it? The apogee of his career had been reached in his first year with Montreal, an eye-blink removed from cop days, and he hadn't scaled that playoff crest again. It ate at him. The big five-oh had come and gone. He was financially set and needn't ever work again. But what was a healthy middle-aged man to do with the rest of his life? So scant were the opportunities, demand overwhelmed by supply, that Burns—two years on the blocks—even considered coaching U.S. college hockey. There had been one alluring job prospect when it appeared Paul Maurice was on the bubble in Carolina. Burns told friends if the 'Canes didn't win their game that night, he'd been lined up as replacement. But they did win, Maurice survived to be cashiered another day, and the window of opportunity slammed shut.

These were some of the matters that Lamoriello, the Meadowlands Mega-Mind, had arrived to kick around, speaking frankly in that New England "ayuh" accent, with its occluded *R*s and dropped gerunds, a mélange of "Rhode Island, New Jersey and Quebec," as the Devils' czar describes it. He was in the market for a bench boss, having canned yet another, Kevin Constantine, but the Jersey franchise had quite specific requisites: the Devils *desideratum*. This was not a team in convulsions, a disaster to be overhauled, turning its imploring eyes to a miracle-working coach like Burns. No cleanup in Aisle 5. They'd won the whole enchilada two years earlier, in 2000, and had come within a game of repeating in 2001, though there was a first-round exit, passionless and punchless, from the 2002 playoffs. Jersey was rarely far from the inner circle of contenders. As a franchise, the Devils had their own way of doing things, which wasn't flashy or histrionic. Psychologically, they were outliers, marching to a monotonous drum beat, anonymous and controversy-free. Except for their devotion to a defensive doctrine, Jersey was the antithesis of a Pat Burns club: even-keeled, almost anal.

Yet Lamoriello liked the cut of Burns's jib, sensed there might be a mutually beneficial alignment here, if this candidate could dispel his doubts. "Pat was without question one of the best bench coaches in the game, in the way he could adjust on the fly, in what he demanded from his players. We were a team that had the talent to be a success, but we'd slipped a little. We'd felt too good about ourselves, thinking maybe we were better than we were. We needed somebody strong to change that attitude. I said to Pat, 'The one thing you haven't done is you haven't won a Stanley Cup. In my opinion, this team has a chance, but it needs a certain type of coach. And it doesn't need, maybe, the coach that you've been up to now. It needs *you* to change. When I say change, not change what you know but maybe change certain things about the way you are.'" The way you *ahhhr*.

Burns listened and was almost too eager in trying to convince that he could reinvent himself. Lamoriello shook his head. He wasn't getting it, this keen-to-coach fellow. "I think he was surprised at how straightforward I was. Pat was an insecure person—most people didn't realize that. He couldn't understand why he was in the position of not coaching. I said, 'It's simple: you were a coach who wore yourself out and you wore on the players. Because you get them to a point where they can have success, and then you lose them.' He didn't know why that happened. But it's easy to do. It's because when you start getting better and better, you begin to think, 'It's me.' And you forget it's the players. As soon as they recognize that you think it's you, and *you* think it's you, then you're in trouble."

Burns had never had such a conversation with a GM, someone who seemed able to look into his soul and not like everything, but not recoil either. He felt stripped, naked, and a little bit reborn. "I wanted him to look at things differently, to trust me," Lamoriello continues. "I told him what he had to do was love his players a little more rather than show that he was tough. Tough is what you do, not what you say. And you've got to let the players love you back."

Uncharacteristically, Burns divulged things, secrets he'd shared only with the most intimate of friends, unburdening. "He had scars," says Lamoriello. "Scars don't go away; they heal, but they don't go away. How you live with them determines the person you become." Lamoriello explained the ethos of his distinctive team and the "Devils way"; that he didn't believe he had all the answers, but he had enough; that Burns could disagree when he felt there was merit, could argue as heatedly as he wished, with the general manager and the players, but there would be no tolerance for grudges or backdoor manipulation, and no spiting of individuals that might poison the environment.

In Lamoriello's concept of "team," the coach was an important component, but he shouldn't be the star and he mustn't be a bully. "One thing about a team that has success: you have to give up your own identity. That was basically the conversation in New Hampshire. I said, 'Pat, if you're willing to give up your identity to bring your tools—because you do have the tools—you'll be a hell of a coach with us. They'll respond, these kids, because they already know how to win. They've won before. Right now, they need the push and the hold—you have to push them as far as you can, but never far enough that you can't catch 'em. If you want to push them and lose them, it's not going to work.'"

Lamoriello shared the wisdom of his vast experience. If things go south, he cautioned, don't panic; that will only freak out the players. Don't harp on what's going wrong; emphasize what should be done to make it right. "You can't have players worrying about what you're thinking. When you reprimand a player, remember that you're not reprimanding the person. You've got to separate the two. If you're not happy with a guy as a player, when he gets on the bus, that doesn't mean you don't look at him, you don't say good morning. You look at him. That's what I mean about loving. If you're talking with them in your office about hockey, don't bring up their behaviour off the ice and say you're a horseshit player too. When a reporter writes bad things, the worst thing in the world you can do is say something to them about it. Just look him or her in the eye and say good morning. You're going to gain a lot more respect, and they're going to think about it. Pat needed the same thing that he needed to give the players. He needed to be kicked in the ass and loved."

They had probed one another, neither finding the other wanting. This will work just fine, Lamoriello concluded. "Pat, before you decide, make sure this is the job you want." There was at least one other team making overtures that Lamoriello knew of. "It should be the Devils, but I want you to think about what we've talked about here.' It was never about contracts or money, that stuff wasn't even an issue. It was about Pat, me, the team, and winning."

On that June 2002 afternoon, both men oblivious of the hours passing, the sun's rays slanting across the porch, they made a tacit covenant. It was the beginning of a beautiful friendship.

Burns embraced the "Devils way." The night before training camp opened, he shaved off his Vandyke beard because Lamoriello didn't allow chin hair on his team. For good measure, he even got rid of his signature moustache. Jersey's new coach was ready to drop the mask. He took over a team that had retained the imprimatur of Jacques Lemaire, whose conservative style led the Devils to their first of two Cups at the tail end of the millennium. The club was loaded with veteran talent, had a well-stocked farm system and was anchored by the consistently brilliant goaltending of Martin Brodeur. They were getting long in the tooth on the back end, captain Scott Stevens and Ken Daneyko both thirty-eight years old. The real problem would be scoring goals, with Bobby Holik having bolted to the Rangers, Petr Sykora dealt away and Jason Arnott gone, too. This was hardly a new conundrum for Burns, however, long accused of an aversion to offence—which wasn't strictly true. An examination of his record shows that forwards with flair, such as Doug Gilmour, had their most productive seasons under Burns. He simply demanded accountability at both ends of the ice. But there was unlikely to be defence-first grumbling from a squad nurtured on the virtues of the neutral-zone trap.

At South Mountain Arena in East Orange, Burns arrived for the first morning of training camp before 7 a.m. "I was dying for everyone to get on the ice. It's like you've never missed a day. I wouldn't call it nervous, but you're anxious, pumped." Mindful of Lamoriello's advice, he was polite yet discreet with local media, unwilling to engage in typical Burnsian patter, stressing that he had evolved and adapted—somewhat—from the relentless authoritarian of olden days. "I've calmed down since then. I still believe in discipline. I still have that same desire to win. I'll let players do what they want to do, but they can only push me to a certain extreme." There would be fewer one-on-one interviews and, Burns had resolved, no cult of the coach. No commercial endorsements, either.

Outwardly, he appeared the same, if slightly trimmer of figure and clean-shaven for the first time in twenty-seven years. He bellowed during drills ("There's a difference between being loud and being mad"), pounded on the boards with his stick, ordered delinquents to give him ten pushups pronto and, when mistakes were committed, had all players drop flat on the ice and roll in the shavings, a weird little exercise he'd adopted way back in juniors. But this was a team on the same general wavelength as their coach: defensive-zone coverage, neutral-zone pressure and offence when chances permitted.

Brodeur, then as now the cornerstone of the franchise, had known Burns only peripherally. He'd been a kid and Canadiens fans when Burns coached Montreal, accompanying his photographer father to the rink, and had later listened to Burns's hockey commentary on radio and TV. "When he took the job in New Jersey, I didn't know him, but I knew him, you know? And he turned out to be exactly as he appeared—a pretty adamant guy and not two-faced. Pat is Pat. By watching him coach, the way he spoke, such a confident person, it made you feel good."

Brodeur recalls their shared passion for motorcycles. "He's the one who came with me when I picked up my first bike. He took me to the dealership and rolled along beside me when we left because it was the first time I was riding it." Burns, no idiot, quickly made an ally of Brodeur. Sometimes, when he thought the team was veering towards complacency and needed a smack upside the head, he'd give Brodeur advance warning—watch this—then arrange his face into boot-camp sergeant demeanour. "One day, we were sitting, just talking, and Pat says, 'Go sit down—I've got to snap at the team now.' So he comes into the dressing room and he throws the Gatorade bottle down, starts breaking sticks. Oh my God, it was funny. Then he looks at me, like, 'How was that?'"

Mostly, Brodeur was impressed by how smoothly Burns blended into the Devils culture. "Coming into our organization, well, Lou's not the easiest guy to deal with. Pat didn't feel threatened being around someone who had that much power. So, as players, we didn't have to feel threatened about the big guy; we just had to worry about pleasing our coach. We kind of forgot about Lou overlooking everything with his eagle eye. Pat was the boss. New Jersey is different from other places in the league, with the way Lou does things.

"Pat got there and he definitely had to clean himself up, shave the goatee, cut his hair." Brodeur chuckles. "That was probably the hardest thing for Pat, because he didn't look like a biker anymore. But he embraced it. He became one of us."

Burns debuted his thirteenth season as an NHL head coach with a road win over Ottawa and another against the Columbus Blue Jackets at home. At every turn, Burns avoided talking about himself. His postgame press conferences were terse, two-minute affairs. The only controversy erupted when head case Mike Danton was sent back to Jersey from a road trip after he'd offered candid comments to a newspaper about his limited ice time, and that was a Lamoriello decision. Burns had banned Danton's odious agent, David Frost, from practices. (Years later, during Frost's trial on charges of sexual exploitation, Burns was revolted that the decertified agent and former junior coach had compared himself to Burns.)

The Devils won six of seven in early October and boasted the league's stingiest defence, but attendance at Continental Airlines Arena was abysmal, the venue often less than half full. "I looked up, and there didn't seem to be a lot of people," Burns noted. "For a 6–1 team, that was surprising."

Through their first twenty-five games, Jersey had a 15–7–1–2 record, winning eleven of those in matches decided by one goal. They held down first place in the Atlantic Division. Yet Burns was steadfastly dour, casting his withering gaze from behind the bench. "Don't judge me by my bad mood," he attempted to explain. "I'm not a pleasant person to be around. You probably wouldn't like to be my friend."

His mood fluctuations, which ran the gamut from A to B, amused Brodeur. "He'd come in with the hat pulled down over his forehead and this expression on his face, you'd know—'Oops, he's pissed, practice is going to be hard today.' Other days he'd be happy, so we were happy." Either way, all the players were attentive to Burns's instructions. "He wasn't a technician, it was more raw than that," analyzes Brodeur. "He'd say, 'This is what we've got to work on.' Lemaire was a coach who could pinpoint something on the ice like it was a carpet, tell us, 'Listen, this is where you need to stand.' With Pat, it was like, 'Uh, stand right around there somewhere.' His approach made everybody feel comfortable, like we didn't have to be on our toes all the time." One morning, amidst a practice tirade, Burns got so wound up that he forgot the name of his backup netminder, Corey Schwab, sputtering: "You! Goaltender! Get in the net!" That cracked everybody up.

Burns then made news when he took a verbal shot at Glen Sather, the Rangers GM who'd given him no more than a courtesy callback when seeking a new coach. The Manhattan team that garnered all the ink had missed the playoffs in five consecutive years. "The Devils have high standards. That's the difference," sniffed Burns. "We have a standard to live up to every year, and a couple of teams in our area don't have the standards we do."

He'd taken the Lou liturgy to heart. Sometimes they locked horns, but, true to his word, Lamoriello would not allow indisposition to linger. "If I had something to say, or if he was upset, he never let it go to a third party. If he didn't like something that I did, he'd tell me and we'd try to correct it. If I didn't like something he was doing, the same thing, eyeball to eyeball. Then leave it there. Don't get me wrong: Pat wouldn't take it easy with me, either. But I'd say, 'Pat, come on.' And he'd smile. He was stubborn, to the point where, in the past, he might not have trusted someone who told him 'You're wrong.' That's what he got better at. With the players, too, sometimes they just needed a little guidance. Pat was a person who could hurt you with the things he said. I told him, "Do you like it when someone talks to you like that?' Or I'd go right back at him. But from the very first day, it was total honesty between us."

In early January 2003, the old Burns escaped from his cage when reporters noted that skilled players such as Patrik Elias, Joe Nieuwendyk and Scott Gomez were merely shadows of their former selves and blamed the coach's static system. Burns lashed out with an obscenity-studded diatribe. "Do you think I'm telling the players not to score goals? That's horseshit. Everybody's job is to score goals. Do you think there's a coach in the league who says, 'Don't score goals because this is a defensive system'? Wake up and smell the fucking coffee." Opposing players who criticized New Jersey's suffocating tendencies Burns dismissed as "crybabies." With his own players, if wayward on the ice, Burns was unafraid of applying the benching timeout, even with his stars. He scratched Gomez from a game. Infuriated, Gomez responded by tallying points in his next five straight.

The excoriated system of airtight defence was winning games, and that's all that mattered. By the All-Star break, the Devils hadn't lost a game in regulation time at home for a month. Burns pummelled dominance at the Swamp into his players' heads, said he could live with .500 on the road. In March two consecutive losses was considered a mild slump by Jersey standards. The Devils finished the regular season 46–20–10–6 with 108 points—second highest in team history—the Atlantic Division title, and seeded second in the Eastern Conference. It had been a superb year one for Burns, who admitted to being physically and emotionally drained on the cusp of playoffs. "I find it more difficult the older I get." But he'd been on his best behaviour, lobbing only the occasional incendiary at reporters, whom he ceaselessly considered the enemy. "I like to throw a shot back once in a while . . . can't bite my tongue. I just feel better. People around here think that I'm supposed to make friends. I'm not here to make friends. I'm about as bouncy as a hunk of clay."

In the first playoff round, Jersey played Boston, and here was intrigue. Not only was this the club that had last fired Burns, but GM O'Connell, after ditching Rob Ftorek with nine games remaining in the season, had gone behind the bench himself. Against Burns, he was hopelessly outmatched, though Burns tried to squelch that storyline. "I worked for Harry Sinden. I didn't work for Mike O'Connell. This is not about revenge. The game isn't being played behind the bench."

For game one, it was exceedingly played behind the bench, Burns coping with the abrupt loss of Gomez (to whiplash) and Nieuwendyk (walloped in the back of the head by Bryan Berard). He shuffled his lines insanely, the Devils held the Bruins' Joe Thornton—101 points in the regular season—in close check, and Jamie Langenbrunner scored both goals as the Devils won 2–1. In a scrappy game two, Langenbrunner again potted the winner, and the Devils were 4–2 victors, taking a 2–0 series lead as the action switched to the FleetCenter. Brodeur posted his fourteenth shutout in seventy career playoff games, Jersey handily dumping the Bruins 3–0. A Boston columnist opined, "The Iraqi army has a better chance of making a comeback than the Bruins do."

The anticipated sweep was avoided when Boston chased Brodeur from the net—a rare sight—in a 5–1 thumping. Even more exceptionally irregular was the absence of Daneyko from the lineup. The veteran— Mr. New Jersey—had attended the franchise's inaugural training camp twenty years earlier and played in 165 straight playoff games, the third-longest such streak in NHL history. Now, a fortnight from his thirty-ninth birthday, Burns had taken the gutsy step of scratching him, reasoning that Daneyko was labouring from a painful hit to the ribs from P.J. Axelsson in game three.

Daneyko was back in for game five and Jersey closed out the Bruins at the Swamp 3–0. That launched the Devils into a second-round encounter with the surprising Tampa Bay Lightning, coached by John Tortorella to the top of the Southeast Division and victorious after overcoming a 2–0 deficit against Washington in their opening series. Typically, Burns used Tampa's admiring press as ammunition in his "the whole world is against us" mantra. "Nobody wants to see us win, except our fans. They would like to see Tampa win. 'Hey, let's see these guys win, they're the Cinderella team.' Every year, there's a team that puts on a glass slipper and turns into Cinderella, and all of a sudden everybody falls in love with them."

Even the home-love for Jersey was underwhelming, with thousands of empty seats at the Meadowlands for each of the first two games, which the Devils took 3–0 and 3–2. Game two was decided by Langenbrunner in the third overtime period. In Florida, the visitors erased a three-goal deficit but lost 4–3 to the Lightning on Dave Andreychuk's winner after Burns was prevented from completing a line change that left him with four forwards on the ice. Scott Stevens left the game early, hit in the ear with a slapshot. His courageous turn in game four, wearing a plastic guard to protect his stitched-up left ear, inspired the Devils into a commanding performance. Scott scored a power-play goal, too, in the 3–1 victory—the "cherry on top," said Brodeur.

Finally, for game five at the Meadowlands, the near-sellout crowd came to life, banging thunder-sticks throughout a marathon affair that went into triple overtime before Grant Marshall dispatched the Bolts 2–1. Marshall had actually missed the bus carrying the team from their hotel to the rink— it left fifteen minutes early—and had to literally run after it, teammates laughing as they watched out the back window. "If I'd known it was going to go three overtimes, I'd have stopped and called a cab." Now the Devils had to contend with Ottawa, the most potent team in the league that year. Because he grew up in the region, Burns was even more of a media magnet during the Eastern Conference final. The Senators were coached by Jacques Martin, another local fellow and the man whose team had defeated Burns's Olympiques squad in the Memorial Cup back in 1986. One paper pounced on a Burns quote that was played across the front page: "We'll win." This immediately evoked memories of Mark Messier famously promising a victory before the Rangers' semifinal against Jersey in 1994, a vow fulfilled as New York went on to end a fifty-four-year Cup drought. Burns didn't dispute the quote saying only that it was taken out of context. He'd been praising the Sens, complimenting their magnificent season. "Then I'm asked, 'Well, the way you're talking, you don't have a chance to win?' I say, 'Oh, we'll win.' Of course, they blow a big headline up the top, 'Burns promises win.'" He grunted. "You can't win."

The highly anticipated matchup opened in Ottawa's Corel Centre,

Devils losing 3–2 in overtime, the first time they trailed a series that spring. Lamoriello took his squad back to Jersey for the day off—Mother's Day, as it happened—before game two, which was widely mocked, some speculating the move was intended to sequester Brodeur from interrogation about his scandalizing marriage breakup. Before leaving town, Burns spent three hours visiting with his mother at the retirement home where she resided. In any event, the Devils got their split upon returning to Ottawa, an impressive 4–1 win.

Back at the Swamp, both Brodeur and Patrick Lalime were awesome in duelling goaltending displays, Jersey eking out a 1–0 decision. Burns lauded Brodeur: "Without him, where would we be? I have run out of words to say about him." The Devils prevailed commandingly in game four, 5–2, to take a 3–1 series lead. But whoa, not so fast—Ottawa had reserves of tenacity and oodles of talent. Rookie Jason Spezza, making his postseason debut, tallied a goal and assist, lifting the Senators to a 3–1 victory in game five. It was at this point that details of Brodeur's marital split were uncovered by the media after his estranged wife, Melanie, filed divorce papers. Her itemized complaints of adultery—dates, places— were reported, gleefully in some quarters. Brodeur had become involved with a woman (now his wife) who'd formerly been married to Melanie's half-brother. His personal problems were grist for public taunting and tabloid sensationalism. "Pat was very supportive of me during that time," says Brodeur. "It was so tough because here we are, in the middle of the playoffs, and there's all this gossip flying around, everything coming out. I wasn't distracted when I was playing. Hockey is the place you hide. The distraction was outside the game. Pat took care of me, and his wife, Line, took care of my girlfriend. It wasn't like he told me, 'You've got to do this and you should do that.' He was just there for me. He'd been through a lot in his own personal life, so maybe he could relate. I needed people around me to help me through it. Pat just said, 'I'm here for you.' That was the beginning of the relationship we built outside of hockey."

With an 11–4 record, 4 shutouts and a 1.67 GAA, Brodeur clearly had no problems between the lines. In so keenly contested a series, he had to be better than merely awfully good. Jersey hadn't lost two straight games in the postseason and was 8–0 at the Meadlowlands, but that streak was halted in game six, claimed 2–1 by the Senators in overtime. The series would be decided in a game seven at the Corel Centre.

Ottawa had more skill, but the Devils, arguably, had more will, and some motivational gimmickry from Burns. Hours before game time, he noticed some trailers set up outside the arena to be used by converging media should the Cup final unfold in Ottawa. This struck Burns as presumptuous and he exploited the scene to fire up his troops, stopping the team bus to direct their attention towards the offending vehicles. "You see those trailers? We're going to send those trailers back because there is not going to be a next round!"

The Devils got on the board first, but lost Nieuwendyk early to a hip injury. Burns went into the medical room during intermission and discovered his thirty-five-year-old two-time Stanley Cup champion in tears, unable to continue playing. "I went back in the room and told the players we have a rangy old veteran on the other side who would love to help you out. He's got a tear running down his eye right now. That seemed to pump up the team. Everybody rallied around each other."

Up 2–1 in the third, Burns paced back and forth, smacking players on the shoulders, exhorting them to go harder. "Pat was so passionate on the bench about 'Let's take it to them!' and 'They're on the ropes!'" said Brodeur afterwards. "I've never seen him that emotional unless he's yelling at the referees—or Gomer [Gomez]." When Jeff Friesen's turnover led to Ottawa's tying goal, Burns consoled rather than flayed. Friesen responded by scoring with 2:14 left to give New Jersey the game 3–2 and the series 4–3.

The drama cranked up even further in the Cup final between Jersey and the Mighty Ducks of Anaheim, though many lamented the prospect of head-to-head slogging between two D-addicted teams. It would undoubtedly be a battle of nerves between two Quebec-born goalies: Brodeur and Jean-Sébastien Giguère, who'd been at least equally spectacular in the playoffs, with a shutout streak of 213 minutes and 17 seconds. Most nerve-wracked among spectators was Carol Niedermayer, mother of Duck Rob and Devil Scott. The biggest name on either team's manifest, however, was Burns, reminded every day that there was no Cup on his resumé. "I'm not important in this," he maintained. "This isn't for me. What I want is for this team." Behind the other bench was Mike Babcock, rookie coach, in the same position where Burns had been as a baptismal boss with the Canadiens in the '89 final against Calgary.

Well-rested Anaheim had zip offence in game one, Brodeur recording his fifth playoff shutout of '03 and Friesen, ex-Duck, accounting for two of Jersey's three goals. Again, Burns sat out Daneyko, as he had in four games against Ottawa. This was excruciating for the battered veteran, though he didn't whine. Teammates appreciated Daneyko's dismay but were also in awe of a coach who had the guts to make that call. "It's not easy to make a move like that when you know that Dano is the face of the franchise," says Brodeur. "Dano was not just a regular player. We're talking about a guy who'd been in the organization forever, and the fans loved him. But it just wasn't working, and it had to be done. We needed our best players to be in the lineup. You've got to tip your hat to Pat for being able to make that decision."

For game two, the Ducks showed a soupçon more determination, but the result was exactly the same: a 3–0 loss. As the series moved to the Arrowhead Pond, Giguère pointed an accusatory finger at his teammates. "I would be very disappointed if not everybody shows up with lots of emotion. That's what's been lacking and that's unacceptable. We have to play for the moment. When is the next time this is going to happen to us?"

Thus aroused, Anaheim showed the mettle that had brought them to this juncture, winning 3–2 in overtime, Brodeur giving up two soft wanderlust goals. In game four, thirty-nine-year-old Steve Thomas was the overtime hero for the Ducks in a 1–0 nail-biter. Critics clucked about a lack of goals diminishing the finals, yet this was good hockey for the discerning eye, if disastrous for the broadcasting network. Jersey unshackled its alleged gunners 6–3 at Continental Airlines Arena in a rollicking game five.

Running out of topics in their largely unsuccessful attempts to engage Burns in a to-and-fro conversation at an off-day scrum, reporters queried the coach about people he most admired. He listed Scotty Bowman, Bill Parcells, Bob Knight and General "Arnold" Schwarzkopf, mixing up his Normans and his Schwarzeneggers.

Anaheim battled back from the brink in game six, humiliating the Devils 5–2 at the Pond, captain Paul Kariya surviving a patented body slam from Scott Stevens that left Kariya unconscious and motionless on the ice for nearly three minutes. "I didn't know if he was alive," said Brodeur. "He just didn't move for a while." With 11:23 remaining, Burns pulled Brodeur in favour of Corey Schwab. Brodeur was, er, jiggy with it, assured he would be starting game seven, Burns simply anxious to give him a little extra rest.

It had been a complete home victory series. "All year, Pat had preached about being good at home, dominate at home. This is where we were going to win. And that's what happened," said Brodeur. To the media, Burns presented a modest but confident face, focusing attention on his players. "This team has accomplished a lot. I haven't accomplished a thing. It's 'we.' That's the way we've done it all year long."

Nine months of labour had boiled down to one deciding game for the Stanley Cup, in an arena lacking in charm and, often, patrons. And Burns, the softie, pulled out one last trick: he reinserted Daneyko into the lineup. "The most important game and Dano came back," says Brodeur. Informed at a team dinner that he'd be playing—but cautioned by Burns to keep that under his hat until game time—Daneyko had to leave the room so he could burst into tears privately.

Game seven was New Jersey's exclamation point to the playoffs, an imperious 3–0 triumph, Friesen contributing two goals and twenty-three-year-old rookie Michael Rupp, filling the void left by injured Nieuwendyk, scoring the first, which was the winner, a kid's hockey dream come true. Before the opening faceoff, Burns had gazed up at the crowd and then taken his own emotional pulse. "I thought I would be a lot more nervous than I was. I thought I was going to be a nervous wreck, and I wasn't." It was his ninth game seven in a thirteen-year coaching career, pulling Burns into a tie with Scotty Bowman and Mike Keenan.

Yet even in the greatest moment of his professional life, Burns didn't shake his signature scowl. Someone asked him about the "beauty" of a game seven. "You call it a beauty? I don't know how pretty it is. I don't know if I'd go out on a date with it very often."

Brodeur's third finals shutout notwithstanding, the Conn Smythe Trophy for most valuable player went to Giguère, who didn't smile upon accepting it. Nor was Burns even nominated for a fourth Jack Adams. But, at last, he'd won the only silver hardware that mattered. Off to the side during the on-ice hoopla, hands stuffed in his pockets, Burns wondered why he didn't feel a surge of elation. "Gee, it doesn't look like this on TV." He watched Gary Bettman present the Stanley Cup to Devils captain Scott Stevens, who hoisted it overhead and began the traditional handoff, player to player, including Niedermayer, who'd changed into full uniform. This was the embodiment of all their toil, the hardest trophy to capture in professional sports. Finally, the jug reached Burns. He planted one tender smooch on the Cup, then lifted it in the direction of his family in the stands. "I was glad to see them up there," he said later. "My son Jason and my daughter Maureen came in from Montreal, drove all the way down. My wife was there, friends and family from Quebec. I pointed the Cup at them because sometimes you forget the people who are behind you, who were there when things don't go so good. The last couple of minutes, it was really exciting, not for myself, but because I was afraid to disappoint people, disappoint my family, disappoint the fans. I owe a lot to Lou."

In the dressing room, drenched by champagne, amidst the hoots and hollers, Daneyko gave full credit to the coach. "He just kept the pedal to the metal all year long and didn't let us get complacent. That was probably what was missing from the club the last few years. He came in from day one and was a no-nonsense guy, did some things that sometimes you don't understand. I guess that's why he coaches and we play. Probably one of the toughest coaches I've played for, but well worth it."

Addressing the media, Burns allowed himself a bit of triumphalism. "There are a lot of people in this room who counted me out, who said I was old-fashioned and couldn't coach anymore. I was out of hockey for two years and you said I would never be back. Well, I've won something now."

After a long night of revelry, Burns drove his family to the airport. In a candid coda, the coach acknowledged that, many times across the seasons, he'd pretended the Cup was a coup he didn't need to validate his career. He'd lied. "I said it often. No, I never believed that."

The victory parade—which in New Jersey was a tailgate party in the parking lot of the Meadowlands complex—had to be put on hold for a day because the Nets were still contesting the basketball playoffs and traffic control was an issue. When staged, upwards of twenty thousand gathered to enjoy the "Devils way" spectacle. Thereafter began the Cup's summer odyssey, a sweet NHL tradition whereby each player gets to have his way with the trophy for a day. It travelled to Alaska with Gomez, was transported in a thirty-two-foot Hummer on a team outing to Hoboken, appeared as guest on *The Late Show with David Letterman* and *Live with Regis and Kelly*, opened the New York Stock Exchange one morning, nestled in the lap of a giant Buddha statue at an upscale restaurant, went on a three-hour cruise around Manhattan Island, and attended golf tournaments and the NHL draft.

When his turn came a month into the summer, Burns stood Stanley in the back of his pickup and drove it to a yacht club in Magog, where a shindig for family and friends was held. A frail Louise Burns, matriarch of the clan, attended. "My ninety-year-old mother was sitting there, touching the Cup with her hands shaking. It choked me up." Son claimed to have seen the trophy reflected in his *mère*'s eyes.

That's when the joy finally overwhelmed.

Chapter Nineteen
Chance and Fate

"I've never backed down from any fight."

IT WAS POURING RAIN, miserable, when Pat Burns went on his last motorcycle run with the Red Dogs. He and his buddies were huddled under a bridge on the New England seaboard, shivering, waiting for the downpour to ease up a little, enough to at least see the pavement ahead. But Burns, brooding, was gazing into an even more bleak immediate future, just down the road. He turned to his friends. "This is my last trip, guys."

Late spring of 2010, it was, and what a tortuous road it had been: six years of sickness, hospitals, debilitating medical treatment, chemotherapy and radiation and surgery, tentative hopes for recovery, then the demolishing verdict that he hadn't outrun cancer, that he wouldn't beat it. Once, twice, Burns had fought back valiantly, summoning all his physical and mental resources for the battle of his life—the battle *for* his life. And each time, after a period of apparent remission, the invasive cancer cells had returned, from colon to liver to lungs.

Burns was terminally ill. He was dying.

"Even then, he didn't show his hurt," says Martin Brodeur. "You had to really know him to figure out what he was feeling inside. He gave it everything he could, but it came back again and again. That last time, I think in his own mind, he probably thought: 'Just take me.'"

How abruptly priorities change when confronted with one's own mortality, the finiteness of it.

The Stanley Cup glow lingered over the club at training camp in September 2003. They were guests at a reception in the Rose Garden at the White House, and President George W. Bush had even given them a peek at the Oval Office. Less happily, Burns's name had popped up in the Montreal murder trial of two Hells Angels when police testified that the coach's unlisted private phone numbers had been discovered during a search of the suspects' homes. He brushed off the controversy, claiming to have no idea how the defendants had obtained the numbers. In fact, Burns had once left a couple of tickets at the Gardens' will-call office in Toronto for a Hells chieftain. But the story, when it trickled out, caused no significant damage to his reputation.

By midseason, Burns was far more concerned with his club's mediocre play, yet confident they would rediscover their pith in the playoffs. As early as January, however, he'd been feeling unwell, unusually tired, dozing off immediately on team flights, which was not at all his normal tendency, so enervated that Lou Lamoriello noticed and asked if everything was okay. Fine, said Burns. For a few months, there had been alarming symptoms of something seriously amiss, but Burns ignored the early warning signs, as many people do—avoidance, not wanting to know, to have their worst fears confirmed. That stalling infuriated Robin Burns when he learned of it later, and makes him mad still. "Pat, you're an asshole," he spits out at the cousin who's no longer around to hear. "Never said a word to anyone."

After a trying, lacklustre season—for Burns, however, on March 30, 2004, his 500th NHL win—New Jersey was preparing to meet Philadelphia in the first round of the playoffs. Players were baffled when Burns missed a practice, a morning skate, a team meeting. "Personal reasons," they were told. "We asked, 'What's going on?' and they told us, 'Oh, he's seeing a doctor about a problem,'" says Brodeur. "Nobody thought it was anything serious."

It was *very* serious. Only at the urging of his wife, Line, did Burns finally share his concerns with Lamoriello, who promptly arranged for team doctors to conduct tests, which led to more tests, which resulted in the heart-seizing diagnosis: Burns had colon cancer and needed to begin chemotherapy treatments right away. Even then, he bargained for time. "I said to him, 'What do you want to do?'" remembers Lamoriello. "'Because I'm going to do what you want, we'll find a way.'" Burns wanted desperately to remain behind the bench for the first round. "Done," responded Lamoriello. "One round. Unless you find you can't do it." Then Burns would step away, whether or not the team advanced.

The Devils, defending Stanley Cup champions, were eliminated by Philadelphia in five games. The following day, April 18, reporters were summoned to a press conference at Continental Airlines Arena, to be enlightened about "a non-hockey-related issue involving the coach." Burns took a seat on the dais, pulled out a handwritten prepared statement, smoothed out the pages, and read the ghastly news aloud to a stunned audience. He had colon cancer that required immediate aggressive treatment.

"The last month or so, I have not been feeling well. There were signs that something was not right, but I was reluctant to do anything because the playoffs were coming up." He apologized to the players for his distraction during the series. "I wasn't the coach I should have been the last couple of weeks, but I had a lot of things on my mind." Only when he spoke of his pride in the team did his voice begin to waver and he fought back tears. "My wish and hope was to see this team continue into the next round and win another Stanley Cup. Even if I was physically not there, I certainly would have loved to see this group of gentlemen do it again." He swallowed hard. "As I learned in the past, chance and fate are a big part of winning. Neither, unfortunately, as I've learned in the past weeks, can be controlled. For those who know me well, I've never backed down from any fight. And I'm not going to back down from this one." He took no questions, and left, disappearing down the corridor with his arm around Line's shoulders.

Lamoriello made it clear Burns was still Jersey's coach and would return in that capacity the following season, health permitting. In any event, it was a moot point—there would be no 2004–05 season. The entire year was wiped out by an NHL lockout. "All my time and energy will be focused on this," Burns had said. He returned the day following his cancer announcement to participate in the formal team photo session then vanished. He immersed himself in a gruelling regimen of daily chemotherapy and radiation sessions, then intestinal surgery in July, then more chemo. Thousands of emails and letters poured in, from hockey people throughout the league, from fans and from complete strangers.

The hospital where he received initial treatment, St. Barnabas, was in Livingston, New Jersey. Brodeur invited Burns to stay at his nearby home, and the coach gratefully accepted. "I told him, 'Come to my house, relax, you'll be better off.' We became close. I have two bulldogs, and Pat loved playing with them." Brodeur's dogs are named Stanley and Vez—as in Vezina Trophy, the first of which he'd won in 2003, playing for Burns.

Doctors were optimistic. The malignant tumour they removed hadn't penetrated the intestinal wall and seeped into Burns's lymph nodes. His cancer was deemed Stage II, which has a 75 per cent "cure" rate without recurrence following surgery. Burns and his wife relocated to their off-season home on a golf course in Punta Gora, near Port Charlotte, Florida.

He continued to receive chemo twice a month for the remainder of the year, many days returning to writhe in his bed, beset by violent nausea. One of the many therapeutic drugs Burns was prescribed had the side-effect of making him keenly sensitive to low temperatures, which would have kept him out of the rinks had there been a season. He later described the horrors of treatment to Rich Chere, hockey writer at the Newark *Star-Ledger*. "The operation was tough, but the second round of chemotherapy during August, September and October was the toughest part. That really made me sick. You couldn't touch anything cold. You couldn't drink a cold glass of water. If you stood in front of the refrigerator and it was open, you had to back off. It was the weirdest thing. I still have numbness in the ends of my fingers and feet. That's going away slowly."

It was a dreadful year, as Line underwent abdominal surgery as well. Then, while Burns was up north, Hurricane Charley struck the Florida coast in August, causing sixty thousand dollars' worth of damage to their house. But by the following spring, Burns had regained much of the weight lost during chemo, was working out almost daily and generally feeling upbeat, buoyant. Doctors were encouraging. Burns—kept on the payroll— was scouting for the Devils, attending NHL and International Hockey League games in Florida. He rode his Harley, played many rounds of golf with Line and returned to Montreal as marshal for the St. Patrick's Day parade, where his father was honoured. Burns had every reason to believe he would be cleared to resume coaching duties at the start of the 2005–06 season, was even fooling around with potential line combinations. And then his world caved in again.

In July, a Montreal radio station reported that Burns had been diagnosed with cancer for a second time, news shortly thereafter confirmed by the Devils. "He will not coach next year," a solemn Lamoriello announced. Larry Robinson would return to the job he'd left after leading Jersey to a Stanley Cup championship in 2000. Burns was shattered. "I was feeling great. I was in top shape with great expectations. Then it showed up again in a CAT scan. That was devastating."

This time, the cancer was in Burns's liver. "I'd been feeling so much better, was going to the gym, looking forward to coaching again and then—*BAM*," he told a friend. "That was the worst part, the worst day, when they gave me that news. I asked the doctor, 'So, what do we do now?' He said, 'An operation and another six months of chemo.' I thought, 'Jesus.'"

He underwent surgery in August, doctors removing a third of the organ. But the liver can regenerate itself, so Burns and his family clung to the best-case scenario. "Fortunately, we got everything. It wasn't a massive attack on the liver," he said. His pal Chris Wood—a pilot who at that time had his own plane—collected Burns in New Jersey, and flew him home to New Hampshire. Lamoriello had picked up Burns at the hospital and brought him to the Teterboro Airport. The patient boarded the aircraft unassisted.

Burns began another agonizing cycle of chemo and radiation. And he adamantly refused to rule out a reboot of his coaching career, at some future date, preferably with the Devils. "It's motivation," he said. "To overcome this sickness, you have to believe. It's hard at times, but I'm going to try to beat this thing." He even managed to find some humour in his situation. "He joked about his colostomy bag," recalls sister Diane. "He said, 'When I fart, I make bubbles.' He was able to laugh about something like that."

Weakened from his treatments, there were some good days, many more bad days back in Punta Gora. A doctor friend who was a hockey fan occasionally drove Burns into Tampa to watch Lightning games. In November, he was in attendance when the Devils pounded the Bolts 8–2 and he visited with the players afterwards. Slowly, his strength—and sprouts of new hair growth on a scalp gone bald from chemo—returned, testament to Burns's tremendous physical resilience and formidably defiant state of mind. As his health improved, he resumed his scouting trips for the Devils, often in the company of Scotty Bowman, who was doing the same as a senior consultant for Detroit. "He lived pretty close to me, so we went to a lot of games together in Tampa and to the other coast," recalls Bowman. This was the coach Burns had most idolized, and now here they were, a couple of semi-retired snowbirds, enjoying their excellent road tour adventures.

Bowman's son, Stan, had been through two bouts of Hodgkin's disease, so Scotty had seen up close the physical trials of treatment. They rarely discussed Burns's illness, though. "I'd ask and he'd say, 'Oh, I'm doing fine.' Then I'd hear he was really having trouble, but he never let on. We'd watch these games together and commiserate when we saw things we didn't like, whether it was the referee's calls or because we couldn't believe what some of the players were doing." They established a close friendship. "He was sort of like me, I guess, because we'd both moved around among teams. And we had the same ideas about player accountability."

The two men gabbed about how damn hard it was to win a Cup—though Bowman had done it a record nine times, which seems inconceivable today. "It's so elusive, winning a Cup," says Bowman. "When you push players—and I did a lot of that, as did Pat—sometimes they end up, not tuning you out, but your voice doesn't sound the same to them after a while. It's probably easier to be a coach and last longer if you're not so demanding. Pat was demanding. His overall record was outstanding, but eventually you're judged on the performance of your team. It's tragic he couldn't enjoy his success longer when it finally came."

Before completing a final cycle of chemotherapy late that year, Burns saddled up his Harley for another trip, dreading the treatment to come. "The stuff's poison, right?" he told a Toronto friend about the chemo. "After the past year, my body's full of poison. It knocks the shit out of me." But it hadn't knocked the fight out of him. "I'm going to beat this thing. We thought we had it beaten once . . ." He was without a shred of self-pity, didn't rail at fate or God about his misfortunes. "I never blamed God, never said, 'Why me?' But this is such an up-and-down disease, mentally. There are days when you're sure you'll beat it, when you feel strong in your head and in your body. Then there are other days when you're nauseous and throwing up, when your stomach hurts so bad, when you're dizzy, when you're so weak you can hardly walk."

He forced himself to get up and out, walking Roxie, smelling the flowers, feeling the warm sun on his face. "Can't just stay in the house and give in." Frequently, he chatted with Lamoriello, loath to speak about his condition but always eager to talk hockey. Burns was profoundly thankful for the organization's continuing support, financially and otherwise. The Devils had his back on a contract—vaguely described as a consultant gig—that extended insurance to cover steep medical bills: $30,000 per chemo treatment, white cell booster shots at $14,000 a pop. "I owe my life to the New Jersey Devils and Lou Lamoriello," Burns stressed. "If it wouldn't have been for my medical insurance, my operations, my chemo, everything, is over $1.5 million."

On December 18, 2005, citing stress and poor health, Larry Robinson resigned as Devils coach. Lamoriello went behind the bench on an "interim" basis—and stayed there for the rest of the season. Within a few weeks of that development, Burns finished off his chemotherapy. When he and Robinson later attended a Devils game in Tampa together—Burns looking hale, with good colour—rumours flared that he was sufficiently fit to take back his old job, possibly at the beginning of the 2006–07 campaign. He didn't squelch the reports, but maintained a cautious posture about his physical recovery. "I don't want to get my hopes up." To a friend, he revealed a troubling detail: "There's still some stuff in there. Doctors said to come back every few months to see what's happening."

When the season began, the coach behind the Jersey bench was Claude Julien.

The next public spotting of Burns was in Toronto, where Wendel Clark had organized a reunion of the '92–93 squad, their old coach the guest of honour, seventeen players crowding into Mats Sundin's private box for a Leaf game, swapping stories. This was the team that Burns remembered most fondly, their framed photograph holding pride of place above the mantel at his New Hampshire home. "I look back on those years in Toronto and, you know, they really were the best. That team, they loved each other, everybody was a family." Burns told reporters he was feeling dandy. "The best I've ever felt. You wouldn't call it full remission because they're always watching. There's never full remission when you have this. It's something they have to watch and watch and watch."

Itching for a return to hockey, Burns stuck a toe back into the coaching waters, at least symbolically, tickled when named as one of four ceremonial skippers—along with Bowman, Jacques Demers and Michel Bergeron—for the annual Canadian junior prospects' game on January 17, 2007. His "Team Red" won the match 5–3 in Quebec City. Buzzed by reporters for an update on his health, Burns said: "Nobody can guarantee it. You live every day with that—that it can come back, and then you face it and punch at it again. You keep your left up and swing with your right. That's all you can do."

Burns was making more public appearances, as if striving to show the hockey world that he was robust and sturdy, even suitable for employment. Primarily, he was intent on living the life he had, which seemingly had been restored to him, without fear of what might happen tomorrow and tomorrow. "If you start thinking like that, you're in trouble. If you get up and think you're going to get sick again, you can't live your life." Together with Luc Robitaille, he was inducted into the Quebec Major Junior Hockey League Hall of Fame in April, arriving in Montreal to enjoy the festivities. He led a fundraising march there to raise awareness of prostate cancer. In Toronto, he was a head-table guest at the annual Conn Smythe dinner to benefit Easter Seals, sharing his insights into the nature of serious illness. "We all say to ourselves, 'It can't happen to me.' I said that for a long time, too, until it creeps up and kicks you right in the ass. I didn't expect it. I felt great. I'd never been sick in my life. I just tell people to make sure they get screened and checked, and don't lose faith. There are some days when, after a round of radiation and chemo, you definitely feel like, 'Is this ever going to end?' or 'Is this the end?' But you have to stand up, and the next day, you feel better, and the day after, you feel better, and then you get it again and you get another treatment and it puts you down. But that's the way it is. It's very stressful, not only physically, but psychologically."

In Jersey, Lamoriello dumped Julien after just one season and, predictably, Burns's name was bandied about as possible replacement, mostly wishful thinking. Burns kept himself hockey-busy, though. In Montreal, he appeared for the relaunch of CKAC as a French-language all-sports radio station. He'd signed on for a morning gig. Repeatedly, Burns was asked, "Are you okay now?" It wasn't a question he could ever answer with 100 per cent assuredness. "It's a cruel sickness. It can harbour and pop out at any time. But I feel strong. If you ask me if I could coach tomorrow, yes I could. I don't want people to assume, 'He's sick, he can't do it.'" Indeed, Burns added, he was fit enough to come back in the fall, if anyone wanted him. Just negotiate with Lamoriello, he advised, because

Burns had two years remaining on his scouting/consultant contract with the Devils. There was even a brief rumour that the Leafs were considering bringing Burns back to Toronto. His response when reached on a golf course in Florida: "Ha. Ha. Ha." How dearly he would have loved that, though. Not that he was dissatisfied with his Devils duties. "Lou handed me the whole southeast to scout. And I get to hit a lot of golf balls while I'm doing it. It's not a bad life."

Apparently spry and chipper, Burns was delighted when named an associate coach on Ken Hitchcock's staff for the 2008 world championships, held for the first time in Canada. The tournament would be a test case for his overall physical and mental stamina. "This is like taking baby steps back into it, and I sure am excited," Burns enthused. It was real hockey, patrolling the narrow space behind a real bench. There was nothing tokenistic about the assignment. When Canada opened the tournament in Halifax on May 2, it was Burns's first stint behind a bench since the Devils had been eliminated from the playoffs in April of 2004. Canada earned silver, defeated 2–1 in the gold medal game by Russia.

Was Burns really and truly back? Was that what this signified? Burns thought so. "Coaching is in your blood," he said. "You miss it when you're not there, and when you are there you say, 'Geez, this is tough.' I've been on both ends, so when the fall comes around, we'll have to see, we'll have to check everything out and make sure that's what I want to do."

The scuttlebutt went into overdrive. Burns was headed to the Senators, to the Sharks, to the Avalanche. Burns believed he was headed for the coaching job in San Jose and was quietly rejoicing over a tentative deal that would bring him a $2 million contract. Privately, however, doctors gently tempered his ambitions. "Don't even think about it," Burns's doc-pal in Florida warned. "You won't pass the physical."

All his aroused optimism, his soaring hopefulness, was crushed in December when the cancer reappeared.

It was in his lungs, both sides.

It was incurable.

———

Jason Burns has only a few distinct childhood memories of his father. There was the time when, as a little boy, he got into a shed behind their home and disturbed a wasps' nest. His father rescued him from the maddened swarm, absorbing a whole lot of stings in the process. He recalls, as well, the old dirt bike on which his dad occasionally propped him, steering his son for a gingerly ride in the woods.

More often, though, Jason has to study all the photographs taken by his mom, Danielle, to convince himself that his dad was really present, part of his life in those early years. "I remember him coming home and tossing his hockey gear down the stairs into the basement. But that's pretty much it. There aren't many memory souvenirs. I can't remember sitting at the table with my mom and dad. I can't remember being with him at Christmas. When I was little, he was working as a detective and he was coaching Midget AAA and he was scouting. So he was never there."

As an adult, Jason is the spitting image of his father, a strapping, barrel-chested fellow with the same hazel eyes, the same Burns monobrow and a similar passion for hockey. He apprenticed as a welder, and for a time ran his own company, but didn't like the business management part of it. Now he's a firefighter in Gatineau, has coached a Junior C team, works on-ice with youth in a high school hockey program and does hockey commentary for a local radio station. Married to a schoolteacher, he became a father in late 2011. As Jason candidly admits, what he learned from his own dad about fathering is how *not* to do it. He loved his father fiercely, but is wistful about a relationship that was sporadic in its bonding moments, the son always yearning for an intimacy that the father was incapable of allowing. Jason didn't even meet half-sister Maureen until he was about twelve years old, though they would become and still remain close. Hockey always came first in Pat's life. As he was the first to acknowledge, parenting was not his forte. "My dad was so hard to seize, to figure out what he was thinking. We did click a little more when I got older. We tried to catch up a bit. But it's never the same. You can't bring your childhood back."

The years when his dad was coaching in Toronto had their highlights for Jason. "He'd bring me on road trips with the team. I'd even be on the bench. That was cool. That's the love part of my dad. He showed me a bunch of stuff that most Canadian kids can only dream of. But there was also that other part where he was distant. I was always a bit scared of him, to be honest. I never knew what answer he'd give me. Well, it was mostly no, like if I had a favour to ask or money that I needed for something. Or he'd come back and say yes, but make me feel really bad about it. I always wanted to see more of him, spend more time with him, because he really was fun to hang around with. I told him that at the end, when he was really sick: 'I'm going to miss hanging around with you, Dad.' He was a good friend, but not a great father."

Jason knew his father as a penny-pinching man, which is perhaps understandable in someone who grew up without financial security. Burns always worried about the money running out, never certain there would be another coaching job, another fat contract. While he was perfectly willing to pay for his children's education—sent Jason to a private school as a teenager, though the boy didn't like it and left after just one year—he was stingy about big-ticket items that he viewed as indulgences. "That was a choice he made, not to spoil us with toys," says Jason. It was his mom who bought him his first car, a used '86 Honda Accord. Upon graduation from high school in 1995, Dad gave him an '88 Toyota. He never bought his son a motorcycle, nor did he give him one of his own.

Some of Burns's miserliness is just plain incomprehensible. For game seven of the Stanley Cup championships, Jason drove to Jersey, picking up Maureen on the way. Jason sought reassurance that his dad would provide tickets for them. "He said, 'Uh, I'll see.' You'll see? Here I am, driving seven, eight hours, to see this game and he's going to *try* to get me tickets?" When Jason and Maureen arrived, they discovered their father's close buddies all had tickets to the game, no problem. Clearly, that still bothers, that he had to plead to be allowed inside the crowning glory of his father's career.

But Jason has some of his father's stubbornness, which he demonstrated that night, after Jersey won the Cup. "I demanded to go and see the press conference after. I followed my dad around. I wasn't going to let him say no. I remember meeting him under the stands and giving him a big hug.

'Wow—you just won the Stanley Cup!' And he said, 'Yeah, it's pretty cool, eh?' I drove back to the house with him later. We were alone in the truck and still we didn't say much. We always had trouble talking."

Jason grew up thinking his dad was spooning out their time together, limiting accessibility even in the summer weeks they'd spend together in Magog. "He didn't like having to carry around the burden of children. He didn't like the responsibility of children. We'd spend a lot of time driving around in his truck, but even then we didn't talk much and hardly ever about personal things. We'd talk about hockey mostly. When I was young, I'd only see him maybe three or four times a year, for a week maximum. So I didn't want to spend time arguing, 'Why don't you do this, why can't you do that?' I didn't want to get off to a bad start and waste the whole week. I was always careful about what I said, because he'd get pissed off. And he could be a bitch about it—not talk to you for a whole day if he was mad. He was a big baby that way."

He accepted his father's emotional limitations, but regrets the distance they never quite managed to close, even when serious illness mended some of the breach. Burns was actually more paternal towards some of his most beloved players than he was with his own son. "I couldn't give him what those guys gave him. I was not the one who was going to win a hockey game for him. What could I give him? I couldn't go out and buy him a motorcycle. And the little things I could afford, he already had. I could only love him, but I don't think he understood the love I wanted to give him."

Terminal cancer would heal some of that emotional remoteness, but not all of it. "A bit," says Jason. "He said to me a couple of times that he hadn't been a good father. He knew. What I think is he never really tried to make it up. I told him, at the end, 'Maybe you waited too long to say it.' But that's all right. I love him. Oh yeah, I love him a lot."

Chapter Twenty
A Surge of Affection

"He let us love him."

PATRICK ROY was having his Number 33 sweater retired at the Bell Centre. Not just raised to the rafters and honoured, but withdrawn from the numerical canon, never to be worn again by a Montreal Canadien. "I have come home," the legendary goaltender, thrice a Vezina Trophy winner, told the crowd that gave him a five-minute standing ovation on November 22, 2008. He'd wanted all—well, nearly all—his former coaches to attend the ceremony. Pat Burns was in the house.

Earlier that afternoon, they'd had a quiet moment together at the brunch arranged for Roy. "It's over," said Burns, revealing what only a handful of family members and friends knew. The battle he'd waged against cancer for so long would not be won. "As much as that was a happy day for me, I was hurting inside," Roy recalls. "Pat wasn't angry, no. Maybe he kept that inside. From what I saw, he seemed very much at peace. It's what he told me, that he was at peace. It was pretty much the first time I felt he was very open with me. I thought he looked good, but he knew that the end was starting. I don't want to say I was privileged that he shared this. But it made me so appreciative of that moment, because I knew it was probably the last time I might be with him."

The sad news that Burns was facing a third battle with cancer was broken in January 2009 by *La Presse*, the French-language daily. When reached by the paper, Burns had little choice but to confirm the diagnosis, though he would have preferred to keep this very private matter confidential for a while longer. "I know what you people are like in Montreal. You're capable of dramatizing everything, if it suits you. The truth is simple: the cancer has returned. But never fear: I'm still alive. I'm not in great shape, but I wake up every morning, I play golf, I ride my motorcycle and I work, despite the illness. I haven't given up."

Terminal illness is a foreign country. The clock starts ticking down on all of us from the moment of birth. But knowing the end of days is imminent, that there's no more to be done, attempted, is obliterating. It is a grieving for oneself, a glimpse of what the world will be like when you're no longer in it. Burns had only a short time between learning that his condition was incurable and having that knowledge become public, being transformed into the Dying Man. He wished that was not so. He recoiled from pity. And yet he was touched by the outpouring of love and support.

He had been a tough guy all his life, but dying with grace, on the few terms he could still control, required a different kind of strength, a hard softness, a relinquishing and resignation that ran contrary to the essence of Burns. "You could never show him that you were feeling sorry for him," says Lamoriello. In the many hours they spent together over nearly two years after lung cancer was detected—a far longer period of endurance than doctors had expected, because Burns did not go gently or feebly to his fate—Lamoriello witnessed a kind of metamorphosis, the one gift the disease imparted. "He mellowed. Quite frankly, in my opinion, Pat released a lot of things that he'd harboured, what he'd hidden away. He appreciated that he had just so much time to find out that he was a good person, that he was okay. I always felt that he was, but Pat didn't. I think that's what kept him going for so long, seeing how people really felt about him, realizing, 'I'm not disliked.' Because of the experiences he'd had in life, he'd mistrusted everybody. He got his trust back in the end. He became comfortable in his own skin."

Burns let his children into his life to a degree of intimacy and compassion that had been beyond his capacity before, most especially with daughter Maureen, as willful in nature as her father. Burns had been mostly a figment father when she was a child, had a more stable relationship with son Jason. With both, though, he'd tried to atone in later years, each spending long summer stretches in Magog. He became close, as well, with wife Line's children, Stephanie and Maxime Duval, especially Stephanie, who visited frequently. When their mother moved to Boston to be with Burns, her then-teen kids resided primarily with their father, an advertising executive in Montreal.

"Pat and my mom were such a good fit, a great match," recalls Stephanie. "The first I met him was at a restaurant. He told me after that he was nervous about meeting us, but I never felt that. He wasn't paternal towards me, because I already had a father. He took his place as my mum's husband, not my father. It was kind of perfect, because I never had to struggle with a two-dads situation. But he became a wonderful friend. I could go to him for advice about things that I wouldn't want to share with my dad or my mother. He had a different approach, and always a very interesting one. Pat knew how to say things politely but with the gloves off. I could talk to him about anything—work, life, men sometimes. It was like having a close girlfriend, but with a man's opinion, you know?"

In the years of sickness, particularly after the cancer came back a third time, all the children—now adults—drew closer to Burns, providing an emotional buffer. "Pat was sick, but he didn't make it dramatic or morbid," says Stephanie. "It wasn't at all hard to be around him. He was just himself. He never said, 'Why has this happened to me?' He wasn't angry—at least, I didn't see that. What I saw was his strength and his courage. He got a lot of comfort from having his family around him, his kids and his grandson." Maureen had a little boy, Samuel. "I remember our last motorcycle ride together. It was in New Hampshire, just from the restaurant to the house. Pat was so sick by then. But it's something I'll never forget, hanging on to him on that bike."

In the last year of his life, Burns got rid of all the motorcycles—sold one to Larry Robinson. The only Harley remaining in his New Hampshire garage belonged to a friend. Burns insisted on returning it personally by riding the bike back to Magog. Many tried to dissuade him from making the trip. "What's the worst that can happen?" he shrugged. "I'll crash and get killed?" Pal Kevin Dixon met him at the Vermont border anyway.

Sheer stubbornness kept Burns active, doing the things he enjoyed for as long as he was able, continuing to scout games, too. He needed to feel useful, that the small service he could provide to the Devils mattered. Inoperable cancer would not slow him down until all reserves of strength were depleted. "Right now, I'm just enjoying the time left," he told reporters who encountered him at a game in Tampa. "The crying and everything, that's all finished. That's over." He also rejected any further chemo treatments because it was about quality of life, not quantity, now. "I told my family, 'That's it. We've done all that. Let's just enjoy what we have here.'" It was a decision he would later revisit and reverse because he did want more time, even the little bit that more chemotherapy might permit.

Serious illness is not mind over matter, though. Burns couldn't will himself to remain robust. Frailness set in, his voice increasingly raspy from the ravaging of his lungs. Yet he continued with his morning radio show because he loved talking about the game, watched as many matches as he could on the dish—and in person when possible—stayed *au courant*. Hockey was a comfort, a solace. And the radio show was wildly popular in Quebec, despite Burns's strained vocal cords and frequent pauses to catch his breath. "I tuned in just to listen to him and changed the channel after," says Félix Potvin. "He was so well connected, knew everybody in hockey," says columnist Réjean Tremblay. "He was one of the most interesting commentators on radio, a huge hit, and good." Benoît Brunet, a full-time broadcaster himself now, adds: "I always listened to his show. Pat was straight up. He went straight to the point. Even at the end, he was still watching games, talking about teams, making his point understood. He didn't have to use twenty sentences to do it, either. That's why people liked the show. He talked hockey and made himself understood to the ordinary person."

———

The surge of affection for Burns, quite startling to him, expressed itself in a spontaneous, grassroots campaign to have the coach inducted into the Hockey Hall of Fame, which just a year earlier had announced new voting procedures to make the selection process less restrictive. An online petition amassed more than seventy thousand signatures within a fortnight. Burns certainly didn't spend his time waiting for a call from the Hall—which never came, not in his lifetime. When the 2010 inductees were announced, the name Burns was conspicuous in its absence. He did not receive the required fourteen votes from a panel of eighteen that included Scotty Bowman, Lanny McDonald, Mike Gartner, Bill Torrey, Serge Savard and Harry Sinden. Reporters and the citizenry were outraged. Who among that august assembly didn't think Burns had the proper qualifications? That would never be disclosed because the selectors had all signed a letter of confidentiality restricting them to comment only on those who'd been anointed.

"It makes me mad because Pat should be in the Hall of Fame," says Savard. "But the thing is, you don't get there just because you're still alive. The committee is made up of six former players, six journalists and six former managers—a pretty good mix. We were ranked number one among all sports in terms of process for those elected to the Hall. The votes just weren't there." Cousin Robin says Burns didn't take the rebuff to heart. "Pat said the people around him were more disappointed about it. He reiterated that every time we met: 'Please tell everyone that I wasn't upset. I have nothing against the inductees who were chosen, I applaud them.'"

There was no shortage of other honours, encomiums and accolades for Burns or in his name, however. Gatineau announced the creation of an amateur sports fund offering training bursaries for coaches. And the town of Stanstead, on the Quebec-Vermont border, 150 kilometres southeast of Montreal, revealed that a new rink, the Pat Burns Arena, would be built on the grounds of Stanstead College, open not just to students at the pricey academy but everyone in the region. Burns had once coached in the dilapidated old rink.

The impetus for the Pat Burns Arena came from his friend Chris Wood, who'd originally been approached by the college chairman to help with efforts to upgrade a facility that was going to be condemned, such was its advanced state of disrepair. "All right, I'll make a deal with you," Wood challenged. "If you name the arena after my good friend Pat, I'll get involved, I'll bring the project to Pat, and if he endorses it, we'll move forward." Told of the scheme, Burns was deeply moved. "The Red Dogs used to play hockey there, in the old arena," says Wood. "Pat would drive up sometimes when he was in Boston to join us."

Prime Minister Stephen Harper was among the dignitaries on hand when the arena development was formally announced in March 2010, with two-thirds of the $8.4 million budget covered by the provincial and federal governments, largely due to the tireless campaigning of Senator Jacques Demers, who emceed the proceedings. In his remarks, Harper harkened back to the '93 Leafs team. "My favourite memory was Pat taking the Leafs all the way to the semifinals. Which goes to show that, with the Maple Leafs organization, a great coach can take a team a long way, but only God can work miracles."

Burns had been collected from Florida by a private plane sent by another friend. Doctors had urged him to avoid flying and crowds because he was acutely susceptible to infection from any virus floating around. He wouldn't hear of missing the event.

For a public that hadn't seen him in a while, Burns's thin and fragile appearance was shocking. He looked like precisely what he was: somebody in the latter stages of lung cancer. But the radical transfiguration was jarring and distressing to many who remembered the coach as robust. Burns had always been such a physical presence. He commanded space.

"I know my life is nearing the end, and I accept that," Burns told the dozens of invited guests, speaking in an unrecognizably threadbare voice. "Excuse my voice," he apologized. "I don't have the thundering voice I used to have to get players going on the ice anymore." Addressing the youngsters from local minor teams who'd been invited to the ceremony, Burns wistfully acknowledged he would likely not be around to see the arena completed. "But I'll be looking down on it. Maybe there's a Wayne Gretzky or a Mario Lemieux or a Sidney Crosby sitting here. A young player could come from Stanstead who plays in an arena named after me."

It was an emotional afternoon. Burns didn't shrink from the truth, not for himself and not for his family in the front row. "As your life gets closer to the end, you realize that your body gets weaker, your mind gets working hard, but your heart gets softer. As you get closer to family, you get closer to God . . . There are things you realize along the way, all the great people you've worked with. I've told myself and my kids that when you look back, you don't cry because it's over. You're happy because it happened."

Burns returned to Florida immediately afterwards. Two weeks later, doctors' fears realized, he was hospitalized with pneumonia. Yet he recovered and was released. For those around him, the waiting game had begun, alarm spiking with every rattling cough and hint of fever. But it wasn't just abiding for Burns. He hungrily seized at experiences, each day that remained, as if filling his own album of memories, freeze-framing the moments.

He couldn't know the timing of his death, but he did know the place. He'd arranged for it.

Burns no longer owned property in Magog. In August, he rented a house there, but stayed in it with Line just a short while. His dear doctor friend from Florida, aware that Burns was in severe pain, delicately counselled that it was time for palliative care. On Labour Day, Burns moved into a Sherbrooke hospice, La Maison Aube-Lumière, for the close-observance ministrations Line and Pat's family could no longer provide. He decorated his room with photos of his hockey teams and other treasured mementos, including a Bible sent by the Leafs. On weekends, he checked himself out to spend time with friends and loved ones in the world beyond. It was on one of these excursions—while shopping for groceries, actually—that Burns heard he'd died.

The false rumour was pinballing around Montreal, gathering momentum on radio stations and then hurtling out into the blogosphere. It began with an employee at the palliative facility who'd entered Burns's room and discovered it empty, the bed's linen stripped—because it was being *changed*—and tipped off someone in the media. In Toronto, Cliff Fletcher strolled into the coach's room at the Leafs' practice facility and received a call from a news outlet, seeking comment on the death of Burns.

"I walk outside and all of a sudden, there's fifty media around me. I'm expressing my condolences. Then somebody said, 'Hold on, hold on, he's alive!' So I break off because I've got to call Pat. He answered his cell. I told him, 'Pat, I've got to apologize. Let me tell you how this happened.' Pat said, 'Those bastards in the media, they want me dead.' He was as feisty as ever." Fletcher, mortified, issued a press statement, apologizing profusely.

Burns took matters into his own hands. He contacted a handful of friends in the media, talking to reporters from the *Toronto Star*, CKAC in Montreal and Bob McKenzie at TSN. "They're trying to kill me before I'm dead," he growled. "I'm not dead, far fucking from it. They've had me dead since June. Tell them I'm alive." For the offenders who'd contributed to the erroneous news of his passing, picturing Burns enjoying a good guffaw out of the incident may have salved their conscience. He wasn't amused. He was hurt.

It was in express retaliation for that false rumour, in defiance of a pending outcome he could not alter, that Burns made another dramatic public appearance in early October, showing up for the groundbreaking of the Pat Burns Arena. Those close to Burns tried to dissuade him. "I said to my husband, 'He'll never make it,'" recalls his sister, Diane. "But he wanted to prove that he could." Burns was just a husk of the man he'd been, with sunken cheeks, walking unsteadily on spindly legs, wrapped in a blanket when he took his seat. Making only one brief remark to reporters—"I'm still alive"—he was helped to place a foot on the edge of the shovel and pressed it a few centimetres into the softened earth. "That was his stub-bornness and competitiveness showing," says Fletcher. "I'm sure 90 per cent of people in his situation, at that stage of the illness, would not have been able to get up there." He'd shown them, he'd shown them all.

Among those who witnessed this display of resilience were former players Guy Carbonneau, Stéphane Richer, Dave Ellett and Doug Gilmour. "It's more than courage," said Richer. "He's a guy who never gives up—he will never give up till the end." Ellett was distraught. "I'd never seen the devastation of cancer before, so it was shocking to me." A heartbroken Gilmour tried to hold back the tears. The players had picked Burns up in an SUV, transporting him to the sod-turning event. "He got into the car and I didn't recognize him anymore," says Gilmour. "He wasn't Pat anymore."

Returning Burns to the hospice, the players lingered to reminisce, aware they'd never see him alive again. It was a melancholy afternoon until Burns lightened the mood. "When we were inside and got a chance to talk about the old times, it turned into a hell of a day for him," says Ellett. "He was pretty doped up, but his mind was still there. He never lost that—and his humour. We laughed, rehashed old times."

The grains of sand were rapidly running out of the hourglass, though. Jason Burns drove down every weekend from Gatineau. Maureen was always nearby. In his final weeks, Burns was visited by other players, some clearly seeking to make amends, to repent for ancient arguments and harsh words rued. Richer came again seeking a kind of absolution and received it. "We were both crying. Towards the end of the conversation, he asked me about my mom and dad. I'm the one who was supposed to be there supporting him, and yet he was supporting me."

Burns called all his siblings together for a final family meeting while he still had the ability to speak. "We all went together in a van," remembers Diane Burns. "I said to the family, 'The one thing he doesn't want you to do is to cry in front of him, so don't. It's going to be a shock to see him, but keep your emotions to yourself until we leave.'

"Pat was sitting up, having his cereal. He didn't want to talk about death; that wasn't the conversation he wanted to have. I asked, 'Pat, do you have any pain?' He said no, he was on heavy medications. He never complained, not one word of complaint. But he said, 'I'm fifty-eight and I've got the body of a ninety-year-old."

To Robin Burns, he admitted: "It's hard to believe that this is the end, but I'm ready. I've accepted it." He'd had many quiet conversations with a young priest, confiding his regrets and his fears of what lay beyond. He took solace from the priest's words and from the family Bible next to his bed. Burns was surrounded by gentleness in those difficult weeks. Daughter Maureen stirred admiration in many as she patiently helped feed her father, caressed his cheeks, straightened his bedclothes and plumped his pillow, unfaltering before the degrading realities of dying. She mothered him. "He let us love him," says Diane. "He let Maureen love him. Jason always loved him. He let Line come in more, closer. He let me in a lot more than ever before in the past."

"They had good conversations," says Robin Burns. "I'd told Jason, 'Go take a tape recorder, sit down with your dad, talk to him, ask questions, because you're not going to get another chance.' There was no doubt in my mind that they'd all had issues. Pat was an absent dad for a lot of years; he had baggage. But at the end, he made peace with God and everybody in the family. As terrible as it was that God took him at an early age, he at least had that opportunity."

As his body broke down, it was frustrating and humiliating to rely on others. "It was so hard for him to be in that condition," says Jason. "I'd help him to the bathroom. Sometimes, he'd fall. I'd have to pick him up. He'd always been such a big, strong man. Now he depended on all of us. We'd sit around watching hockey games, not really talking much. But I enjoyed that time together with my dad, just being with him. It was good for me. I think it was good for him, too."

When Lamoriello came to see him, the last time, Burns could no longer speak, communicating only with his eyes. "By that point, it was like, 'Go to sleep, Pat, don't wake up again,'" says his closest friend, Kevin Dixon. But he was unyielding to the very last ragged breath.

Pat Burns died on November 19, 2010.

Tributes poured in. At the Bell Centre, where the Habs were hosting the Leafs, a video montage of Burns depicting all his mood-ring faces—fierce, glowering, snickering, wryly smiling—was shown on the scoreboard, his image projected onto the ice, to the poignant strains of Lennon and McCartney's "In My Life."

In Newark, at their new arena, the Prudential Center, where Burns had never coached, the Devils selected Sarah McLachlan's "I Will Remember You" as haunting musical accompaniment to their video homage, and players wore "PB" patches on their chests. Then they drilled the Capitals 5–0, snapping a three-game losing streak. That, Burns would have savoured. It felt as if he hovered above it all, not quite gone, a testament to his life force.

At her home in Gatineau, Diane Burns opened a closet and smelled cigarette smoke. No one in the household smoked. Her brother had smoked on and off, but gave it up completely when he became ill, enjoying only the occasional cigar until cancer treatments deprived him of any sense of taste. "I felt him there, spiritually. It was comforting."

Burns had asked for a small funeral, conducted by a parish priest. What he got was a grand affair on an epic scale, a funeral fit for a statesman, at the magnificent Mary, Queen of the World Cathedral in Montreal—a stone's throw from the Bell Centre—presided over by a cardinal, Archbishop Jean-Claude Turcotte, fervent Habs fan, who returned from Rome for the occasion.

"Here's your family and look at your friends," Robin Burns marvelled in his eulogy. "Not bad for a tête-carré from St. Henri." "Squarehead," it meant—a Québécois colloquialism for anglophones.

Very nearly all of hockey royalty was in attendance: a fleet of NHL managers and coaches, the entire New Jersey Devils team, former players and the game's dignitaries—Jean Béliveau, Dickie Moore (Burns's favourite player, his name engraved on five consecutive Cups from the

Canadiens' championships in the '50s), Gary Bettman, Yvan Cournoyer, Ray Bourque, Doug Gilmour, Wendel Clark, Patrick Roy, and on and on. Leather-clad bikers from riding clubs he'd initiated in various cities, and maybe some real Hells and Nomads too, but not wearing their colours. The policing brethren were well represented, from olden days and the present. Senator Jacques Demers, who described Burns as "a confrère," and Quebec premier Jean Charest, dozens of reporters—some of whom had managed to penetrate the coach's irascible façade. All 1,200 seats in the basilica were filled by people Burns had known, and hundreds more he'd never met—ordinary folks who wanted to pay their respects to a man they'd liked and admired because they recognized he was one of them, a working-class hero who'd risen to the top and never forgotten his roots. "He didn't put on the dog," says Robin Burns.

It was a long service, two hours, and trilingual—French, English, Latin. There was both solemnity and lightness, reminiscences and jokes, the music that he loved, and Robin Burns evoking the child-Burns in short pants and propeller hat. Lamoriello recounted a phone conversation from two weeks earlier, when the Devils had been in a funk. "I asked how he was doing. He said, 'To hell with how I'm feeling, I just watched you play.'" A vivid splash of colour was provided by the red gloves worn by Maureen and Stephanie—Devils red—in contrast to mourning black. When all were seated, Line Burns entered, cradling a miniature replica of the Stanley Cup containing Burns's ashes. That was a grace note Burns had specifically requested, and Lamoriello had seen to it, getting one customized with the Devils' insignia. "That's when I really knew how much winning the Stanley Cup had meant to Pat," he says. "He wanted that urn, and he wanted the logo on it." The vessel sat near the altar with a flame flickering over it during the service. Afterwards, loved ones stopped to kiss the urn as it was placed in a hearse.

That evening, a coterie of family and friends gathered to celebrate Burns's life in a venue and manner more appropriate to the dearly departed, a wake held at the Irish Embassy pub. Only the next morning was it discovered that thieves had broken into Line's SUV, parked nearby, and made off with a slew of personal effects: Burns's watch, family photos, two suitcases containing clothing, even bed linen from the cancer hospice, and a dozen jerseys autographed by all thirty NHL teams, intended for auction to help raise funds for the Pat Burns Arena. Because Burns's wallet was also taken, the culprits would have known precisely who they were robbing. Everybody was on the lookout, with someone even tipping off police to a homeless man spotted wearing an NHL sweater. Jason and Line Burns pleaded for the return of the items, no questions asked, and police warned they would be monitoring pawnshops; it would be near impossible to move the swag without attracting attention. Within a few weeks, six of the jerseys and two suitcases were recovered—returned via a media go-between— apparently surrendered by a contrite criminal. In fact, underworld elements had made it their errand to shake down sources, putting out the word on the street that the stolen goods had to come back. An individual known as "The Negotiator" made the arrangements. His identity remains a closely guarded secret. Suffice it to say that the outlaws Burns always semi-admired had come to the aid of the former cop.

The sports world can often be mawkish, bathing in bathos, in thrall to its legends of the game, especially when the endings are sad. Burns would have cut through that crap, in his own plain-spoken fashion. Yet in truth, he too was squishy at the core, emotional and sentimental. His game face was not his real face.

"He was a blue-collar guy, someone who worked like hell to become successful," says Cliff Fletcher. "He wasn't spoon-fed. He wasn't highly educated. He was just one of the masses, and people gravitated to that."

"He had a tough façade, but he was sincere," says Wayne Gretzky. "People recognized he spoke from the heart. Pat had a big heart."

Claude Lemieux, who long ago set aside their disagreements, salutes the Horatio Alger arc of Burns's life, from humble beginnings to hockey luminary. "There are coaches that have been more successful and had a bigger impact on the game, but they're not going to be recognized because they don't have that kind of historical story. Pat was a great story."

Bob Gainey played for him, coached against him and remembers him with esteem. "He touched a lot of very important places in the hockey world—three of the Original Six teams. He left a mark that resonates with a lot of people that he touched, whether directly, on the back of the jersey to get them over the boards, or with eye contact through the TV camera."

His old detective partner, John Janusz, watched the Pat Burns narrative unfold from up close and afar. He remains proprietary. "The Canadiens had him. The Leafs had him. The Bruins had him. The Devils had him. But he's still our coach, the Gatineau boy. The rest of the world can share him and remember him, but he's ours. We never let him go."

Jason Burns had to let go of his dad as a larger-than-life physical presence. But the father is in the son's DNA and in his heart. "His demeanour, the way he talked and acted, how hard he worked. He was always entertaining, fun to be around. Even at the end, he found ways to laugh.

"I like to remember our summers in Magog, water-skiing, boating and fishing. Those were great times because he was relaxed. Not a day goes by that I don't think of him. I wish he was still here to guide me, especially with the coaching and the hockey part of my life. I wish I could give him a call and chat about a bunch of shit. I miss when he'd answer the phone and say, 'Duuude, what's up, my man?'

"I miss him, my dad."

So does hockey—the game Pat Burns loved, and which loved him back.

Requiem

PAT BURNS COACHED 1,019 games in the NHL. His teams won 501, lost 353, tied 165. In 149 playoff games, he won 78 and lost 71. He was named coach of the year three times, with three different clubs. In 2003, his New Jersey Devils captured the Stanley Cup.

And those are the least of his accomplishments in a life ended too soon, at the age of fifty-eight.

His ashes are interred in Georgeville, a little town on the shores of Lake Memphremagog, just up the road from a plot of land he bought in his first year with the Montreal Canadiens.

The gravestone reads simply:

Patrick J. Burns

1952–2010

Devotion. Discipline. Courage.

Acknowledgements

EXPLORING THE LIFE of Pat Burns has been a journey of privilege. I am grateful to the many people who shared their insights and memories. I'm also indebted to the written record amassed by journalists who covered Pat's career. I've plundered their work shamelessly. In particular, I'd like to note the reportage of beat writers in the four NHL cities where Pat coached.

My thanks to Patrick McCormick—a dear friend—for his skillful close editing of the manuscript, and all the errors that he caught. Any bloopers that remain are down to me.

I'm obliged to *Toronto Star* editor-in-chief Michael Cooke, who gave me the book-leave. Thanks as well to everyone at Doubleday Canada, especially editor Tim Rostron, who pushed too hard but brought me in on deadline.

I'd still like to start over, though.

Rosie DiManno
May 27, 2012

Photo Credits and Permissions

About the Author

Rosie DiManno is a news and sports columnist with the *Toronto Star*. She was friends with Pat Burns from his coaching days in Toronto to the end of his life. She is the author of *Glory Jays, Canada's World Champions* (1993), about the Toronto Blue Jays.

Index

Broadhurst, Chris, 182

Brodeur, Martin, 256, 257–58, 261,
    263–66, 272

Brodeur, Melanie, 263

Brophy, John, 70, 71, 138

Brown, Jeff, 167, 201

Brunet, Benoît, 37–38

Buffalo Sabres, 95–97, 245

Burke, Brian, 194

Burns, Alfred Jr. (brother), 3, 6

Burns, Alfred Sr. (father), 1–6

Burns, Diane (sister), 2, 5–8, 55,
    118, 289–92

Burns, Jason (son), xv, 11, 116,
    119–20, 267, 279–81, 284,
    290, 291, 294, 295

Burns, Lillian (sister), 3, 5, 6

Burns, Line (wife), 12, 235, 243–45,
    263, 271, 272, 273, 284, 291,
    293–94

Burns, Louise Geraldeau (mother),
    2–3, 5–13, 42, 268

Burns, Maureen (daughter), xv, 10,
    11, 116, 267, 279, 280, 284,
    290, 291, 293

Burns, Pat
    in playoffs with Montreal, 81–88,
        95–100, 107–13
    in playoffs with Toronto, 155–85,
        195–203
    in playoffs with New Jersey,
        260–68, 270–71
    alleged anti-francophone bias,

69, 71–72, 79–81, 92, 122,
    125–26
appointment as Montreal coach, 54
appointment as Toronto coach,
    131–37
arena named after, 286–88,
    289–90
and biker gangs, 20, 270
as broadcaster, 235, 236, 277, 285
and Canadiens veterans, 63,
    65–67, 86–87
childhood, 1, 3–9
as coach of Hull Olympiques,
    22–39
as coach of New Jersey Devils,
    252–68
as coach of Sherbrooke
    Canadiens, 42–51
coaching rivalries, 33, 45–46, 51,
    94, 174–75, 176–77, 180
coaching style, 27–34, 37–38,
    46–48, 241–42, 259, 264
coaching style with Canadiens,
    56, 60–64, 96, 129
coaching style with Maple Leafs,
    138–39, 142–43
command of French, 18–19,
    125–26
conflicts with O'Connell, 244
conflicts with Sinden, 240–41,
    246–47
death reported prematurely,
    288–89